Quality TV

QUALITY TV
Contemporary American Television and Beyond

· ·

edited by
Janet McCabe
and Kim Akass

I.B. TAURIS
LONDON · NEW YORK

Published in 2007 by I.B.Tauris & Co Ltd
6 Salem Road, London W2 4BU
175 Fifth Avenue, New York NY 10010
www.ibtauris.com

In the United States of America and Canada
distributed by Palgrave Macmillan, a division of St Martin's Press
175 Fifth Avenue, New York NY 10010

ISBN (HB) 978 1 84511 510 4
ISBN (PB) 978 1 84511 511 1

A full CIP record for this book is available from the British Library
A full CIP record is available from the Library of Congress

Library of Congress Catalog Card Number: available

Typeset by JCS Publishing Services, www.jcs-publishing.co.uk

Contents

Contributors

· ·

Kim Akass has co-edited and contributed to *Reading Sex and the City* (I.B.Tauris, 2004), *Reading Six Feet Under: TV To Die For* (I.B.Tauris, 2005), *Reading The L Word: Outing Contemporary Television* (I.B.Tauris, 2006) and *Reading Desperate Housewives: Beyond the White Picket Fence* (I.B.Tauris, 2006). She is currently researching the representation of motherhood on American TV and co-editor of the new television journal, *Critical Studies in Television* (Manchester University Press), as well as (with Janet McCabe) series editor of 'Reading Contemporary Television' for I.B.Tauris.

David Bianculli is TV critic for the *New York Daily News* and National Public Radio's *Fresh Air*.

Jonathan Bignell is Professor of Television and Film at the University of Reading. He is the Director of the Centre for Television Drama Studies, established in 2000 to develop research into television analysis and historiography. He has led three major collaborative research projects to date, funded by the Arts and Humanities Research Council, on BBC TV drama in the 1960s and 1970s, British broadcasting in the period 1960–82, and on relationships between US and UK television from 1970 to 2000. He specialises in analytical and archival study of television drama, developing links between academics, archives and television practitioners. He is the author of several books and numerous articles on television drama and has also published on factual television and on film.

Sarah Cardwell is Senior Lecturer in Film and Television Studies at the University of Kent. She is the author of, amongst other things, *Adaptation Revisited: Television and the Classic Novel* (Manchester University Press, 2002) and *Andrew Davies* (Manchester University

Press, 2005), and is co-editor of 'The Television Series' for Manchester University Press.

Peter Dunne, Emmy and Peabody Award-winning producer, writer, and teacher, has written and/or produced, among others, *Sybil, CSI, JAG, Dallas, Knots Landing, Savannah, Nowhere Man, Eight is Enough* and *Dr. Quinn: Medicine Woman*. His book, *Emotional Structure: Creating the Story beneath the Plot* (Quill Driver Books, 2006), is based on his writing courses at UCLA.

Michael M. Epstein is Professor of Law at Southwestern Law School in Los Angeles, where he teaches courses on media and entertainment law. A lawyer with a PhD in American Culture, he is an editor of the American Bar Association's *Journal of International Media and Entertainment Law* and serves on the editorial board of *Television Quarterly* at the National Academy of Television Arts and Sciences. In addition to his collaborations with Jimmie L. Reeves and Mark C. Rogers, he has authored numerous articles on a variety of subjects, including telecommunications law and policy, the entertainment industry and attorney representations in American culture.

Jane Feuer is Professor of English at the University of Pittsburgh. She is author of *The Hollywood Musical* (Indiana University Press, 1993), *Seeing Through the Eighties: Television and Reaganism* (bfi, 1995) and co-author of *MTM Quality Television* (bfi, 1984).

Karen Fricker is a lecturer in the Department of Drama and Theatre, Royal Holloway, University of London. She completed her PhD at the School of Drama at Trinity College, Dublin, in 2005, and has published essays on her doctoral research subject, the québécois theatre director Robert Lepage, in *Contemporary Theatre Review* and *Staging Nationalism: Essays on Theatre and National Culture* (McFarland, 2005). Her current research focuses on theatre and globalisation; and on the Eurovision Song Contest, particularly Irish Eurovision fandom. She is the founding editor in chief of *Irish Theatre Magazine* (1998–2005), co-edited a special issue of *Modern Drama* on Irish theatre criticism, and writes about theatre for the *Guardian* (UK) and *Variety* (US).

Ian Goode is Lecturer in Film and Television Studies at the University of Glasgow.

Dermot Horan is Director of Broadcast and Acquisitions for RTÉ, the Irish public broadcaster. As such he sits on the board of the television division of RTÉ, and is responsible for the following areas: programme acquisitions, scheduling, on air presentation and promotion, press and publicity, marketing, programme sales, merchandising and licensing. His high-profile acquisitions for RTÉ include *ER*, *The Sopranos*, *Desperate Housewives*, *Lost*, *Ally McBeal*, *24*, *The West Wing* and *Friends*.

Peter Kaye is a refugee from a career in Hollywood music and is currently working on his PhD entitled 'Harmonic progression and emotional content in the motion picture/music phenomena' at Kingston University, Surrey.

David Lavery holds a chair in Film and Television at Brunel University, London. He is the author of over 100 published essays and reviews and author/editor/co-editor of 11 books, including *Reading Deadwood: A Western to Swear By* (I.B.Tauris, 2006) and *Reading The Sopranos: Hit TV from HBO* (I.B.Tauris, 2006) in the 'Reading Contemporary Television' series. He co-edits the e-journal *Slayage: The Online International Journal of Buffy Studies*, and is one of the founding editors of the new journal *Critical Studies in Television*.

Mark Lawson writes about television, politics and culture for the *Guardian*. He presents *Front Row* on BBC Radio 4 and *Newsnight Review* on BBC Television. His latest novel is *Enough is Enough: Or the Emergency Government* (Picador, 2005).

Geoff Lealand is Associate Professor in Screen and Media Studies at the University of Waikato in New Zealand. His teaching and research interests include children and media use, journalism, national cinemas, issues of the local and global, and television studies. His choices for quality TV would include series such as *The Simpsons*, *Six Feet Under*, *Brass Eye* (UK) and *Eating Media Lunch* (NZ).

Janet McCabe is Research Associate in TV Drama at Manchester Metropolitan University. She is author of *Feminist Film Studies: Writing the Woman into Cinema* (Wallflower, 2004) and co-editor of *Reading Sex and the City* (I.B.Tauris, 2004), *Reading Six Feet Under: TV To Die For* (I.B.Tauris, 2005), *Reading The L Word: Outing*

Contemporary Television (I.B.Tauris, 2006) and *Reading Desperate Housewives: Beyond the White Picket Fence* (I.B.Tauris, 2006). She is managing editor of the new television journal, *Critical Studies in Television* (Manchester University Press), as well as (with Kim Akass) series editor of 'Reading Contemporary Television' for I.B.Tauris.

Máire Messenger Davies is Professor of Media Studies and Director of the Centre for Media Research in the School of Media, Film and Journalism at the University of Ulster, Coleraine, with special responsibility for policy research. A former journalist, with a PhD in Psychology, she has taught in universities on both sides of the Atlantic. Her books include *Television is Good for Your Kids* (Hilary Shipman, 1989; reprinted 2002), *Fake, Fact and Fantasy: Children's Interpretation of Television Reality* (Lawrence Erlbaum, 1997) and *'Dear BBC': Children, Television Storytelling and the Public Sphere* (Cambridge University Press, 2001). Together with Roberta Pearson she has been conducting research on American television, using *Star Trek* as a case study, to be published in a forthcoming book by University of California Press.

Robin Nelson is Professor of Theatre and TV Drama at Manchester Metropolitan University. He has published widely on arts and media topics, and his books on TV drama include *Boys from the Blackstuff: The Making of TV Drama* (with Bob Millington) (Comedia, 1983) and *TV Drama in Transition: Forms, Values and Cultural Change* (Palgrave Macmillan, 1997). He is currently working on a monograph, *State of Play: Contemporary TV Drama* (Manchester University Press, 2007).

Roberta Pearson is Director of the Institute of Film and Television Studies at the University of Nottingham. She is the co-editor of *Cult Television* (University of Minnesota Press, 2004) and the co-author of *Small Screen, Big Universe: Star Trek as Television* (University of California Press, forthcoming). She is also currently working on an edited collection on *Lost* for the 'Reading Contemporary Television' series.

Jimmie L. Reeves is Associate Professor of Mass Communication at Texas Tech University. In addition to articles on subjects ranging from Mr T to *The X-Files*, *Twin Peaks*, *The Sopranos* and *Seinfeld*, he is the co-author of *Cracked Coverage: Television News, the Anti-Cocaine Crusade, and the Reagan Legacy* (Duke University Press, 1994).

Mark C. Rogers is Professor of Communication at Walsh University in North Canton, Ohio. He has previously collaborated on articles about *The Sopranos, Twin Peaks* and *The X-Files*. He is also the author of a number of articles about the American comic book industry.

Ashley Sayeau writes on popular culture, politics and women's issues for a variety of publications, including *The Nation, Salon, Dissent, Boston Globe* and *Philadelphia Inquirer*. Her work appears in various anthologies, including *Reading Sex and the City* (I.B.Tauris, 2004), *Reading Six Feet Under: TV to Die For* (I.B.Tauris, 2005) and *The W Effect: Sexual Politics in the Bush Years and Beyond*, edited by Laura Flanders (Feminist Press, 2004). She is currently working on a 'cultural autobiography' about growing up in the American North and South. Visit her website at: www.ashleysayeau.com.

Robert J. Thompson is Director of the Bleier Center for Television and Popular Culture and Trustee Professor at the Newhouse School of Public Communication at Syracuse University. He has written or edited six books on American TV.

Acknowledgements

We are indebted to our contributors – Robert J. Thompson, Karen Fricker, Sarah Cardwell, David Bianculli, Robin Nelson, Ashley Sayeau, Jimmie L. Reeves, Michael M. Epstein, Mark C. Rogers, Peter Dunne, Dermot Horan, Ian Goode, Geoff Lealand, Jane Feuer, Jonathan Bignell, Máire Messenger Davies, Mark Lawson, Peter Kaye, David Lavery and Roberta Pearson – for turning in such absorbing chapters, adhering to strict deadlines and pushing our thinking on quality TV further than we could have hoped.

We are extremely grateful to David Chase and the BBC for kindly granting permission to reprint the transcripts of Mark Lawson's interview with him. Thanks also to W.G. 'Snuffy' Walden for taking time out of his busy schedule to talk to Peter Kaye. Gratitude to *The Irish Times* for consenting to the reprint of Karen Fricker's review of the American Quality Television Conference.

We would like to acknowledge Trinity College, Dublin, and in particular the School of Drama and the Samuel Beckett Centre, for generously hosting the conference. Special thanks go to Professor Brian Singleton for inspiration and support as well as Francis Thackaberry, Ann Mulligan and Michael Canney for invaluable administrative and technical support. Thanks must go to our student helpers and, in particular, Sara Keating for her sterling efforts and hard work during the conference. We would also like to thank the Visual and Performing Arts Fund at Trinity College, Dublin, the Communications and Cultural Studies Research Committee at London Metropolitan University, Dublin City Council and the Cultural Division, Department of Foreign Affairs in Dublin and especially Michael Sanfrey, for generously providing funding for the conference.

Thanks to those at I.B.Tauris and Palgrave who have supported the project. Thanks also to Jessica Cuthbert-Smith for managing the project in its final stages.

Babies, family demands and changes in jobs have conspired to delay this project. Throughout, though, our families have endured with us the frustrations and patiently supported us. We owe an enormous debt of gratitude to them: Mike Allen and Olivia, Jon Akass, Daryl and Caitlin.

Last, but absolutely by no means least, our fellow conspirator and inspirational editor Philippa Brewster, who waited so patiently for this manuscript and *still* believed it would arrive. Over the years, she has stalwartly believed in our projects and encouraged us to bring them to fruition. We appreciate her consummate professionalism, her wise counsel, her intelligent observations, her incorrigible sense of humour and are so very proud to call her our friend. It is to her, with love, as always, that we dedicate this collection.

Preface

Robert J. Thompson

. . . .

Over 10 years ago, I wrote a book about 'quality television'. It was a very short book. There weren't that many shows to write about. A lot has happened since then.

Television's Second Golden Age documented the first phase of 'quality TV' on the American broadcast networks and, as it turned out, it was published just as a new phase was kicking in. That first phase stretched from the debut of *Hill Street Blues* in 1981 to the cancellation of *Twin Peaks* in 1991. 'Quality' shows were very specialised offerings of the networks during this period. There were only a few of them, and they were most conspicuous. Series like *Hill Street Blues*, *St. Elsewhere* and *Moonlighting* really stood out next to their generic contemporaries like *CHiPS*, *Trapper John, MD* and *Murder, She Wrote*. In fact, quality TV back then was best defined by what it was not: *Knight Rider*, *MacGyver* and the rest of 'regular' TV.

Then, in the early 1990s, something remarkable happened. *NYPD Blue* and *ER* reached Nielsen's top 10, and suddenly the quality TV aesthetic, which had been making modest inroads on the primetime schedules for several years, started spreading like a virus. Demographically conscious producers and network executives were now employing the quality TV style in a massive repackaging strategy across generic lines. It was a retooling comparable to the switchover to colour three decades earlier. 'Quality TV' had become a super-genre, a formula unto itself.

By the turn of the century, quality was busting out all over the networks. As far as hour-long dramas were concerned, it was hard to find a show in the autumn of 2000 that *wouldn't* have fallen into the category of 'quality TV' as defined in the 1980s. *The Practice*, *Ally McBeal* and *Boston Public*; *Buffy the Vampire Slayer*, *Angel* and *The X-Files*; *Once and Again*, *Judging Amy* and *Providence*; *Law & Order*, *The West Wing* and *City of Angels*: the quality style was everywhere. In fact, traditional TV series like *Walker, Texas Ranger* and *Nash Bridges* were looking pretty lonesome. The very shows against which we used to define quality TV were disappearing.

Needless to say, cable – both pay and basic – became an important player in this second phase of quality television. In fact, by the 1990s, cable had emerged as the principal test kitchen for innovation in television. It should be remembered, however, that cable followed broadcasting's lead, not the other way around. While the networks were ushering in the revolution of quality TV in the 1980s, cable was experimenting with TV series that could hardly be called 'quality'. As NBC was redefining the medium with shows like *Hill Street Blues*, HBO was still testing the series waters with such undistinguished programmes as *1st & Ten* and *The Hitchhiker*. It wasn't until *Tanner '88* and *The Larry Sanders Show* that HBO started raising its bar, years after network TV had begun setting new standards.

Once they put their minds to it, of course, the folks at HBO often outdid their network counterparts. The phrase 'an HBO-style series' has, in fact, now trumped 'quality TV' as a description of high artistic achievement in the medium. HBO's hubristic slogan picked up on the old idea of defining quality by what it isn't: 'It's not TV. It's HBO'. With no concerns about ratings (subscribers are what count), advertisers or federal regulations, HBO realised it could do what it pleased, and pretty much did. The string of series that included *Oz*, *The Sopranos*, *Sex and the City*, *The Wire*, *Curb Your Enthusiasm*, *Six Feet Under* and *Deadwood* went beyond anything imaginable in the old network era in terms of content, narrative complexity, language and lots more. Subsidised by hits, HBO could occasionally even defy its audience with fascinating but often incomprehensible art-house offerings like *K Street* and *Carnivàle* that the networks, even in the trippy days of *Twin Peaks*, would never have touched. Still, most of HBO's creators and producers had cut their teeth in broadcast TV – and had there been no *Hill Street Blues* there probably would have been no *Sopranos*.

Basic cable has also emerged in the past few years as a somewhat surprising venue for new iterations of quality TV. Who would have guessed 10 years ago that a basic cable channel like FX would be winning Emmy awards and critical acclaim with original programming? Still, after a daytime schedule crammed with reruns of *Spin City* and *Dharma and Greg*, FX has been slipping in high-end primetime series like *The Shield, Nip/Tuck, Rescue Me* and *Over There*. Midway between the freedoms of pay cable and the restrictions of broadcasting, basic cable channels like FX and Comedy Central have created new territories of television content.

At the very highest levels, broadcasting executives worried about their networks' futures in the face of *The Sopranos*. One response was to lean heavily upon the procedural dramatic franchises like *Law & Order* and *CSI*, which seemed to do just fine without cursing, nudity or scripts that sounded like they were written by comparative literature majors. The other was to load their schedules with reality TV, in which the cursing could be bleeped and the nudity (what little there was of it) could be digitally blurred. Though networks would probably be best to leave subject matter like organised crime to the pay cable channels that can do it justice, there are areas of quality TV in which broadcasting can still excel. *The West Wing*, for example, was probably a better show on NBC than it would have been on HBO. This highly stylised series turned out to be as much about language as it was about politics. Broadcast limitations forced the drama to come not from the use of forbidden words but from the complex gymnastics of syntax.

The DVD industry has also put important new forces into play for quality TV. In 1981, not everyone had a VCR, not many of those who did were efficient enough to record every episode of their favourite series, and not many of those who did that could find the right tape when they wanted it. The DVD changed all that. Unlike the home-video industry, which released small numbers of series episodes, the basic unit of release on DVD is an entire season, sometimes an entire series. Producers now make shows with the knowledge that each episode might be viewed and scrutinised over and over again.

The precise definition of 'quality TV' was elusive right from the start, though we knew it when we saw it. These shows were generic mongrels, often scrambling and recombining traditional TV formulas in unexpected ways; they had literary and cinematic ambitions beyond what we had seen before, and they employed complex and sophisticated serialised narratives and inter-series 'mythologies'. Back in the 1980s we breathlessly celebrated these new aesthetic approaches and challenges being taken on by a medium that had changed very little since the 1950s. But by the century's end, these innovations had become formulas.

About 12 years ago, I defined 'quality TV' with a list of a dozen characteristics. Now I can find a lot of shows on the air that exhibit all 12 characteristics but in the end, aren't really all that good. Also, I can find some spectacularly innovative programming – the first season of *Survivor*, for example – that aggressively resists the category of 'quality TV'.

What does 'quality TV' mean now? How is it adjusting to the multi-channel universe? Is the new television aesthetic developed in the 1980s continuing to transform the medium in positive and interesting ways? The essays that follow examine the state of the art of quality TV 25 years after its first appearance.

Introduction

Debating Quality

Janet McCabe and Kim Akass

. . . .

> How did the wasteland get so beautiful?
> Jonathan Storm, *Philadelphia Inquirer* (quoted in Harris 2006: 36)
>
> Judgements about the quality of television are made in a great many
> ways all the time – in speech, in newspapers, in practice – and on
> television . . . Judgements are being made – let's talk about them.
> Charlotte Brunsdon (1990a: 89, 90)

The initial impetus for this book came out of a conference we
organised at Trinity College, Dublin in April 2004. Something had
been happening on American TV, and we wanted to understand
the significance of this new wave of critically acclaimed drama
hitting our screens. Titled 'American Quality TV', the forum was
conceived, in part, to kindle discussion about the current state of
American television, and, in part, to debate ideas that had gained
currency within the academy about the term 'quality' in relation to
television (Feuer 1984; Brunsdon 1990a: 67–91; Corner 1994: 141–8;
Thompson 1996; Nelson 1997, 2006: 58–71; Jacobs 2001: 427–47;
Jancovich and Lyons 2003).

Instead, we unwittingly stirred up a minor storm. Even the call
for papers provoked reactions that we had not quite anticipated.
Misconceptions prevailed; charges of essentialism were levied.
Departmental meetings had colleagues sniggering, calling 'quality
television' an oxymoron. Others queried the criteria, while a few
quibbled over our examples. A television executive whom we had

invited to participate went as far as to question the relevance of such a conference, suggesting that we were behind the times and a tad naïve.

And maybe we were.

Looking back, it seems quite an audacious title. But, mindful of the debate, we were also being deliberately provocative, for there is something inherently divisive about the term quality – its meaning, its use, which often finds colleagues compelled to apply quotation marks as qualifiers around the word.

Even before a definition can be made, almost any discussion involving quality cannot escape issues of value judgement and personal taste. In her 1990 seminal article on the problems of quality published in *Screen*, Charlotte Brunsdon observes that 'any interrogation of what is, and could be, meant by 'quality' in a discussion of television' involves 'discourses of judgement' (1990a: 67). Pierre Bourdieu's highly contentious work (1986) on hierarchies of taste offers her a means of understanding why 'to have preferences which run against the hierarchy involves people in endless self-justification . . . or else in the polemic assertion of other hierarchies' (Brunsdon 1990a: 75). Given the traditional ephemeral nature of the medium, its relative novelty and its appeal to the mass audience, debates on taste and judgement are thus inevitably handicapped. Brunsdon insightfully identifies a central problem: 'there are *always issues of power* at stake in notions of quality and judgement – Quality for whom?, Judgement by whom?, On whose behalf?' (1990a: 73; emphasis ours).

Nonetheless, the controversy intrigued us and prompted this latest undertaking. Bringing together leading scholars, writers, industry insiders and practitioners, *Quality TV: Contemporary American Television and Beyond* invites debate on the term 'quality television', primarily in the context of American small-screen fictions. Each contributor aims to make sense of what quality TV means to our present television cultural zeitgeist. Striving to find appropriate methodologies, apt writing styles and different ways of talking about this notoriously contentious term, this collection emphasises difference and deliberately promotes discordant voices. It asks, what are the criteria used to define quality – taste, personal judgement, commercial success, industrial conditions, aesthetic values, product differentiation? Who defines it, and who has the right to intervene and judge what we mean by quality? Who is perceived as producing it, what are the attitudes of those behind the scenes, and for whom is it meant? Does quality mean the same in different cultural contexts, in different televisual 'flows' (Williams 1974)? Is it, indeed, an appropriate term at all?

It cannot be stressed enough that no easy answers emerge, and it is with this in mind that Karen Fricker's review of the conference for *The Irish Times* is reprinted. Its inclusion is meant to flag up those issues – those theoretical blockages, subjective factors and critical difficulties – expressed above. What follows in the rest of the collection are a number of timely and thought-provoking responses. From a range of very different perspectives, and cognisant of the difficulties involved in articulating the very term quality, authors provide varying accounts in an effort to explore different meanings, alternative definitions and fresh approaches to thinking about and studying quality television.

This book takes as its starting point 1996. That year saw the publication of Robert J. Thompson's *Television's Second Golden Age*, where he argued that 'Quality TV is best defined by what it is not. It is not "regular" TV' (1996: 13). Surveying a new type of programming that emerged in 1981 'thought ... better, more sophisticated, and more artistic than the usual network fare' (12), he set out a debate for defining quality that scholars have been disputing ever since. Furthermore, just as Thompson was analysing the 1980s institutionalisation of unique televisual primetime network shows like *Hill Street Blues*, *St. Elsewhere* and *thirtysomething*, something new was happening in American television. Changes in broadcast delivery, new systems of production and distribution, economic restructuring based on brand equity and market differentiation, and the rise to prominence of Home Box Office (HBO), whose tagline 'It's Not TV. It's HBO' characterises its quality marker, defines the post-1996, post-network era. For these reasons, Thompson has been invited to review the last 11 years in the preface to this collection.

Part 1, 'Defining Quality: Critical Judgements and Debate', deals with conceptual matters. Sarah Cardwell begins by noting 'that the recent high visibility of "American quality television" and the scholarship that focuses on it has opened up new possibilities for thinking about the question of quality versus good television'. She argues that this demarcation should train the television scholar's mind 'upon the act of critical judgement or evaluation' – a subject that up until now 'has been sorely neglected'. British academics, she notes, have long struggled with the term 'quality' (Caughie 2000; Brunsdon 1990a, 1997), either identifying it as having a privileged relationship with the real or annexing it to traditional high cultural forms like theatre and literature. Conversely, American TV scholars have fewer problems, partly because of the lingering tradition of evaluative criticism. Implicit in her discussion of textual features and aesthetic values – texts requiring close scrutiny not only as 'artefacts of popular culture' but also 'rich, complex artworks' – is that American quality TV has given a renewed impetus to discourses of evaluation and criticism.

Whereas the scheme for transforming quality into academic discourse has long demanded both critical and emotional distance (as observed by Cardwell), the discourse of TV journalism has always been concerned with making critical judgements about television (McArthur 1980: 59–61; Caughie 1984: 109–20; Poole 1984: 41–61; Lawson 2006b: 104–7). Personal opinion and a clear subjective voice are established imperatives; furthermore, as Brunsdon articulates, 'different taste codes and expectations of television are daily inscribed in newspapers in ways that casually employ targeted, but rather mixed criteria of judgement' (1990a: 82). Writing about quality television for the last 30 years, American television critic David Bianculli confirms how personal criteria and emotional response are central to his professional role and writing practice as a TV critic.

Notions of quality are nothing new, but instead have a long history. Robin Nelson, in his contribution, charts traditions of cultural value and what defines a quality TV artefact, both in the UK and the USA. Identifying shifts in criteria for evaluating television small-screen fictions as well as changes in social, economic and industrial discourses that have an impact on such thinking, he argues that the quality debate has an ever-changing history. His conclusion is that notions of quality are 'an open narrative of the broad cultural and institutional context of the evaluation and the valuer, rather than a closed resolution answering the question of worth for all time'.

The final two chapters in this section investigate the politics of quality in American television. Both explore how discourses of quality are often necessary before newer discourses can be properly articulated and/or accepted. Each chapter looks at how the term is often evoked at moments when television is attempting to utter the new and broadcasters are aspiring to locate a desirable demographic profile, namely those with disposable income so desired by advertisers. Ashley Sayeau's chapter considers how TV has been used to promote or dismiss women's rights as women were recognised as an important segment of the audience for networks. Looking back over the history of American sitcoms, she considers how quality granted programme makers permission to talk about, as well as propagate knowledge of, the changing place of women in American society. Our contribution looks at how HBO's original programming pushes the boundaries in broadcasting content by shrouding the modern illicit within a discourse of quality and making it somehow respectable. We describe how courting controversy has been institutionalised by HBO, in its unwritten rules, and embedded in and through its original programming, as a distinct feature of its cultural cachet, its quality brand label, its exclusivity, its difference from standard network fare and (until recently) its leading market position.

Cultural values influence institutional policy; business strategies affect programmes. Part 2, 'Defining Quality: Industry, Policy and Competitive Markets', explores cultural and institutional discourses of quality in terms of policy-making decisions, broadcasting mandates and production demands. In 1996, television programme makers and executives were confronted with a highly competitive market, one where economic survival and business success were dictated by factors that could never have been imagined before the arrival of multi-channel television and the cable revolution. Satellite transmission meant cable went from local to national, and even global. It gave rise to a diversity of new cable channels, from the superstations to those specialising in niche entertainments. 'Cable economies differ from broadcasting enough to make such diversity and niche-orientation possible' (Hilmes 2003b: 63). The new post-1996 era was driven by consumer demand and customer satisfaction as well as being shaped by digital technologies and technical innovations, and new ways of distribution in terms of international sales and global syndication.

Back in 2001, Scott Sassa, then president of NBC West Coast, and responsible for overseeing primetime hits like *The West Wing* and *Law & Order: Special Victims Unit*, is quoted as saying, 'The big lesson from cable is that people will watch what they want because they have choices, so you increasingly need to aim for a niche' (Friend

2001: 90). Jimmie L. Reeves, Mark C. Rogers and Michael M. Epstein develop such an idea in their chapter, where they discuss quality in terms of the 'political and economic ramifications of television in the age of digital reproduction'. Market forces in terms of quality control and brand equity, and the conversion of cultural currency into economic capital, are all considered through a case study of cable channel Comedy Central and its flagship programme *The Daily Show*. Key to their argument is the suggestion that '"quality control" . . . ranks as one of the organising principles in the logic of post–late capitalism'.

'Simply to survive producers now have to create and realise ideas that sell,' argues David Liddiment, creative director of All3 Media. 'Capturing the public imagination with innovative programmes that serve purposes other than delivering commercial impacts or increasing share is not necessarily at the top of their agenda' (2004: 4). Award-winning writer and producer Peter Dunne assesses professional codes and practices for making quality programmes as he charts his experiences of working in the American television industry over the last 30 years. Familiar with conflicting demands and the compromises that need to be made, he writes on how quality is ultimately censored by economic pragmatism, industrial trends and financial constraints. Offering an insider's account (often from bitter experience), he talks about the politics of producing quality drama: who has the power to commission it, who has the money to make it? This last question is something later picked up and developed by Máire Messenger Davies.

The last three chapters in this section look at quality from different national contexts, and the competing demands that can change the definition of quality as a TV product moves from one television flow into another. Long gone are the days when American programmes were cheap fillers on Irish and UK screens argues Dermot Horan, Acquisitions Director for Irish public broadcaster RTÉ. Now they are the most expensive television he buys. Citing the cyclical nature of quality television, Horan contemplates the demands placed upon him when he is acquiring individual programmes as well as package deals from America. What he has to consider is how they will be placed across the entire network schedule, cognisant of how they will function for the brand identity of individual RTÉ channels and attract particular audiences. Despite changes in taste and a preference for the local, as well as spiralling costs for quality series,

Horan concludes that quality for him is ultimately always about ensuring programmes that will attract 'an upscale audience, with plenty of spending power'.

Janet McCabe has written that the UK minority terrestrial Channel 4 has long made use of American television small-screen fictions like *ER* and *The West Wing* to define and strengthen its own corporate identity as it repositions these shows as quality (2005: 207–23). In recent times, the rebranded Channel 5 has increasingly relied on a similar strategy to elevate its institutional status within the British broadcasting context. Tim Gardam, writing in the London *Evening Standard*, confirms this trend, saying that the 'best American drama on British television is now on Five' (2006: 39). Citing *House, M.D.* as an example of how the channel is finding ratings success over other terrestrial channels, he suggests that it is overtaking Channel 4 in finding the more 'adventurous' US shows. It is a point developed by Ian Goode in his chapter, as he looks at how the 'America's Finest' campaign has resuscitated the fortunes of the UK channel better known for late-night soft porn and football. Goode argues that these programmes are inherently signalled as quality, used, as they are, to endorse a quality brand for a previously inferior channel.

Foreign territories may now bid huge sums for American programmes, using them to brand channels and locate a quality demographic, but all television markets are subject to state intervention, government regulation/de-regulation and national policy debates. Definitions of quality in this context are inherently conservative in terms of a need to protect indigenous markets as well as preserve cultural values and national identity. Geoff Lealand takes up such debates, and updates his thinking on quality television in the context of New Zealand, where he identifies what is meant by quality in a national context where American television is marginalised and the local output dominates. Public service broadcasting prevails and guides standards on programme strategy and practice. Criteria for defining quality and judging what it is are deeply embedded in this remit, made visible in and through cultural policy, government funding and guidelines.

Moving the discussion on from critical arguments and institutional concerns to focus specifically on the televisual product, Part 3, 'Defining Quality: Aesthetics, Form, Content', deals with textual and aesthetic matters. The first two chapters define quality textual and aesthetic components, and begin with Jane Feuer engaging with many of the issues she first raised in her 1984 seminal account, chronicling the influx of American television programmes produced by MTM Enterprises. Identifying a complex politics at work involving the producers, programme makers and audience, Feuer contends that, 'In interpreting an MTM programme as a quality programme, the quality audience is permitted to enjoy a form of television which is seen as more literate, more stylistically complex, and more psychologically "deep" than ordinary television fare' (56). In Robert J. Thompson's opinion, 'without MTM Enterprises . . . there would likely have been no second Golden Age of television . . . [in fact the company] went on to define the standard of quality in the television industry' (1996: 46).

In 1996, Thompson listed specific defining characteristics of quality TV, to argue that 'quality [drama] has become a genre in itself, complete with its own set of formulaic characteristics' (16). Feuer, in this collection, revises and advances the debate with an analysis of what constitutes quality today. Focusing on two drama series considered 'quality' – *The West Wing* and *Six Feet Under* – her chapter reveals the complex definitions in play but rooted in a longer tradition of quality American drama. For Feuer, *The West Wing* makes claims to quality status, representing how primetime has institutionalised past definitions of quality brought to television that will appeal to a mass audience while creating something new, something 'not TV' in fact. *Six Feet Under*, on the other hand, aspires to creating quality through absorbing élite modernist art conventions to make a uniquely televisual product for a more select audience. Innovation here has recourse to older, more established art traditions. It leads one to ask if co-opting prestigious cultural affiliations is necessary before the new can be formulated and accepted into something different, something innovative and groundbreaking.

Innovations in production techniques have enabled TV series to produce visual effects similar to ones that were once only seen in Hollywood movies. Moreover, as more homes install widescreen, plasma and HD (high-definition) television sets and state-of-the art Dolby sound systems, consumers demand content that keeps up with these advances. Such innovations have further contributed to television now becoming a medium that rivals film for entertainment. Offering his perspective on quality TV, Jonathan

Bignell develops such an approach to suggest that industrial and institutional factors have contributed to the creation of a high-end television aesthetic. Analysing how *mise-en-scène* relates to generic components of the contemporary US police/investigation series, and *CSI* in particular, Bignell understands quality in terms of television style and its appeal to a media-savvy audience.

Underlying the centrality to contemporary debates of *Hill Street Blues* as establishing the quality television drama as a uniquely televisual form is the emergence of the writer-producer. Michele Hilmes credits the pioneering cop show and its creator Steven Bochco with defining new standards of quality that inaugurated, she argues, 'one of the most creative periods in traditional broadcasting [with] "producer/auteurs" able to exercise a greater degree of creative control over the programmes than they had before' (2002: 305). Talking about Bochco, she says:

> As one of television's premier auteurs in a fragmented business that provided few forms of continuity, his name had begun to mean more in terms of genre, quality, style, and audience than did the name of the network his show appeared on. The stamp of the author – even when actual authorship was somewhat removed by the production practice of television – gave a program a degree of authenticity and legitimacy absent from television's earlier decades (312).

Transformations taking place within the industry, as broadcasters 'struggled for ratings in a multi-channel, fragmented audience environment' (Pearson 2005: 11), are responsible for the above and discussed in the three subsequent chapters, which explore how the writer-producer functions as a protector, guarantor and organiser of quality in the post-network, post-1996 television age. Interrogating ideas of television authorship and professional practice, and interviewing writer-producers who worked on the *Star Trek* franchise, Máire Messenger Davies 'raises issues of authorship, value and the nature of creativity in an industrially mass-produced medium: television, with particular reference to the contributions of writers'.

'All great shows flow from the pen of a writer,' writes John Rash, Professor of Communications at the University of Minnesota (quoted in Harris 2006: 36). A bold statement indeed, but it does seem that in recent times American broadcasters are once again emphasising the importance of authoring as a means of distinguishing their products from regular TV. Using the idea of the author as brand label of quality and exclusivity, they are institutionalising the writer-producer as a strategy. HBO, for example, financially supports and trusts – or so its aggressive marketing campaign tells us – its creative teams to come up with something special and to produce 'quality'. Reprinted in full is Mark Lawson's BBC4 interview with David Chase, creator of *The Sopranos*. Chase has emerged as *the* TV auteur of the TVIII age; or, as Chase himself says in the interview, a brand. This is, then, followed by an interview with another television auteur, W.G. 'Snuffy' Walden, who has emerged as a leading musical auteur of primetime quality. He talks here to Peter Kaye about scoring *The West Wing*.

As we edge closer to a shift from analogue to digital, consumers are enjoying ever more control over content, with more choice about what to watch, where to watch it and when. Mark Lawson, discussing how TV box sets are now dominating the DVD charts in the UK, even warranting their own 'separate hit parade' (2006a: 5), says 'the fact that the majority of the most popular boxed shows are cultish American dramas confirms . . . [that shows like *The Simpsons, Friends, The West Wing, The Sopranos, Sex and the City*] are shows that have played on minority channels in Britain, their audience eventually reduced to a core audience that is demographically likely to have included the kind of income-rich, time-poor viewers who like to believe that they are in control of their own lives' (7). The television-viewing experience may have been transformed with the box set, but, as David Lavery argues, the companion book also enriches it. Giving context to hours of television, investing it with prior narratives and backstories, the quality companion book adds additional weight, nuance and significance to the narrative of shows like *The Sopranos* and *Six Feet Under*.

When this manuscript was submitted, America's networks had launched 25 new shows for the autumn 2006 schedule, an unprecedented 16 of these were dramas and most had multi-layered storylines and complex characters involved in ambiguous moral dilemmas. *Studio 60 on the Sunset Strip*, created by Aaron Sorkin (and cancelled after only one season), portrayed life behind the scenes of a top TV comedy show, and gave the writer complete creative control, something he had never had on *The West Wing*. *The Nine* tells the story, through a series of flashbacks, of a hostage-taking during a bank robbery; another was *Six Degrees* (also cancelled after the first season), which linked six seemingly unconnected Manhattan dwellers; and *Heroes* deals with a group of teens struggling with their newly discovered superpowers and the trials and tribulations that follow. It is certainly no small coincidence that these shows built on the immensely successful formula instigated by breakthrough ABC hit *Lost*. Roberta Pearson, in her afterthoughts piece, examines the phenomenon of the castaway series as she looks forward to the post-television era – and asks if this new TV age will 'see an increased valuing of authorship, a further re-evaluation of cultural hierarchies, with television seen as cinema's equal or superior, a rise in the critical and commercial stock of genre shows, [and] even more emphasis upon international distribution'.

'The enormous success of the dense and literate *Lost* has stimulated networks to develop shows of a similar complex nature' contends Robert J. Thompson (quoted in Harris 2006: 36). Ever since *Hill Street Blues* in the early 1980s, American TV has been known for producing intelligent high-quality shows, but rarely have so many quality shows been released at once. This anthology is published at the very moment when something new seems to be happening again. What we hope is that definitions of quality offered in this collection will stimulate fresh questions as we enter the post-analogue, post-*Sopranos* age.

'Quality TV' On Show

The Irish Times' review of 'Quality American
Television' international conference, held at
Trinity College, Dublin in 2004

Karen Fricker

It sounds like a scene from *The Simpsons*: a bunch of intellectuals
spending a whole weekend shouting at each other about what
defines quality on television. 'Is network versus HBO a false
dichotomy?' wonders one participant. 'The structured ambiguity
of *Six Feet Under* self-identifies with modernist art and literature,'
opines another. Still another: 'Is *24* an anti-feminist text of male
resentment and/or a rebellion against female emancipation?'

A lot of big words, and, in a few cases, some fairly over-inflated
and surprisingly defensive arguments. But by and large, the
conference at Trinity College, Dublin achieved its aims of advancing
understanding of its subject – 'American quality TV' – within
television and media studies, and certainly provided a fascinating
vantage point for this outsider into the internal dialogue of a fast-
advancing and contentious field of study. The conference was
organised by lecturers Janet McCabe of Trinity College, and Kim
Akass of London Metropolitan University, under the auspices of
their two institutions and the Department of Foreign Affairs. Some
75 participants from eight countries came together to debate one of
the hotter questions in contemporary media studies – what actually
defines the field now known as 'American quality TV'?

The term came into circulation after the publication of American
academic Robert J. Thompson's 1996 volume *Television's Second
Golden Age: From Hill Street Blues to ER*, in which he laid down 12

criteria for inclusion in the field, among them that American quality TV breaks the rules of established television; it is produced by people of quality aesthetic ancestry outside the field of television; it attracts a blue-chip audience; uses ensemble casts and multiple, overlapping plot lines that indicate literary values; includes social and cultural criticism; and creates a new genre by combining old ones (1996: 12–16).

In other words, is American Quality TV better than crappy old ordinary TV? There is certainly more than a whiff of élitism and dismissal around Thompson's criteria; it could be argued (and was, vehemently, all weekend) that in Thompson's terms, American Quality TV is TV that wishes it weren't television at all, but something 'better' and more artistically worthy. Part of the problem is that Thompson chose a word to describe the field that seems to contain a value judgment, when in fact the best way to use the term 'quality' may be simply as the delineator of a certain kind of television programme that is currently in vogue.

If we are to understand American Quality TV as a genre, then, the most useful short definition of it came from American freelance writer and conference participant Ashley [Sayeau]: 'politically engaged, often independent TV that aims to enlighten, as well as to entertain'. The golden children of this 'new golden age'? *Buffy the Vampire Slayer, Angel, The Sopranos, Sex and the City, Six Feet Under, The West Wing, ER* and, to the surprise of many, *24*, which was the subject of more papers – seven – than any other programme. What was perhaps most troubling about the conference to me was the emphasis in many papers on the aesthetic and formal qualities of the programmes discussed, often at the expense of any consideration of their content, and the ways they might play into real-life relations of power and politics.

Television is, after all, a vastly influential medium, and the conference was convened to discuss programmes created by the world's most powerful nation. As Rod Stoneman – former CEO of the Irish Film Board and now director of the Huston School of Film and Digital Media at the National University of Ireland, Galway – pointed out in one of the weekend's most politically engaged (and, sadly, shortest) contributions, American television is one of 'the most important sites of contestation in today's world . . . there is a lot at stake'.

Television disperses images and ideas that affect and shape how billions of people see themselves and each other; one of the weekend's more eye-opening contributions was that of Barbara Villez from the Université de Paris 8, who argued that watching *Ally McBeal* has shaped her students' understanding of not just the American, but the French legal system – that is, her French students regularly seem surprised when it's revealed to them that their own legal system differs radically from the fictionalised American one they see on their TV screens. Scary – but sadly believable.

Given this, papers on topics like 'Genre Hybridity in *Angel*' had the smack of frivolousness about them, and the assertion by keynote speaker Jane Feuer, of the University of Pittsburgh, that her discussion about how cinema and theatre use their formal qualities to 'deflate' television was 'political', felt downright risible. However, according to many at the conference, this is a necessary phase in the intellectual field of television studies, which started out as a discussion mainly of ideology and is now moving through a necessary phase of aestheticism.

Because we live in a time in which all the master systems of understanding have broken down, in which ideas like 'meaning', 'reality' and 'value' have been called into question, with what set of criteria do we start to reassemble a language with which to evaluate how a book, play, or indeed television series creates meaning? The answer of Roberta Pearson, from the University of Nottingham, and Máire Messenger Davies, the incoming chair of Media Studies at the University of Ulster, is head-wreckingly simple: talk to the people who make the shows themselves.

For their forthcoming book about *Star Trek*, Pearson and Messenger Davies interviewed many of the creative personnel behind the highly successful science-fiction franchise – a Trekkie's wildest fantasy, to be sure, but also a way of working towards an understanding of the television industry's internal value systems. On the same panel, Robin Nelson of Manchester Metropolitan University offered useful insight in the evolution from the big-three networks' insistence on 'least objectionable programming' to the cable and digital era, in which the focus has shifted from distribution to production and to membership channels which need appeal only to their subscribers.

The weekend's best papers – as with any good scholarship – offered specific and focused arguments that referenced established critical theory and made tangible connections between the programmes they were discussing and the ways in which we, as viewers, see the world. Conference organisers McCabe and Akass offered a subtly argued paper about the 'problematic' mother–daughter relationship in *Six Feet Under*, a programme whose starting point was literally the death of patriarchy in the form of father Nathaniel's unexpected contact with a fast-moving bus.

On the same panel, Ashley [Sayeau] provided useful background about the 'older sisters' of today's 'quality heroines', arguing that Mary Tyler Moore, Maude, Murphy Brown, and even Wonder Woman reflected the changing circumstances of women's place in American society and at some times helped to advance that status. Trinity's Eric Weitz delivered a fabulously entertaining paper, which attempted a definition of 'quality humour' through a discussion of, and well-chosen clips from, *The Simpsons*. My world was perhaps most rocked by the argument of Paul Woolf from the University of Birmingham about the sponsorship of *24* by the Ford Motor Company: what happens to the series' putatively anti-war status, wondered Woolf, given its rampant product placement of gas-guzzling Ford Sports Utility Vehicles, which have been controversially pinpointed as contributing to the War on Terror by a centre-right-wing American lobby group?

On its final panel, elegantly chaired by a real-life television personality – *The Late Review*'s Mark Lawson – the conference's focus shifted to the local with an impressive and surprising paper from RTÉ's director of broadcasting and acquisitions, Dermot Horan. The American programmes that had provoked so much critical energy all weekend are actually of waning interest in Ireland and across Europe, revealed Horan; the current trend internationally is towards local programming, and local remakes of international 'brands' such as *Who Wants to be a Millionaire?*, *Pop Idol* and *Big Brother*.

And so, shouldn't we really be talking about the 'other' major television trend, the spectre of which hung thunderously over the conference all weekend – reality TV? After all, as Jane Feuer now had the chance to argue, reality programmes are 'radically new, for better or worse, and more in touch with the cultural moment'. Doesn't *The Bachelor*, in its way, really have more to say about 'the horror of modern life' than *Sex and the City*? Oh God. I feel a conference coming on.

Original appeared on 12 April 2004 and reprinted here with kind permission of *The Irish Times*.

PART 1

Defining Quality
Critical Judgements and Debate

1
Is Quality Television Any Good?

Generic Distinctions, Evaluations and the
Troubling Matter of Critical Judgement
Sarah Cardwell

· ·

What is 'quality television'? Is it the same as 'good television'? If
not, what relation do they bear to one another? Viewers, critics and
scholars persistently draw curious distinctions between quality and
good television, and yet simultaneously find themselves implicitly
asserting overlaps between the two. This chapter draws out a range of
features by which the two categories might be distinguished, while
acknowledging some of the ways in which they are interrelated,
and questions the usefulness of demarcating the two. The recent
high visibility of 'American quality television' and the scholarship
that focuses on it has opened up new possibilities for thinking
about the question of quality versus good television. Ultimately,
and invaluably, these issues focus the television scholar's mind
upon the act of critical judgement or evaluation, broadly conceived
– a subject that has been sorely neglected in the field until now.

It is clearly unrealistic to hope for an immediate clarification,
let alone resolution, of complex and abiding concerns regarding
the role of critical judgement within television studies. Indeed,
unsurprisingly, when we are determined to speak more carefully
and reflexively about quality and good television, about evaluation
and critical judgement, about criteria and discrimination, our
understanding of television as an art form appears to be complicated

rather than simplified. However, the process is invigorating, for we are also able to lay out some tentative distinctions and to be more precise, honest and reflective in our assessments of programmes. Television studies has for too long lacked sufficient attention to detail in conceptual matters (and indeed in textual analysis). The aim of this chapter is therefore to proffer some claims regarding quality and good television in order to provoke the reader through exposing and perhaps unsettling his or her assumptions about the evaluation of television programmes. Polemically, this chapter urges that we all examine more closely and disclose more honestly our own systems and criteria of judgement, and engage more deeply with those television programmes we deem worthy of such engagement.

Quality: A Generic Classification

In the week that my television students watched the 1995 classic-novel adaptation of *Persuasion*, one student responded intriguingly with the statement, 'I could see it was quality television, but I didn't like it'; when questioned further, he suggested that he found the programme 'boring'. His reaction, which is by no means an atypical response to artworks, including television programmes, raises some interesting questions. Perhaps the central question is this: if the student did not enjoy the programme, if he did not value it, or experience it in positive ways, why did he say it was 'quality television'? What does it mean to call something quality television?

The most reasonable answer here is that the student had identified certain textual characteristics that signify or represent high quality; in fact, when pressed on this matter, he acknowledged that the programme was carefully constructed, well acted, well filmed and based on a good story adapted from a classic novel. In view of these assessments, the student felt that he 'should' have liked it – and yet he did not. So he tempered his own, intuitive response with a statement about how he could see that the programme was of high quality.

What this instance exposes is one aspect of the intricate and sometimes rather curious system of judgement we use to assess texts. We are able to conclude that something is of high quality based not on our own experience or critical judgement of it, but on our recognition of particular aesthetic features it contains. At this level, to label something 'quality television' is more like making a generic classification: it is comparable to agreeing that a certain film is a Western. This part of the process is more dependent upon the observation and apprehension of textual qualities than on our immediate, subjective responses, emotions and evaluations. Thus, in spite of feeling 'bored' by *Persuasion*, the student wished to assert that it was quality television and to credit it with several praiseworthy characteristics.

A further facet of commonplace conceptions of 'quality' is also evident here: to label something with the word is not necessarily synonymous with offering a personal endorsement; we can make a distinction between categorising something 'generically' as quality television, and offering a considered evaluation that the same programme is 'good'. Quality television may be perceived as being good *for* its viewers – morally or educationally edifying – but it may still be experienced as worthy, dull, conventional or pretentious.

The assessment of a programme as *good* television, in contrast – while it is indeed determined by that programme's particular aesthetic qualities – is more aptly defined by the audience's experience of it. Good television is rich, riveting, moving, provocative and frequently contemporary (in some sense); it is relevant to and valued by us. It speaks to us, and it endures for us. If the student had enjoyed the programme, he would perhaps have described it as *good* television as well as quality television.

I shall elaborate further on this distinction between quality and good television later. At this point one final observation is necessary. The student's response also suggests that the recognition of quality and the perception of 'value' (i.e. the generic classification and the personal evaluation) are hard to separate completely. If a programme is regarded as being quality television, viewers may feel more compelled to give it a chance, to remain more open to seeing its attributes for themselves. That is, critical evaluations may be more subjective, based on our own experiences, our feelings of like or dislike,[1] but they are also framed by broad, culturally specific understandings of what is considered good quality. In the case of *Persuasion* cited above, the student was aware of at least two previous 'evaluations' of the programme. First, he was aware that it was considered quality television, and this implies not just certain generic features but also a broad cultural consensus that the programme exhibits potentially impressive characteristics – it is regarded with a certain 'seriousness'. Second, the student knew that I had chosen to screen the programme on my television aesthetics course; he could therefore assume that I considered it to have significant enough merits to warrant its study. This guided him in seeking out the qualities of the text that I might have chosen to value, rather than dismissing the programme on the basis of a personal preference. He sought to 'balance' his view, in recognition of the critical evaluation of another, significant person and that of a wider milieu. This is a microcosmic instance of a viewer being aware of what we could call a 'critical community', which determines what is to be classified as quality, and which appears to imply that we ought also to find those high-quality texts *good*, and value them appropriately.

Problems with Quality Television

So what are the 'generic' traits of quality television, and why have they come to be regarded as potentially valuable or good? Interestingly, classifications of quality television appear to be deeply affected by national context. Contemporary British quality television differs from its American counterpart; similarly, the critical community of scholars and critics appears to take a different stance towards these two groups of programmes. The stance most commonly taken towards *American* quality television enhances the possibilities for future television scholarship.

Academics writing about British quality television seem to exhibit a level of discomfort with their subject matter.[2] They seek to maintain not so much a *critical* distance as an *emotional* distance from such programmes. It is intriguing to note the underlying struggle in such academic writing: scholars fluctuate between taking up a rather superior stand over these programmes, regarding them as somehow manufactured, mediocre, trying too hard, and yet simultaneously exhibiting a sympathy with and respect for some of their key features – especially those of 'realism' and attention to detail.

There is perhaps a concern that quality television is a commercial wheeze, an over-priced product that, at root, is little different from its cheaper variations (the unfortunate modern connotations of the word 'quality' that have been endowed upon it through its being appended to far too many mediocre boxes of chocolates and other consumables). Such a fear – or prejudice – is evident in John Caughie's claim that quality television is actually 'a middle-brow term' (2000: 210); he hopes to undermine its supposed pretensions to grandeur and cut it down to size. There is an élitist tone in his criticism, which is not to say that he is incorrect, but simply to note that, in assimilating all quality television to the mediocre, Caughie reveals his anxiety about seeming to admire such programmes. The middle-brow is regarded as inauthentic – neither proudly popular or plebeian nor firmly highbrow and artistic. Instead it panders to the middle ground – and to the middle classes, who have not fared well within television studies, given the Marxist history of the field and the prominence of theorists who hold special scorn and the sharpest criticism for any work with bourgeois aspirations or connotations.[3]

Caughie's implication that quality television is not necessarily *good* television is useful, though, for it also reveals a laudable desire to make precisely that distinction I outlined above: between quality television (the generic product) on the one hand and good television (serious drama, worthy of his critical attention) on the other. Charlotte Brunsdon echoes this when, revisiting the topic of quality and good television, she clarifies her own understanding of the difference between the two, positing a similar distinction, and suggesting that 'the point about this adjectival/generic distinction [quality television] is that it makes it possible to think about bad "quality television" and indeed good non-quality television' (1997: 108). That is, by recognising quality as a generic description rather than a term of positive critical evaluation, we are able to engage more straightforwardly and with fewer reservations in the evaluation of all television.

What one may take from the study of British quality television, therefore, is the reasonable and useful desire to avoid assuming that quality television is synonymous with good television; this respects the commonplace experience of viewers, as is shown by my student's response to *Persuasion*. Yet this has been accompanied by a broader reluctance to establish what the key features of quality and good television are – and especially to engage with the question of what good television is (Caughie, Brunsdon and Jason Jacobs are notable exceptions here).[4] Unlike critics, whose jobs depend upon their making discriminations between and evaluations of programmes, television studies scholars have been far too unwilling to stake their claims about individual programmes. Relatively comfortable with the categorising of programmes as 'quality television', even if uncomfortable with the connotations of that label, scholars have chosen to accept the notion of quality television while avoiding tricky claims about what is actually *good*.

American Quality Television

Those scholars writing about American quality television appear to be less perturbed by the quality/value[5] debate, and seem to be more comfortable offering unequivocally positive evaluations of quality programmes. Less concerned with distinguishing quality television from good television, scholars have been far more willing to accept the categorisation of a programme as quality television as an indication that it is also *good* television worthy of study. There is little of the reticence or ambivalence found in British writing on, for example, classic British literary adaptations when one reads articles about American contemporary quality television.[6]

For example, Christina Lane, in her essay on *The West Wing*, writes:

> Following the tradition of 'quality programs' such as *NYPD Blue* and *ER*, Warner Bros.' *The West Wing* dramatizes the moral ambiguity and complex, layered relationships between the private and public spheres. Drawing on numerous 'quality' conventions and styles, the NBC program employs ensemble casting, mobile camerawork, densely packed visual fields, hot splashes of light, accelerated pace, and narrative velocity in order to dramatize the complex questions it asks... *The West Wing* launches a number of contradictory positions while maintaining, through three-dimensional characterization and mastery of dialogue, a moral center that subtly and precariously stands up to repeated challenges (2003: 32).

Here, quality is initially spoken of as a set of conventions and stylistic features. This, however, is quickly accompanied by Lane's positive evaluation of the programme and her desire to present it as worthy of critical attention – it is depicted simultaneously as being *good* television. This reflects the more widespread practice when scholars deal with American quality television rather than British quality television: there is a greater acceptance of the commercial and cultural association between quality and value – that is, scholars appear more willing to assume that American quality television is likely to warrant serious critical attention and that American quality television is also good television.

Lane thus conflates quality with value: she couches her critical judgement in terms of 'quality', condoning an association between the two. But there is still some anxiety evident in her writing. Throughout her essay, Lane puts the word 'quality' in inverted commas, following the predominant tendency in television studies. This suggests an excessive caution, as if she is afraid to lay her cards on the table and assert her critical judgement. It is as if to say that she esteems the programme but that, if push came to shove, she would not impose that view upon others. It is to put inverted commas around the very practice of critical judgement (I shall return to this later).

Lane writes of the traditions and conventions of quality television as if these were widely known and recognised. Although 'quality television' is not a genre in a true sense, she is correct to assume common awareness of continuities within this group of programmes. The call for papers for the 'American Quality Television' conference, which inspired this collection, offered a list of programmes as potential texts for discussion. These were: *St. Elsewhere, Hill Street Blues, thirtysomething, Twin Peaks, The X-Files, Buffy the Vampire Slayer, ER, The Sopranos, Sex and the City* and *Six Feet Under*. My immediate, instinctive response was to spot omissions and challenge wrongful inclusions. Why wasn't *The West Wing* included? Why had they listed *Buffy, ER* and *The X-Files*? Friends and colleagues eagerly contributed to this discussion of the programmes the list 'should' have contained.

The first thing indicated by my and others' responses is that we shared an experience and awareness of the generic nature of quality television. I and my interlocutors accepted the concept of such a list of programmes, and felt that the list constituted a coherent 'set', like a genre, in which there are texts that, although different, belong together in some way. There was a sense of connection, continuity, even development, across the group. This explains our reactions, our attempts to amend and refine the list; we perceived that there existed here a sense of 'group identity' that typified contemporary American quality television.

How can this identity be defined? What is creating it? As with a generic group, are we able to determine particular aesthetic features – elements of style, for example – that connect the programmes? How else could they be classed together, given their disparate subject matters, as a 'strand' of television? And most pertinently, what clues are provided in the word 'quality', which is suggested as the connecting feature of the group? What does an indicator of quality look like? If we can determine this, we can determine the reasons that this set of programmes might coherently and logically be grouped together.

Continuing with the generic analogy, let us consider how one might classify programmes as quality television on the basis of their exhibiting certain textual characteristics of content, structure, theme and tone. American quality television programmes tend to exhibit high production values, naturalistic performance styles, recognised and esteemed actors, a sense of visual style created through careful, even innovative, camerawork and editing, and a sense of aural style created through the judicious use of appropriate, even original music. This moves beyond a 'glossiness' of style. Generally, there is a sense of stylistic integrity, in which themes and style are intertwined in an expressive and impressive way. Further, the programmes are likely to explore 'serious' themes, rather than representing the superficial events of life; they are likely to suggest that the viewer will be rewarded for seeking out greater symbolic or emotional resonance within the details of the programme. American quality television also tends to focus on the present, offering reflections on contemporary society, and crystallising these reflections within smaller examples and instances. The 'everyday incidents' that are the stuff of more straightforward, non-quality soap operas and sitcoms are here transformed by a suggestion that they may be read symbolically, reflexively or obliquely in order that broader truths about life or society might be found.

Returning to the example of *The West Wing*, Lane correctly notes the high production values, weighty themes and careful characterisations and performances that imply that we are in the presence of 'quality television'. Further features are present in the programme that indicate that the audience ought to classify it thus, such as the foregrounding of the creative impulse and artistic vision of the creator and original screenwriter Aaron Sorkin, which adds prestige and a sense of artistic integrity, and suggests that the series should be more highly valued.

Other aspects encourage an intense level of audience appreciation and engagement, such as the complex narrative structure, its intricate themes, its use of erudite, technical, oratorical and even poetic language, and its fast-paced style. We are shuttled between scenes, between moments; this implies a more developed creative vision and technical skill, and reaffirms the necessity that the viewer concentrate. This higher level of engagement is considered to be another feature of high-quality television. It also places the viewer into the active position that one takes up when making a critical judgement. The programme encourages us to interpret and evaluate it.

It is clear that *The West Wing* shares with soap operas and other melodramas an interest in interpersonal relationships. But *The West Wing* offers a more intricate, eloquent and ambiguous exploration of these. It also presents characters as social and political actors, as players within a larger scheme, not just as emotional individuals. The series foregrounds their interrelationships as fluctuating, changing, subtle and profoundly affected by bigger things: politics, ethics, work, history and so on. Take the credit sequence as an example: we see black and white photographic shots of characters, which echo official news or documentary images, as well as moving shots that capture the real person 'behind' the official role. This is especially true of the last three shots of the president, where we move from an official shot, to him as seen by his team, to him alone, unaware of being observed. This movement promises us privileged access, right up to the top of the hierarchy and the president as fulcrum; it promises that the programme will bring us closer to the human beings behind the news stories. Consider, too, the music: it is inspiring, grandiose, overstated. This reflects the idealistic framework of the series. The programme presents a kind of perfect public sphere in which ideals and principles are central, and the characters are under pressure to negotiate these ideals in the face of the gritty realities of real, political life. The programme itself is not idealistic but it engages with ideals. This is captured here in the credits. The powerful, inspiring music integrates with the images of active, concerned characters to reflect carefully and honestly the kind of dynamic that informs the action. The credits have stylistic integrity, accurately and expressively revealing the programme's concerns, themes and emphases.

These qualities can similarly be found in other examples of American quality television. Consider, for example, *Six Feet Under* and *Nip/Tuck*. Each of these programmes exhibits a similar 'glossiness' of style and a seriousness of content at a thematic level. Rather than focusing solely on a series of events, these programmes draw out thematic connections, subtle interrelations and echoes between those events. Each programme tackles contemporary inflections of themes that have affected humankind for centuries: death, dying and, conversely, life and living, in the case of the former, and the relationship between our selves and our bodies, our identities and our images, in the latter. Interestingly, each of these programmes echo the form of *The West Wing*, for they posit a relationship – couched often but not always in terms of a disparity – between the mythic or ideal and the actualities of everyday, lived life. In proffering particular instances of life and death, *Six Feet Under* presents protagonists who encounter the difficult experience of reconciling ideals and beliefs about life and death with the more prosaic experience of these things. In *Nip/Tuck*, the stark, clinical reality of carving 'better' bodies out of our original ones is examined alongside all the dreams, hopes and insecurities that are wrapped up within those bodies, suggesting that an individual's personhood is not reducible to, but is inextricably involved in, the body that contains it. The reflective and thoughtful qualities of these programmes thus arise because they place the ideal (in its primary sense) alongside the real – and this is one of the key features that distinguish them from soaps, which are firmly committed to examining the real.

These shared thematic preoccupations are also suggesting shared aesthetic choices, though the programmes are stylistically diverse. Fragmentation in the form of abstraction is commonly employed, for example, allowing the focus to be narrowed to a small detail that is nevertheless connotatively rich and encourages interpretative work on the part of the viewer. This technique is especially clear in credit sequences, which also exhibit an 'art film' aesthetic. Of course, many television credit sequences employ fragmentation, and some employ it in the form of abstraction, but most credits do not objectify or defamiliarise to the extent seen in quality television.

The opening of *Six Feet Under* is a good example of such defamiliarisation. An opening chord chimes and a large black crow flutters across the top right-hand corner of the screen against an unusually deep blue-green sky. The camera tilts downwards, framing a solitary tree, beneath which is an expanse of dark earth. The limited palette of colours, blanket lighting and lack of shading mean that perspective is unclear, and this image feels flattened. Two hands are framed at the bottom of the image, large in front of the background; they are clearly some distance forward of the tree and, because of the flattened effect, they seem to be in another plane altogether. As a further chord chimes, the two hands move upwards, straining their grasp on one another, and then pull sharply away from one another, as if torn apart against their will. The movement subsequently slows as the hands continue to move apart, but more slowly, as if drifting, floating in space. The use of non-naturalistic colours and composition, and the music that coincides carefully with the movement on screen, suggest a strange 'staged' quality, implying that the image is there for a symbolic purpose – it asks to be interpreted. The hands that are torn reluctantly and suddenly apart, and gradually fade from one another, present in abstraction an image of the experience of death. Yet the image is not reducible to this verbal meaning but expresses the meaning in a particular and emotive form.[7]

Abstractions and defamiliarisation are also found in the credit sequence for *Nip/Tuck*, in which perfectly constructed shop dummies exhibit occasional and unnerving signs of life, and gradually blend to form a real, 'perfect' human being. The sudden, pulsing jolt of an apparently inanimate white plastic hand lends an eerie quality to the credits, while the accompanying fast, low drum beat implies a frantically beating heart, conveying the sense of a threat perceived by a real, living, fragile body. As in *Six Feet Under*, the opening credit images play with perspective and depth, using white shapes on white backgrounds so that the bodies are in one moment two-dimensional drawings, in the next moment three-dimensional models. Defamiliarisation and abstraction again lead the viewer to interpret and ruminate on the question of human and social identity, and their relation to the bodies that are distorted in pursuit of artificial perfection.

So What is Good Television?

The purpose of drawing out such shared features was simply to suggest that these three programmes fit together into the category quality television – rather than to support a claim that the programmes should be highly valued as good television. To notice a programme's signifiers of quality is not to assert anything about its value.

Yet I believe these qualities also make them good. That is, I would argue that many of those attributes that define quality television are also ones that may relatively reliably contribute to making a programme a good one.[8] They do so because such attributes enable the viewer to watch the programme repeatedly and to draw and revise various interpretations, and those interpretations reveal the programme to be coherent at the level of *stylistic integrity*. In good television there is a high level of synthesis and cohesion between stylistic choices and the programmes' 'meanings'. The way a camera moves, the moment at which a cut is made, the choice to frame a character in mid-shot rather than close-up, the use of a cello rather than a violin on the soundtrack: each of these stylistic choices can be found, upon repeated viewing, to be coherent with the programme as a whole and the moment in which they are contained. Further, the 'meanings' that may be drawn from the programme – the experiences and reflections with which they provide us – enable us to regard our lives slightly differently, especially in terms of the relationship (of whatever kind) between the physical and practical elements of life and the ideals and ideas that are not customarily visible but that are nevertheless determining.

Why are such programmes 'good'? Why are they 'better' than programmes that do not sustain repeated viewings because they lack stylistic coherence and/or thematic importance? These are questions that have concerned aestheticians for centuries. A tentative and personal response would be that these programmes are capable of raising our thoughts and observations above an immersion in the prosaic and quotidian, yet in doing so they may shed light upon, reassess and reshape the significance of the ordinary and the everyday, and they can do this repeatedly. As valuable artworks, the programmes exhibit endurance and flexibility, providing the viewer with the potential for active discovery and ongoing reflection.

It can be seen then that many of the features of American quality television outlined above are also features that may be used to define 'good' television. It is not that a particular pace or style of camerawork, or level of detail in the *mise-en-scène*, or type of performance, or particular set of themes, make a programme good – though these things may make it quality television – but that the way in which these things are integrated can create a coherent whole that has stylistic integrity. Moreover, lest this seem too broad, let me emphasise that this is not a simple matter of style 'coordinating with' or reflecting the themes or central concerns of the programme. Such correlation can be found in quiz shows and cookery programmes. Good television also avoids making redundant stylistic choices. Take, for example, use of simple repetition, such as the chords that herald the closing of a soap opera such as *EastEnders*, or the opening of a new round of questions in *Who Wants to be a Millionaire?* in contrast with the more thoughtful use of near-repetition or reiteration found in the formal strategy of *Six Feet Under*: each episode opens with a death, thus repeating a structure, but in order precisely to reveal the individual and unique nature of each iteration within that structured form.[9] This suggests that qualities such as subtlety and reinvention, as opposed to formula and repetition, contribute to the possibility of fulfilling repeated viewing and interpretation.

Good television also requires one further crucial element mentioned previously. Good television is television that we *experience positively*: we find it engaging, stimulating, exciting, original and so on. We might also evaluate a programme on the basis of its moral qualities or ideological framework, given that those aspects affect our ability to view repeatedly and engage with the work. So, good television, though constituted by textual features that open up the potential for rich, repeated viewing, requires something special for its classification: it requires the subjective experience of an appreciative viewer who feels something towards it. Unlike quality television, we cannot simply categorise good television on the basis of a cursory viewing; we must experience and respond to it. Quality television can be found through a reasonable level of attention to the text – the seeking out of particular textual features. Good television can only be discovered through the exercise of critical judgement, a personal decision based upon our considered, sympathetic and (ideally) disinterested response to the details of a text.[10]

Thus the distinction between quality and good television rests upon the notion of evaluation or critical judgement, and this in turn depends upon the existence of an individual subjectivity taking up an appropriate attitude towards the work.

Quality Television versus Good Television: Where to From Here?

We have seen that one can claim that a programme ought to be classified as quality television, and that one can also make claims for the value of a text (i.e. offer a critical judgement of how good it is), by referring to textual attributes within the programme. These two types of claims are often conflated, but actually involve different things. To determine quality one need only refer to details of the programme and show that they exhibit fundamental defining features. To determine real value – to make a critical judgement and try to persuade others of it – one must both interpret the programme and evaluate it according to explicit criteria.

'Quality' is not synonymous with value or how good something is; it is closer to being a set of generic traits that distinguishes a group identity. In scholarly writing on British quality television, this distinction has been made relatively clearly; in comparable writing on American programmes, however, quality television is often conflated with good television. Although the latter approach may seem conceptually imprecise, perhaps it is a positive step towards a rather radical solution to the quality/value problem. We would not speak, after all, of 'quality' art in the same way that we speak of quality television, as if it were a generic category. We would speak of good and bad art (and all the shades of grey in between). Perhaps the notion of 'quality television' is so nebulous that in the end it is not particularly useful. Perhaps the recent scholarship on American quality television reveals that what many of us really want to write about is good television – but we seem afraid to do so.

Some television scholars *do* write overtly about good television – even if they deploy other terms for it. Writing about the problem of value, Caughie justifies his use of the term 'serious drama' as a demarcation for the particular set of programmes he has chosen to study: 'If we were to concede a single scale of values which contained both *King Lear* and *Coronation Street*, it would be difficult to argue for the seriousness of soap opera' (2000: 21). He hopes in time to 'whittle away at the scare quotes [around 'serious drama'], to unhedge the bets, and to justify the claim that the tradition of television drama I am concerned with is serious in particular ways' (23). Caughie states that he does encounter comments from students on his television course who expect 'soap opera, crime series and hospital melodrama' (3), but he resists, and persists with his category of 'serious drama'– partly, he says, to be 'provocative' (ibid). This is the kind of provocation that is needed in the field.

If television studies limited itself to dealing with quality television, the field would be narrowed and impoverished – especially as there are examples of 'bad' quality television, and conversely of good non-quality television. However, television studies would be enriched if more scholars focused on good television. If we disposed of the idea of 'quality television' and reinstated the notion of 'good television', what might we achieve?[11] We would have to initiate a serious, thoughtful and constructive debate about evaluation and critical judgement. We would have to tackle the prevailing concern that hampers this field, that evaluation is merely personal opinion, that no real agreement can be found, and that therefore evaluative discussion is fruitless.

Perhaps the first thing to recognise is that no one need accept anyone else's evaluation, interpretation or indeed classification of a text unless there is coherent, persuasive evidence for it in the text under scrutiny – thus the importance of close textual analysis as an indispensable aspect of evaluation. The one will enhance the other. As Jason Jacobs writes:

> As with the analysis of all art, understanding [our involvement with specific television texts] requires above all concentrated study: minimally, the close observation of texts in order to support the claims and judgements we may wish to make about them. Criticism is a way of articulating why television programmes matter to us and the nature of that significance. Only in this way can we develop meaningful criteria for specific instances of television that may then be applied more generally (2001: 431).

The study of American quality television has already contributed to this project. Alongside more traditional media studies analyses and ideological critiques, scholars have proffered careful and engaged analyses and evaluations of American programmes such as *Twin Peaks*, *The West Wing* and *Six Feet Under*. The best of these studies take the view that the programmes under scrutiny are interesting not only, or not even, as artefacts of popular culture, but that they are rich, complex artworks worthy of sustained study in themselves.

Second, we should make much more explicit the criteria behind our choices of individual programmes. We should recognise that we are making evaluations all the time, and yet by refusing to admit that we are doing so, or by refusing to state any criterion beyond the rather lame answer that a programme or genre is 'interesting', we are avoiding the most vibrant and appealing part of the study of the arts: interpretation and evaluation. As Brunsdon rightly says: 'I do not wish to argue that television studies should be devoted to discriminating between "good" and "bad" programs, but I do want to insist that most academics involved in television studies are using qualitative criteria, however expressed or repressed, and that the constitution of the criteria involved should be the subject of explicit debate' (1990b: 69). The criteria I use above – of interpretative richness and endurance (i.e. the capacity to sustain repeated viewings and concomitant interpretative revisions), stylistic coherence, and thematic seriousness or importance – are propositions. They may have a sound history of critical practice behind them,[12] but they are still open to consideration, confirmation and challenge by other scholars. At least in proposing them I open up the possibility of debate.

Evaluation, with its implications of discrimination, and its emphasis on criteria and 'evidence', is unfashionable within television studies, which has long been characterised by pluralist and egalitarian impulses. It seems as if we nervously avoid serious debate regarding evaluation and critical judgement. Whatever its final merits, the study of 'quality television' usefully brings to the foreground the question of where 'value' is to be found in television programmes, in its implicit connotations of selectivity. The prevailing notion that any evaluation is equally valid, that there can be no reasonable evidence to establish the superiority of one critique over another, is oppressive, for it incapacitates our critical faculties and disables us in advancing discussions of good television within the field. We should be bold and state our critical judgements, not fear them as instruments of oppression. We should free ourselves from the timid inverted commas. Let us openly defend those programmes we believe are worthy of serious, dedicated study and discussion. Let us abandon quality television and embrace good television.

2
Quality TV

A US TV Critic's Perspective
David Bianculli

I've been a TV critic for more than 30 years now; my first professional review, for Florida's *Gainesville Sun*, was a positive assessment of the premiere of NBC's *Saturday Night Live* in 1975. Several decades later, asked to define quality TV as it applies to the United States, I find myself echoing the sentiments of one of our US Supreme Court justices, Potter Stewart, who admitted in a 1964 ruling that perhaps he couldn't properly define hard-core pornography, 'but I know it when I see it'.

Quality television, to me, encompasses everything from the novelistic themes and scope of *The Sopranos* to the silly antics of the medical sitcom *Scrubs*. It includes the puncturing of political and media sacred cows on *The Daily Show with Jon Stewart* and the endlessly analysable clues on *Lost*. It makes room for such important, unforgettable fare as Ken Burns's new series *The War* (a Second World War documentary that doesn't come out for another year, but I've seen enough brilliance at an early rough-cut screening to champion it early), and such giddy goofiness as *The Simpsons*.

Asking what these shows have in common, though, is asking a lot.

First of all, if we can have Doctors without Borders (Médecins sans Frontiers), we ought to have quality TV without borders, too. Some of the best television I've ever seen in the US has been imported:

the most brilliant drama written expressly for TV remains, for me, Dennis Potter's superb British miniseries *The Singing Detective*. Any time anyone tries to argue that TV is not an art form, I ask if they've seen that miniseries (*not*, I hasten to add, the subsequent, vastly inferior movie). Whichever way they answer, my argument's over.

I've also seen riveting, daring, delightfully different television that's never been shown in the USA, while serving, on several occasions, as an international juror at the Banff TV Festival. These ranged from Japanese documentaries on the bombings of Nagasaki and Hiroshima, and on a loving fifth-grade schoolteacher, to a British poetry programme called *Whine Gums*.

Confining myself to home-grown product still leaves a lot to discuss, though. In the USA, quality television came early, but not necessarily often. It came in the 1950s, when Rod Serling wrote the live television drama *Patterns*, and Paddy Chayefsky wrote *Marty*. It came with the perfect early sitcom templates of *I Love Lucy* and *The Honeymooners*, and the weekly genius of Sid Caesar and company on *Your Show of Shows*. In those early years, it also came with the technical playfulness of Ernie Kovacs and the macabre playfulness of Alfred Hitchcock.

What was slower to mature, in terms of excellence, was the weekly television drama series. For far too long, US drama series consisted largely of tales told in easily interchangeable chunks, like cards in a deck that could be shuffled and dealt in any order. The daytime soap operas, borrowing from radio, told stories in sequential, serialised fashion. At night, though, whatever happened to Mannix or Perry Mason one week had no bearing on what happened the next.

When shows and characters began to reflect their own history, that's when TV in the USA truly matured. It wasn't coincidental that when *The Fugitive* ended its character's years-long quest with an actual conclusion – a two-part finale that identified the real killer of the fugitive's wife – the final episode was, for a time, the highest-rated programme in US TV history. It offered closure, and made *The Fugitive*, from start to finish, seem less like a series of shows, and more like chapters in a novel.

That novel approach grew quickly, as did quality TV. Shows like *The White Shadow* injected not only surprise, but unsettling suspense, by randomly killing off a key character – a key ingredient of the current, groundbreaking *24*. By the 1980s, pioneering series such as *Hill Street Blues* and *St. Elsewhere* broke all kinds of rules and boundaries, from the way they were shot to the fates befalling their characters.

Quality TV shows began to flock together, like birds. In 1973, Saturday night on CBS meant *All in the Family*, *M*A*S*H*, *The Mary Tyler Moore Show*, *The Bob Newhart Show* and *The Carol Burnett Show* – every one a classic. On NBC two decades later, the final two hours of Thursday featured *Seinfeld*, *Frasier* and *L.A. Law*. And today, thanks to cable and satellite TV as well as increased broadcast networks, you really can find something of quality on almost any given night, though you have to sort through an awful lot of dross.

So what has quality TV evolved to in the US?

It's turned into *The West Wing*, the first two seasons of which, with creator Aaron Sorkin's razor-sharp wit and tone, are about as good as television can get. It's turned into Larry David's *Curb Your Enthusiasm*, his partly improvised, all-hilarious follow-up to *Seinfeld*. It's turned into the improbably dense, satisfying and consistently entertaining *Buffy the Vampire Slayer*, and its non-supernatural spiritual sister series, *Veronica Mars*. On cable, it turned into the bold brutality of *Oz*, the brilliance of *The Sopranos* and *Deadwood*, the richness of *Monk*, the trendiness of *Sex and the City*, the wildness of *Weeds*, the unforgettable coda to end all codas in *Six Feet Under*, and the complex, sometimes repugnant lead characters of *The Shield*, *Nip/Tuck* and *Rescue Me*. On the comedy front, *Arrested Development* just ended here, and *My Name is Earl*, *Everybody Hates Chris* and *Sons and Daughters* just started. *My Name is Earl*, like *Cheers* and *Frasier*, I suspect is one for the ages, a comedy with such a sweet centre, and populated with such individually striking characters, that it'll be around, and appreciated, for a long time.

Those, to me, are prime primetime examples of quality television. At this point, I can add only one possibly helpful definition of what makes a show worthy of the 'quality' compliment. TV critics, to do their job, must multi-task voraciously, taking notes on one show while writing about another. With most TV, that's easy to do, and short-changes neither the TV creator nor the newspaper reader. But when something comes along that's good enough, complex enough, surprising enough, or just different enough, I'll stop multi-tasking and give the show my full attention. That's my equivalent of 'I know it when I see it'. In my case, I know it when I stop to watch it.

Which, fittingly, is my cue to stop writing. A new episode of *Scrubs* is on . . .

3

Quality TV Drama

Estimations and Influences Through Time and
Space

Robin Nelson

• •

Backstory

Unless it is claimed that values are universal and that quality
artefacts are the same through time and across space, it must be
acknowledged that values and evaluation have a history. Before
addressing the estimation of today's 'American Quality TV', this
chapter draws upon television's history to bring out shifts not only
in criteria for evaluating television but the social, economic and
industrial undercurrents, which may help to explain the swirl of
contradictions on the surface. It is not necessary to revisit in detail
the core traditions in Britain and America with whose television
cultures this chapter is primarily concerned since they are well
documented.[1] But it is helpful, with some backward glances, to
identify key premises. Several core tensions were in play historically
between cultures and within cultures in the broad period from the
late 1950s to the late 1980s. For the sake of brevity, I propose to
set these out more starkly than they have functioned in actuality,
before addressing the continuities and discontinuities into TVIII
(the 1990s and early 2000s).[2]

Britain has been much influenced by its public service heritage
in the BBC, balancing entertainment with high cultural aspirations

and 'seriousness', whilst America, barring a brief early dalliance with classic drama, settled quickly into a commercial, popular culture with least objectionable programming (LOP) adjudged primarily by ratings values. Early British TV drama had its roots in theatre and had a strong disposition to privilege the writer as the locus of a distinctive vision or guarantor of authenticity. America, in contrast, with its television industry developing substantially in Los Angeles, has lived in the shadow of Hollywood film. There has always been a tendency within both the British and American industries to estimate film more highly than television. This evaluation is based partly on the higher production values historically associated with the big-screen cinema image over the poor resolution of the small television monitor; partly on industrial practices in which more time is taken to produce film on the back of better funding; and partly on the domesticity of television, which militates against scopophilic cinematic pleasures.

The privileging of film over television in America is significantly informed by an industrial hierarchy in which film production personnel and practices were kept as discrete as possible from those of television in a situation in which they were in fact close neighbours. The distinction between them was founded on the much higher budgets of film in comparison to television, and filmmakers did not want to be tainted by association with a cheaper, and allegedly inferior, product. Notions of quality in the European film industry were sustained in the wake of modernism by the auteurist director's vision. Such films carried something of the cultural cachet of the authored TV drama, but crediting the vision of the director rather than the writer. Even though this cachet may not have applied to industrial Hollywood, it has always seemed possible to do something interesting on film in a way that the television industry typically seemed to preclude as authored drama diminished even in the British tradition. If anything distinctive was achieved in American television, it was perceived as being against the grain of the industry, as being, in Robert J. Thompson's seminal formulation, 'not regular' (1996: 13) or following 'a noble struggle against profit-mongering networks' (14).

There are strong undercurrents in this broad sketch review that make assumptions about the industry, viewers, television texts and the processes of creativity. In respect of textual production, the distinctive vision of a special individual – a film auteur or a playwright – has been seen in critical discourse, as noted, to guarantee authenticity and independence of viewpoint in a liberal romantic tradition that carried over through high modernism into early television. Whilst film might sustain such quality, the industrial processes of early television, racing to supply the rapacious schedules but static and studio-bound with its cumbersome cameras and cables, allegedly could not. In addition, the tried and tested television programming – repeating formulaic codes and conventions with only minor adjustments – appeared to serve the needs of LOP culture but, almost by definition, could not be distinctive. Ratings appeared to confirm broadly the satisfaction of audiences with LOP output, though the crude mechanisms of Nielsen in America and BARB (Broadcasters' Audience Research Board) in Britain were not capable of sophisticated distinctions. Thus, viewers were conceived and measured in mass numbers although, in Britain, there were occasional overtones of a 'common culture'.[3]

The critical traditions in both Britain and America have valued sophisticated texts. But, in spite of John Reith's early aspirations for the BBC, television was typically thought to be incapable of achieving such textual richness.[4] Historically, Reith's aim to bring high culture to the masses in Britain was tempered with the introduction of commercial television in 1955 and with subsequent softening of BBC policy aiming to 'make the good popular and the popular good' rather than sustaining a diet of serious, educative programmes that viewers increasingly chose not to watch.[5] Nevertheless, there was a sense at least until the 1990s, as television executive Michael Grade has observed, that the legacy of BBC public service kept the UK commercial sector honest.[6]

In respect of quality in American television, two views share a similar standpoint that, left entirely to the market, television is disposed to entertainment. In the first, negatively expressed account, Neil Postman argues that the American television medium is:

> a beautiful spectacle, a visual delight, pouring forth thousands of images on any given day. The average shot is only 3.5 seconds, so that the eye never rests, always has something new to see. Moreover, television offers viewers a variety of subject matter, requires minimal skills to comprehend it, and is largely aimed at emotional gratification ... American television, in other words, is devoted entirely to supplying its audience with entertainment ... [and] has made entertainment itself the natural format for all experience (1987: 88–9).

Searching for positive value, in contrast, the American Viewers for Quality Television propose that a 'quality series enlightens, enriches, challenges, involves and confronts. It dares to take risks, it's honest and illuminating, it appeals to the intellect and touches the emotions' (quoted in Thompson 1996: 13). Despite differences, there is agreement here that, in espousing the LOP values of popular entertainment, American television, with rare programming exceptions, has eschewed the intellect and amused through a relatively superficial emotional engagement.

The Western tradition of privileging the intellect over the emotions might be traced back to Plato,[7] and thus assessments such as Postman's, which denigrate emotional gratification, consign television to be inferior to other modes of cultural production in these terms. But John Caldwell, in inviting us to 'dispense once and for all with the notion that trash is a moral judgement' (1995) opens up a space for re-evaluating all kinds of television pleasures. As a 24/7, domestic medium, television serves a range of functions, some of which are closely associated with relaxing after work. Thus it would be very surprising if all programming aspired to a Reithian high seriousness. Assuming that informative and educative programmes have a value where they do appear, too little has been established critically about the other pleasures television might generate for viewers, not all of which are mindless. Though the scope of this chapter does not afford a full discussion of television's pleasures, as we proceed to address changes in contemporary culture, new perspectives will come into play.

Thus, despite the fact that British television schedules included American imports (and American television has from time to time valued British imports, as we shall see), a difference has been historically perceived between the two cultures which, from those critical positions cited above, sees American television as tending towards trash (negatively conceived), and British television drawn towards 'seriousness' by its public service heritage, but enlivened by the entertainment imperatives of commercial television.

Shifting Foundation; Altered Viewpoints

In the late 1990s and early 2000s, however, critical discourse on quality TV drama has been dominated by the celebration of American quality TV. Even before film buff Peter Krämer famously remarked that 'American fictional television is now better than the movies' (quoted in Jancovich and Lyons 2003: 1), American critic, David Lavery, had published edited collections of critical essays on *Twin Peaks* (1994), *The X-Files* (1996), *The Sopranos* (2002) and (with Rhonda V. Wilcox) *Fighting the Forces: What's at Stake in Buffy the Vampire Slayer* (2002). From the UK, Kim Akass and Janet McCabe have contributed much since 2003 to the critical exposure of American quality TV both in their Dublin conference on the subject in April 2004 and in their own edited collections, *Reading Sex and the City* (2004) and *Reading Six Feet Under* (2005), as well as with their I.B.Tauris series 'Reading Contemporary Television'.

In journalism, too, Andrew Billen, for example, wrote a two-page article for the *Observer* on 28 July 2002 entitled 'Why I love American TV' and subheaded 'British television could once boast the best writers, actors and directors in the world . . . but no longer. The greatest shows on earth now come from the United States' (2002a: 5). Thus the first point of change to note is that American quality TV is currently dominating the discourse and, given the sketch above, an explanation for this apparent turnaround is needed.

It is not the first time that one television culture has been perceived to be better than the other. In the late 1950s and 1960s, for example, British television was highly rated in America. As Jeffrey Miller has remarked, '[already] by 1956 a discourse in which television programs "produced in England" were better than "standard fare . . . produced in Hollywood" was being conducted in the single national publication devoted to American television [*TV Guide*]' (2000: 25). The *TV Guide* of 9 August 1969 argued that Americans 'should envy the British their prime time program balance. It's what we need more than anything else' (quoted in Miller 2000: 25). Though such judgements were made in part from a high-culture point of view in admiration of Britain's public service television values, popular series such as *Secret Agent* and *The Avengers*, produced by Lew Grade with the aim of penetrating the American market, were also lauded (see Miller 2000). At that moment in history, British popular culture, based on the Bond and Beatles factor in the 'swinging sixties', was attractive in America, illustrating that there is an element of fashion in the evaluation of television. Just as New York has a cachet in *Sex and the City* today, so London was sexy in the 1960s.

Beyond mere fashion, underlying changes have been highly significant, however, in technological, financial, industrial and cultural approaches to television over the past two decades. First, a matter on which there is broad consensus: production values in television have improved significantly. Digital technologies in particular have not only produced a higher resolution, more stable image and surround sound for television, but have offered production techniques approximating those of cinema. As John Caldwell reports, '[computerised], frame accurate editing allowed broadcast television a dynamic and rapid editing style impossible to achieve with the low-band control-track editing equipment' (1995: viii). The result is a better quality of visual imagery, enhanced by the capacity for sharper editing and digital treatment in post-production. The quality TV product is typically shot on 35mm film or HDTV and, whilst it may not have Hollywood cinema budgets, it is much more highly funded than its television precursors. *The West Wing*, to take an NBC network example, cost US$400,000 per episode. In addition to a cinematic look, the final television product can be enhanced with special effects by digital treatment. Different film stock (super-8mm, 16mm and 35mm), video and computer graphics can be mixed and treated in post-production since they can readily be dropped into digital format.

Whilst technology is never solely determinant of value since other factors are always in play, digital technologies have undoubtedly blurred the boundary between film and television in terms of both production processes and technical quality of product. Thus the former denigration of television in the face of cinema has itself been revalued and established film directors who earlier would not have worked in television, now frequently opt to do so.[8] At the reception end, large, widescreen digital monitors are available to carry the cinematic image into the domestic space. Purists may still argue for the distinctiveness of the big screen, cinematic image, and other interest groups may extol the virtues of black-and-white television or the atmospheric qualities of videotape. But commentators today (Caldwell 1995; Lury 2005) broadly agree that the improved imagery has fostered an aesthetic dimension in television that approximates the visual aesthetics of cinema.

The industry, notably in the form of HBO, takes a similar stance. Indeed, HBO's tag line, 'It's Not TV. It's HBO', consciously references the cinema box office and draws a stark contrast with network television's LOP strategy. Advanced digital and satellite technologies have completed the unsettling of the network era oligarchy in America and promoted global television markets. Multi-channelling has fundamentally shifted the perception of markets away from the mass to micro-cultures. In niche markets, television is no longer simply a regular broadcast medium, but offers appointment viewing on a variety of platforms to busy professionals who select the best entertainment for their limited leisure time. Accelerating through the 1980s, demographic targeting of segments of the market, perhaps small in number but great in wealth, has become the dominant approach. Select groups feel themselves to be distinctive in culture and thus choose cultural goods (of all kinds) to affirm their status. Industry economics in a competitive, multi-channel environment happily resonate with a demand for distinctive product by the most desirable demographics, as opposed to LOP for the masses.

In the dislocations caused by the break-up of the American network era's distribution oligarchy and the consequent proliferation of outlets, Fox Television muscled in to create a fourth network.[9] In the emergent multi-channel environment, analysts broke the audience down into target market segments, each supposed to be seeking a different product. As Fox market analyst Andrew Fessel recounts:

> There was a very strong theme of very repetitive complaints about the three networks that indicated to us that if we had innovative programming, if we had programming that focused on particular age groups, if we had programming that pushed the edge ... then we thought we could really appeal to a very strong interest and need (quoted in Kimmel 2004: 22).

Fox executives effectively rebranded youth itself, working 'to sell [advertisers] the values of 18–34 and how they were very sophisticated and upgrade' (Fessell, quoted in Kimmel 2004: 117). Fox produced innovative, urban, high-energy alternative programming such as the teen drama *21 Jump Street* (which discovered Johnny Depp), *Beverly Hills 90210* and *The Simpsons*, aimed particularly at capturing the elusive target audience of younger males with a disposable income. Fox forged a reassessment of quirky, edgy, visually dynamic television and opened up a space for product that had the potential to resonate with the values of modernist cinema. In sum, a range of industry changes manifests itself clearly from the mid-1990s in the 'must-see' approach to American quality TV quite distinct from the blandness of LOP.

These fundamental changes in television and the value of its products should be located in broader economic and cultural shifts that have seen a marked drift towards a consumer individualism in which everybody is encouraged to assert their right to the satisfaction of their specific needs and wants. As the marketplace has become increasingly global, and television production companies have been absorbed by vast media conglomerates, the merchandising of ancillary products has become a major part of profit making from and through television. A significant number of people now use their television monitors to watch DVDs that they have purchased, free from the interruption of advertisements, and thus television companies have been drawn to consider revenue sources beyond spot advertising. Some, such as the subscription channels, bypass advertisers altogether. Thus, although television is more than ever a commercial medium, the framework of its enterprise has changed, with the result that distinctive programming is required in a highly competitive environment. Whatever exactly quality TV comprises, channels want to be associated with it and, network, cable or subscription, they have rebranded themselves accordingly.

Worldwide, there has been a strong drift away from a public service ethos towards increased privatisation and commercialism (see Steemers 2004: 6). In the early 1990s in Britain, for example, Prime Minister Margaret Thatcher's monetarist commitment to breakdown 'the last bastions of restrictive practice' led to the Peacock Report that upset the historical balance between commercialism and public service in British television culture and shifted it significantly towards the kind of primarily commercial ethos that had informed American television since the 1950s. Peacock recommended that:

> British broadcasting should move towards a sophisticated market system based on consumer sovereignty. That is a system which recognizes that viewers and listeners are the best ultimate judges of their own interest which they can best satisfy if they have the option of purchasing the broadcasting services they require from as many alternative sources of supply as possible (Home Office 1989: 13).

De-regulation and increased exposure to the global marketplace might be thought to instigate a drift away from the serious to the entertaining, at worst invoking again the lowest common denominator thesis in television discourse. There has indeed been an upsurge of 'trash TV', exhibitionist in its visual and emotional excesses and thus, by the high-culture standards of quality indicated above, of questionable worth, Caldwell's cited perspective notwithstanding. There has been much talk of the dumbing-down of television in this context but, in respect of TV drama production, this discourse is scarcely sustainable since both quality and variety of provision have increased over a range of formats. Distinctive product is the name of today's television game in channel branding and 'must-see' television or 'event TV' programming. Thus technology, industrial change, multi-channelling and the fragmentation of the audience have together yielded a range of fundamental industry changes, including a virtual inversion of at least the claims to quality that television now makes of itself.

Qualities of Drama in TVIII

Subscription channels can perhaps take the fullest advantage of their liberation from both advertisers and regulatory constraints to explore new approaches; they can be 'edgy' where LOP was conservative. Because, for example, HBO Premium's target market is wealthy professionals who are likely to be college educated, the best entertainment may sustain aspects of the radically innovative and 'the serious'. In contemporary television, it is no longer an either/or issue. Generic hybridity has gone beyond a device to aggregate different target groups to build an audience (see Nelson 1997) to be used creatively, with one genre consciously played against another. *The Sopranos'* mix of gangster movie, soap opera and psychological drama, for example, plays self-consciously and intertextually with the various contributing discourses and plays them against each other to produce complex seeing (see Akass and McCabe 2002: 146–61). *Six Feet Under*, particularly in season one, deployed strategies derived from surrealist exploration of dreams, death and the macabre, dislocating comfortable viewing positions by playing with time and space. It also blurred genre boundaries between, for example, the show itself and advertising space, historically marked as discrete in television's flow. In short, some HBO Premium output has consciously associated itself not just with film but also with modernist cinema (see Feuer, Chapter 11 in this book). Modernist value criteria may thus again be in play, but it is a matter of judgement as to whether the devices used have been appropriated into mainstream television or whether the counter-cultural potential envisaged by their advocates in the early twentieth century and in the *Screen* debate of the 1970s can still function.[10] But, for the purposes of my narrative here, there is an unquestionable appeal to modernist values that carry a cultural cachet, albeit the alternative values of the avant-garde rather than those of an established 'high culture'.[11]

Though it may all claim to be 'event TV', as Caldwell has alleged (see 1995: 9), not all contemporary television is equally distinctive. It is both possible and helpful to identify through analysis the qualities that TV dramas manifest. Traditional dramas that locate interesting, multi-dimensional characters in recognisable locations with plausible plots moving to a resolution can still invite in contemporary television viewing a 'suspension of disbelief' that, to a greater or lesser extent, engages the emotions and the intellect. The quality of such dramas needs to be judged in terms of aesthetic and production values appropriate to the dramatic mode. Since television fictions in all parts of the industry function in the new TVIII context, it may be reasonable to say that even the more standard fare has raised its production values, althought it may not achieve an individualist, authorial signature. At the upper end of this spectrum, *The West Wing* may be a case in point: it is not radical but its very high production values and its unusual content marks it as special among its kind.

Some TV drama is, of its nature, highly expensive to produce. Period drama, for example, requiring sumptuous sets consonant with its bourgeois materialist setting, has never been cheap but increasingly requires co-production funding to achieve contemporary standards. *Dr Zhivago*, produced by Granada International in conjunction with WGBH Boston and European partners is the epitome of a TVIII version of a period drama, international in its production approach and target market.[12] Its downside may be a transnational feel, lacking the national cultural specificity evident in some British costume drama. Contrastingly, the aesthetics of a documentary drama exploring with a hand-held camera the least attractive aspects of policing on a downtown sink estate (e.g. *The Cops*) needs to be judged against criteria of local resonance. In turn, a self-conscious, postmodern drama making the viewer aware that it knows she is well versed in television's codes and conventions, and that part of the viewing pleasure is enjoying a mutual playfulness, cannot be sensibly critiqued for its lack of plausibility. But it need not be either/or since contemporary texts engaged by sophisticated viewers can function on several levels at once, as, for example, in Buffy the Vampire Slayer (see Wilcox and Lavery 2002).

Most TV drama still meets the traditional requirement of 'followability' and thus linear narrative forms and narrative realism are sustained where they have long been abandoned in contemporary theatre practice. But the drive for episodic narrative closure, though its traces remain, is not as strong as in the past. Since distinctive narrative modes have developed in television's ongoing serial narrative (soap) forms, this is unsurprising. Indeed, the increased teleliteracy (see Bianculli 1994) of viewers corresponds with increasingly oblique narrative modes. Experience of the medium allows people to infer very quickly what in the past would need exposition, and contemporary TV drama is accordingly fast paced and understated.

The most evident feature of TVIII, however, is its visual style. This is not, of course, a single style but a widespread emphasis upon the primacy of the visual, which Caldwell has dubbed 'televisuality' (1995). In respect of questions of worth, the emphasis on the visual as opposed to the verbal-aural in television has inaugurated a new mode of criticism in younger scholars evaluating television in terms of visual aesthetics, previously reserved for cinema texts.[13] Caldwell makes a broad distinction between cinematic and videographic visuals (12) that is echoed in Karen Lury's distinction between two particular functions of television, 'images which dramatise' and 'images which demonstrate' (2005: 15–21ff). With regard to TV drama, it is cinematic images that build this; as Lury puts it, it is the images serving 'to make up the different scenes or "world" of the programme' (15) that predominate. Whilst, then, in videographic modes from CNN to MTV, surpluses of overlaid visual information may constitute a visual aesthetic of excess in its own right, the cinematic use of visuals affords a range of visual styles and looks that are appropriate to different TV fictions. In an era where style is much more important than in the past, the aesthetic worth of television fictions has not only enhanced viewing pleasure but has also afforded an arena for critical debate that would not previously have made sense.

Pleasure Principles

Underlying the tension - brought out institutionally above
- between serious (educative and informing) television and mere
entertainment is a range of implicit value judgements about pleasure.
These circulate around an economy of the pleasure principle and
social constraints upon it, which in industrial societies are located
typically in a work ethic (it is no coincidence that Lord Reith came
from a Calvinist background). Indulgence in pleasures of all kinds
in this tradition is deemed frivolous and, at worst, against God's
purpose. Over time, however, critical traditions such as the work
of Michel Foucault (1989) developed to deconstruct dominant
social forces and bring to light the fact that power, rather than
unquestionable measures of moral worth, was operating to enforce
these judgements. As Michael Williams recognises, new, sceptical
ideas today:

> underpin such widely accepted doctrines as 'social constructivism',
> according to which what people believe is wholly a function of
> social, institutional and political influences, so that 'reason' is only
> the mask of power; relativism, which says that things are only 'true
> for' a particular person or 'culture'; and 'standpoint epistemologies',
> according to which social differentiation by gender, race, class or tribe
> gives rise to distinct 'ways of knowing', there being no possibility of
> justification according to common standards (2001: 10).

Thus where a 'common culture' was thought to function in post-
war Britain, based at least upon a sense of shared values, post-
industrial societies have fragmented into micro-cultures. At the
same time, increasing affluence in the Western culture of consumer
individualism has promoted immediate over deferred gratifications.
The basis for common adherence to any specific social ethic
has accordingly become less secure. In its extreme formulation,
postmodern relativism gives free rein to pleasure, since there can be
no consensus on any constraining ethical imperative.

In the age-old conflict between consumer individualism and
public service, then, the former has gained the upper hand in
contemporary culture. Thus the visual pleasures of television
become a legitimate domain for consideration from several points
of view and, as noted, even the excesses of visual spectacle have been
equally valorised and denigrated in the process of change. Visually
narrated TV fictions might now be taken as valuable in themselves

as well as located in the traditions of visual pleasure afforded by the high-culture traditions of visual arts and cinema, and the pleasures of television are being retheorised accordingly.

That those products in TVIII aspiring to cinema are regarded as the most prestigious has an impact on institutional infrastructures and policy. In the British context, for example, the New Labour government instigated a drive to increase the exports of the cultural products of 'Cool Britannia', having identified a shortfall in the television industry (see Steemers 2004). Apart from the success of BBC Worldwide (the commercial arm of the BBC, inaugurated in the wake of Thatcher's de-regulatory legislation in the 1990s), independent commercial companies have proved to lack the critical mass to generate the funding required for big-budget projects and are accordingly unable to penetrate international markets. Policy makers looked to respond through further de-regulation in the 2003 Broadcasting Act, which relaxed foreign ownership rules and enabled a merger of Granada and Carlton to form a large Independent Television company (ITV). Some believe it is intended that one of the global media conglomerates might buy it and by this means afford British product entry into international markets. In America, relaxation of the 'Fin Syn' and commercial ownership rules supported the development of the Fox Television network and contributed to the strands such as NBC's 'must-see' Thursday night (see Kimmel 2004). Thus, changes in market circumstances yield a disposition to 'quality' products that has, in turn, required institutions to respond to new value circumstances.

Resolution Without Closure

Within a genre or hybrid mode of television it is possible to identify qualities and make a case for any one text being a better example of the genre/mode than another. The real difficulty arises in speaking of quality TV in the abstract, particularly when, today, individual tastes are so bound up with personal identities that any critical imputation that an individual's taste might even be called into question makes hackles rise. Modern critical traditions that have explored the multi-accentuality of signs (e.g. Mikhail Bakhtin's dialogism, see Holquist 2002), borne out by ethnographic audience studies (Morley 1992) that confirm variant readings, suggest that people may gain insights into their lives ('learn from' and be 'informed' by) popular fantasy products from *Star Trek* (see Jenkins and Tulloch 1995) to *Butterflies* (see Hallam 2005: 34–50). Thus, even where there is a disposition to sustain 'the serious' in a public service ethos, engagements between products and viewers need to be considered in addition to the aesthetic value of the product itself. Education today is seen more as a process of negotiation than a reception of tablets of stone from on high.

This is not, however, to uphold an 'anything goes' postmodern relativism, effacing any basis for discrimination. As my narrative indicates, I take evaluation to be a matter of a social and institutional process in which individual judgements are informed by a range of factors. Though consumer individualism is currently queen, cultural estimation, as distinct from personal taste, must imply more than 'well . . . *I* like it', not because of any ethical imperative but simply in terms of language usage. The distinction of American quality TV drama can be identified and understood in socio-cultural and institutional terms, just as Lord Reith's wish to bring 'the classics' into people's homes to improve their lives can be identified and understood in terms of institutional forces of another age.

Is it possible, then, to say in conclusion that the current spate of 'American Quality TV' drama surpasses former output and that, amongst it, *The Sopranos* is the best TV drama ever? To answer this question fully requires detailed analysis beyond the scope of this chapter. It would have to take account of the fact that all identifiable national (and perhaps regional) cultures are known to prefer television reflecting their indigenous circumstances (see Steemers 2004: 6). The pleasures of American culture as mediated through its high-end, cinematic TV dramas would need to be analysed from a range of viewpoints in the various countries that buy in the series. Though this is a complex matter to unravel, particularly in plural national cultures, it is unlikely that any given product, no matter how marked its global visibility, could satisfy all local needs. Thus, in my account, it would be an open narrative of the broad cultural and institutional context of the evaluation and the valuer, rather than a closed resolution answering the question of worth for all time.

4

As Seen on TV

Women's Rights and Quality Television

Ashley Sayeau

· ·

'Whatever happened to men?' asked *TV Guide* in 1953. 'Once upon a time (Before TV) a girl thought of her boyfriend or husband as her prince charming. Now having watched the antics of Ozzie Nelson and Chester A. Riley, she thinks of her man as a prime idiot' (quoted in Spigel 1992: 28). From the beginning, as Lynn Spigel suggests in her essay, 'Installing the Television Set: Popular Discourses on Television and Domestic Space, 1948–1955', many have feared that television would bring subversion to the suburbs by distracting women away from their domestic duties and stripping their husbands of any authority. 'Men have only a tiny voice in what programs the set is tuned to', *TV Guide* grumbled, as if who controlled the television dials might control the world. To counter this, television was regularly promoted as a toy for men or the family more generally. Most often, Spigel points out, women were portrayed as isolated from the group watching television (1992: 13); and rarely, 'almost never', were they shown watching it by themselves (29).

Television complicated the traditional gender order, in part because it promised to bring the outside world home: the public into the private. The 1946 book, *Here is Television, Your Window on the World*, regarded this feat as a sort of utopia. With TV, 'the outside world can be brought into the home and thus one of mankind's long-standing ambitions has been achieved' (Thomas

H. Hutchinson, quoted in Spigel 1992: 7). To a certain extent, this rhetoric supported the isolationist tendencies of the 1950s that viewed the home as no longer just a man's castle, but as a 'kind of fall-out shelter from the anxieties and uncertainties of public life' (6). But for women, I would like to argue, television may have defied its protectionist underpinnings in the upcoming decades – and fulfilled its mission better than (maybe) it ever intended to – becoming not merely a window on the world for women, but a door to it. In this chapter, I would like to give a few instances focusing on the 1970s onward where television and women's politics have intersected. Among the questions considered are: how has women's place in society been negotiated on American TV? How has TV been used to promote or dismiss women's rights? Must television reflect reality in order to be effective, or can fantasy inspire politics as well? And, finally, who decides what is and what is not a quality show?

By the 1950s, American women hardly needed more incentives to stay within the home. In fact, some women's magazines at the time worried that, unable to pry their husbands away from the set, women would never again see the light of day (Spigel 1992: 30–1). The fact that nearly two-thirds of speaking characters on 1950s primetime shows were male, and that in the 1960s only two of the top 10 shows even featured regular female characters did not help (Faludi 1991: 143). Nevertheless, even in these early years, a few shows did manage to speak to women and their imposed isolation. No series did this better than *I Love Lucy*, which featured Lucy Ricardo (Lucille Ball), a spunky, but reluctant housewife, desperately trying to break into the public sphere through her husband, Ricky's (played by Desi Arnaz Jr) nightclub act. As some, including Denise Mann (1992), have pointed out, such shows stressed their ability to relate to women's everyday desires. *The Martha Raye Show* featured so-called 'average girls' encountering Hollywood's leading men. Unlike the Marilyn Monroes and the Liz Taylors, these television stars were viewed as more authentic, more natural than the unreachable starlets of the silver screen (40–69). Of course, this was also a marketing tool of advertisers, who wanted television stars to look normal, because no one would buy the idea that Marilyn scrubbed the back of toilets (55). But nevertheless, it stands to reason that if housewives could believe that Lucy really cleaned her own apartment, then they could also envision themselves desiring to break free of domesticity and share a bit of Ricky's limelight.

Still, by the early 1970s, television had a long way yet to go. At the time, 90 per cent of voice-overs were male and so were 70 per cent of characters (Douglas 1994: 200). Nevertheless, with social movements well underway, people were becoming used to seeing serious events – from the McCarthy hearings to the Vietnam War – play out on the television (143). Women were also becoming more media savvy. In a 1972 *Redbook* survey 75 per cent of readers felt that 'the media degrades women by portraying them as mindless dolls' (200). Two years earlier, hundreds participated in the 'Women's Strike for Equality', which focused largely on boycotting products whose advertising was degrading to women. At the time, 75 per cent of commercials were aimed at helping women keep their houses, their clothes and their bodies clean (ibid).

Consequently, during the 1970s, American television shows became increasingly interested in their own relevance. While masculinity was explored in some of the great American films of the period, like *The Deer Hunter, Easy Rider, Deliverance* and *Apocalypse Now*, television became focused on the changing role of women (201). No one helped this along more than writer and producer Norman Lear, who became well known in the 1970s for his no-nonsense, progressive brand of social realism. Courting controversy, Lear believed that television – which reached 98 per cent of people in 1978 – could influence society if one were not afraid to unveil the bigotry, sexism and other prejudices of everyday life. *All in the Family*, which debuted on CBS in 1971 – and remained in the number one spot for five years – was by far Lear's best-known series. It centred on Archie Bunker (Carroll O'Connor), a racist, sexist, working-class guy and his doting wife Edith (Jean Stapleton), who was always forgiving of Archie's slurs and quips about her intelligence, but who could also – in her soft way – give as good as she got. The couple shared their house with their blonde but increasingly less girlish daughter Gloria Bunker-Stivic (Sally Struthers) and her liberal husband, Michael 'Meathead' Stivic (Rob Reiner). The sitcom, which reached up to 50 million people a week, covered a number of racy female issues, including breast cancer, rape and even menopause. An entire episode is devoted to Edith buying a pair of trousers and another to that beautiful moment when Gloria finally gets the courage to tell Mike off for opposing 'discrimination against the Puerto Ricans, Jews, and every other minority', but not caring about women's liberation ('Gloria and the Riddle', 3: 4).

By bringing the outside world into the home, *All in the Family* fulfilled TV's early promise. The 1970s was a time of tremendous progress for American women. In one decade they gained the right to abortion, to credit, to no-fault divorce, to classified ads that were not sexually segregated. At their best, television shows made these laws come alive. In 1978, *All in the Family* tested the limits of the 1974 Equal Opportunity Act, when Edith, who wants to buy Archie what else but a colour TV, is refused a loan without Archie's signature, in violation of the law ('Edith vs. the Bank', 9: 8). With no money of her own, Edith eventually outwits Archie by asking if her housework for the past 25 years was worth at least $1 a day. When he concedes that it was, she calculates that he owes her $10,000. Eventually she settles for $500, but not before the point is made: the law, while well intentioned, is not always followed and housework is work too. In another episode, 'Mike Faces Life' (7: 7), the series was ahead of the curve when it showed Gloria unjustly – but lawfully – being fired for being pregnant. It would be three more years before Congress would pass the Pregnancy Discrimination Act that would have outlawed this.

These independent, political shows – precursors, if you will, to quality television today – also served a didactic purpose. When Mary Richards (Mary Tyler Moore), a 30-year-old single woman, walked into WJM-TV in Minneapolis in 1970 looking for secretarial work, the burly station manager Lou Grant (Edward Asner) tells her the position has been filled. 'There's another', he taunts her, 'but I figured I'd hire a man for it' ('Love is All Around', 1: 1). Of course, he ends up hiring Mary because she's got 'spunk' and the famous *Mary Tyler Moore Show* is born, but not before certain ground rules are set. Mary is thrilled about her new position as 'associate producer', until she finds the job pays $10 less a week than the secretarial post. But she is not a complete pushover. When Lou asks her religion, she informs him *and the audience* that employers are 'not allowed to ask that when someone's applying for a job'. 'Would I be violating your civil rights if I asked you if you were married?' he continues. 'Presbyterian', Mary blurts out. She stands up to leave: 'It seems to me you've been asking a lot of personal questions that have nothing to do with my qualifications for this job.' To the millions of young women who, like Mary, were deciding to postpone wifedom for the workplace, Susan Douglas (1994: 206) has noted, such a scene was inspirational, but also informative. It is not often that a sitcom tells you of a civil right you did not know you had.

Another example comes from the most explicitly feminist show of the 1970s, *Maude*, which, like *All in the Family*, was produced by Norman Lear. The highly rated series featured Maude Findlay (Beatrice Arthur), the first divorced woman (three times over) on a television comedy. Loud mouthed and proud of it, Maude was a conservative's worst nightmare, spouting off liberal views on everything from rape, divorce, the ERA and, most memorably, abortion. In the show's first season, Maude decides to have a termination when she finds herself pregnant at 47 years old ('Maude's Dilemma: Parts 1 and 2', 1: 9–10). In addition to complaining about the archaic birth control available to women (not even to mention men), the episode personalises what would be a key element of Roe *v.* Wade – a woman's right to privacy. 'For you, for me, and for the privacy of our own lives, you're doing the right thing,' her husband Walter (Bill Macy) tells her. But again the purpose of the episode is largely pedagogical. While allowed in certain states, abortion was not legal throughout the USA when the show aired. So, in pre-Roe *v.* Wade America, when Carol Tranior (Adrienne Barbeau) lets viewers know that 'it's legal in New York now' . . . and that 'it's as simple as going to the dentist', she's giving some pretty helpful tips to viewers.

None of this is to say that the political shows of the 1970s were perfect. Mary Richards was hardly a bra-burning feminist (though she remained single and happy at 37 years old) and Maude – at 5'11" with 'the voice of a diesel truck in second gear', as *Time* magazine put it – fitted the stereotype of feminists as loud mouthed and hyper-masculine (Douglas 1994: 202). The shows were also controversial. Mary created a firestorm of press when she let it slip that she was on the pill ('You've Got a Friend', 3: 11); some affiliates refused to air Maude's abortion, and its network, CBS, is said to have received thousands of letters protesting at the content of the episode. Nevertheless, these shows had a dialogue with a society embracing women's rights as never before or since, and their high ratings throughout the decade attest to this.

Enter, stage right, Ronald Reagan. Reagan was said to have been one of the most loyal fans of *The Cosby Show*, which, as an NBC executive put it, finally 'brought masculinity back to sitcoms' (quoted in Faludi 1991: 154). It starred Bill Cosby as Dr Heathcliff 'Cliff'

Huxtable, the single best father figure ever – funny, always around, full of wisdom and well paid. His wife, Claire Hanks Huxtable (Phylicia Rashad), was a poster woman for the have-it-all lifestyle – a successful lawyer and mother of five. As Susan Faludi points out, by the mid-1980s, gone were all the smart, sassy, independent TV women of the previous decade: 'In the 1987–88 season, 60 percent of new shows had either no regular female characters or included only minor ones. 20 percent had no women at all' (1991: 142). In both the 1970s and 1980s, television spoke to the political climate of the day, with one important distinction: *All in the Family*, *Maude* and *Mary Tyler Moore* gave representation to concrete changes that affected real women's lives, while the shows of the 1980s were only symptomatic of the cultural backlash against women's rights more generally – not, in other words, reality based. Women were even absent from their normal stomping ground, the sitcom, with two-thirds of comedies about single-parent households run by fathers or male guardians, though outside TV Land 89 per cent of single parents were mothers (143). Far from reality, according to Faludi, bogus and sexist producers often thought up these bogus plots. *Cagney and Lacey*, a show about two hard-nosed female cops that explored a variety of women's issues including abortion, domestic violence and sexual harassment, was a welcome relief to the primetime line-up in the 1980s. But, despite very high ratings the show was constantly pressured by male network executives to temper its tone (152). One was quoted in *TV Guide* as saying the heroines 'were too harshly women's lib . . . [they] seemed more intent on fighting the system than doing police work. We perceived them as dykes' (quoted in Faludi 1991: 152).

As in the 1950s and 1960s, we see women being squeezed out of television, only this time they came back fighting. When CBS cancelled *Cagney and Lacey* in 1983, despite high ratings, tens of thousands of letters poured in from angry fans (Faludi 1991: 152). So many, in fact, that the network put the show back on the air. It was not only fans that took this protective stance, but a handful of female writers and producers as well. In her book, *Primetime Feminism*, Bonnie Dow argues that *Designing Women*, which was created and written primarily by women, was another rare show of the 1980s that regularly defended feminist views. Centred on four women, the series, which ran from 1986 to 1993, was often 'driven by conversation rather than events . . . it presented "women's talk"

– frequently devalued as gossip, chatter, or bitching – as meaningful and worthwhile . . . What emerged in many episodes is a variation on consciousness-raising' (Dow 1996: 105).

What we see in *Designing Women*, and increasingly in the late 1980s and 1990s in other shows like *Roseanne, Grace Under Fire* and *Ellen*, are women viewing television as a site of resistance against the dominant conservative cultural climate (208). Consequently, as Dow proves, these shows became increasingly topical. Not content with the hypothetical abortions of times past, *Designing Women* had an episode devoted to the controversial appointment of Supreme Court Justice Clarence Thomas, despite accusations of sexual harassment by a former colleague named Anita Hill ('The Strange Case of Clarence and Anita', 6: 8). In the episode, one of the characters, wearing a shirt that says, 'He Did It', proclaims the case to be about 'equality and respect'. After complaining about other inequalities like the wage gap, she concludes, 'I don't give a damn anymore if people think that I'm a feminist or a fruitcake' (quoted in Dow 1996: 124-5).

No television series at the time had a more direct affect on politics than *Murphy Brown*. Starring Candice Bergen as Murphy, a single, high-powered *television* anchor, the series initiated a firestorm of controversy when it featured Murphy having a child out of wedlock. Most memorably in May 1992 Republican Vice-President Dan Quayle in a speech about restoring family values said, 'It doesn't help matters when primetime TV has Murphy Brown – a character who supposedly epitomizes today's intelligent, highly paid, professional woman – mocking the importance of fathers, by bearing a child alone, and calling it just another lifestyle' (quoted in Fiske 1996: 69).

While *Murphy Brown* didn't exactly pick this fight, the series hardly backed down from it. The show's female creator and producer, Diane English, told *The New York Times* that if Dan Quayle was serious about unmarried mothers, he better ensure abortion remained safe and legal (Fiske 1996: 21–3). And in September 1992, two months before Bill Clinton would defeat the first President Bush, the traditional barrier between television and reality was further diminished when the series dramatised the debate within the show ('You Say Potatoe, I Say Potato: Parts 1 and 2', 5: 1–2). In the episode, Dan Quayle's comments are heard and the fictional anchor Murphy responds to them on her news show.

I doubt that my status as a single mother has contributed all that much to the breakdown of Western civilization ... In a country where millions of children grow up in nontraditional families ... it's time for the vice-president to expand his definition, and recognize that whether by choice or circumstance, families come in all shapes and sizes (quoted in Fiske 1996: 73).

This controversy, I would argue, set off a string of series in the 1990s about non-traditional families, especially ones about older single friends living together, as in *Friends* and *Sex and the City*.

That Quayle would choose to attack a fictional character reveals that many conservatives remain just as anxious about television's ability to transform culture, particularly women's culture, as they were in the 1950s. And they have a point. Perhaps because they have lacked other political outlets, television has often created an alternative space for women to discuss the issues that affect them most. This was very apparent in the 1970s, when sitcoms became one of the ways progressives could promote their causes. As Susan Douglas has pointed out, sitcoms frequently faced news media outlets head-on, which more often than not merely mocked the women's movement. In the 1980s and 1990s, television also found ways to circumvent and even fight the dominant cultural and political trends of the day. Murphy Brown in many ways defeated Dan Quayle, appearing on the cover of *Time* magazine with a button that read, 'Murphy Brown for President'. For many women, it seemed, television characters understood them better than top executives or elected representatives.

Of course, television has a long way to go, I need only reference *The Bachelor*, in which 25 single women go head-to-head over some gorgeous idiot. But, in general, the common accusation in American culture that television – and especially sitcoms – represents the lowest of low culture is overstated. As we have seen, it is often through television – and again especially sitcoms – that women's issues have been most delicately and persuasively addressed. In this respect, dismissing TV as mere entertainment can be seen as a way of dismissing women's issues more generally. We might even want to consider how the term quality TV may contain a gendered aspect to it. While I would agree that HBO shows are of much higher production values than most network shows, it is also true that the title 'quality' is not always equally distributed. Perhaps not here, but, even in my progressive, semi-intellectual circles, it is not easy to convince people that, say, *Sex and the City* is in the same class as *The Sopranos* or *Six Feet Under*. The fact that it is a comedy about four women who have more sex and more money than 'real women', as some critics have said, often precludes people from believing it could have any political bearing. But, like many of the comedies we have looked at, *Sex and the City* has addressed political issues like abortion, the growing abstinence movement and what to do when your progressive boyfriend can't handle your professional success. Instead of simply dismissing these shows, or their more progressive elements, a more critical question would be ask why – from *The Mary Tyler Moore Show* and *Maude* to *Sex and the City* – has society only been allowed to watch women grow while it has laughed at them?

That is not to say, however, that I would like to see the humour, the supposed 'lack of reality', or the spunk taken out of women's popular culture. Doing so would be to make the false assumption that the often funny or fantastical life on television could never be inspirational, particularly when it contrasts it to 'lame', domestic life. Though we have focused on them less, there are many such shows. In the 1960s, *Bewitched* starred Samantha Stevens (Elizabeth Montgomery), a housewife who is imbued with special powers that allow her to do everything from clean the house to influence the town's mayor with a twitch of her nose (Douglas 1994: 123–38). And alongside the political realism of the 1970s were shows like *Charlie's Angels*, *The Bionic Woman* and *Wonder Woman*, about beautiful, superhuman women who could compete with and defeat the boys (193–219). Even the shows we have examined use humour and images of the ideal life to rebellious ends; there is more to *Sex and the City*'s Charlotte York's (played by Kristin Davis) rabbit than meets the eye. As *TV Guide* suggested back in 1953, snickering at men is no laughing matter – at least to the men in power. But to the women laughing and to those watching them laugh, at their beaux, at social expectations, even at their own failings; this can be liberating. Television enables this subversion. The best shows have realised this, including *Sex and the City*; in season six, top-notch lawyer Miranda Hobbes (Cynthia Nixon) finds a new lover, the TiVo ('Great Sexpectations', 6: 2). Unlike most relationships, this device gives her complete control, pausing, rewinding, taping weeks in advance. On the show, we see Miranda with her 'date' – she is dating the machine, understand – watching her beloved romance *Jules and*

Mimi alone, which we know is a rare and seditious thing in TV. She understands we think it is funny and silly of her, but smart viewers know it is more than that. Remember that the only thing her nosy housekeeper, Magda (Lynn Cohen), ever breaks are her TiVo and her other dear *device* – as if television and vibrators equally threatened the social order. Of course, Miranda eventually returns to the real world and finds her true love, Steve Brady (David Eigenberg). But, significantly I think, it is only after he fixes her TiVo that she knows for sure that he is a keeper, as if to say, if you really love the woman, you have to love her TV.

5

Sex, Swearing and Respectability

Courting Controversy, HBO's Original
Programming and Producing Quality TV
Janet McCabe and *Kim Akass*

. . . .

Introduction: Getting Away with Murder

Pregnant exotic dancer Tracee (Ariel Kiley) gets more than she
bargained for when she smart-mouths psychotic mobster Ralph
Cifaretto (Joe Pantoliano). Denigrating a made-man's masculinity
in front of his crew is never wise. What *does* she think she is doing?
Following Tracee into the car park, Ralph seduces her with the
promise of security, family and home, only to cruelly snatch the
'happy ever after' away. He taunts her by saying that if they have
a daughter she too could grow up 'as a cocksucking slob like her
mother'. He spits in her face. She slaps him. He retaliates. 'Does that
make you feel like a man?' she goads. Two body blows to the abdomen
fix the pregnancy. A fist slammed into her youthful innocence,
overpowering her fragility. His sadism climaxes into a violent orgy
of punches, smashing her head repeatedly against the crash barrier.
'Look at you now,' he sneers, leaving her brutalised corpse like trash,
discarded, dispensable, violated. Another goomah bites the dust in
HBO's original drama *The Sopranos* ('University', 3: 6).

The opening of Larry David's co-owned restaurant narrowly
averts disaster when the replacement French chef with Tourette's
Syndrome starts speaking his mind in earshot of the customers

('Grand Opening', 3: 10). 'Fuck-head. Shit-face. Cocksucker. Asshole. Sonofabitch.' Silence falls over the bacchanalian revelry. Larry must think fast: 'Scum-sucking, mother-fucking whore.' Jeff Greene (Jeff Garlin) comes to his aid: 'Cock. Cock. Jissum. Grandma. Cock'. He shrugs – he did his best. Michael York chips in. His clipped British tones incongruously enunciate a foul litany: 'Bum. Fuck. Turd. Fart. Cunt. Piss. Shit. Bugger and balls.' Cheryl (Cheryl Hines) takes a turn: 'You goddamn mother-fucking bitch.' Arriving late following a dental appointment, Jeff's wife Susie (Susie Essman) takes umbrage, thinking Cheryl's words are meant for her. She screams back, 'Fuck you, you carwash cunt,' before taking to her heels and storming out. Another awkward moment is defused when a respectable older male diner chimes in. 'Fellatio. Cunnilingus. French-kissing . . . Rim job.' An elderly woman takes up the chant. 'Crap. Piss.' It is at this point that the entire restaurant descends into linguistic anarchy. Raucous laughter and scatological language create a bawdy carnivalesque atmosphere before the diners toast the success of the restaurant. And a good time is had by all at the end of season three of *Curb Your Enthusiasm*.

Shocking scenes, unforgettable sequences; available *only* in America on premium cable channel HBO, these outrageous TV moments are taken from original programmes considered by many critics and viewers as 'the best of American TV' (Bradberry 2002: 8). But when did incessant profanity and rampant misogynistic violence against a young pregnant stripper pass for the finest in what US television has to offer? How do sequences, like the ones described above, inscribe, and bring into focus, broadcasting practices and policy as well as broader cultural discourses about what is permissible? And how does this pushing the limits of representation elevate the status of HBO as a producer of quality television? This chapter aims to address such questions, an intervention designed to illustrate the manner in which courting controversy has been institutionalised by HBO, embedded in and through its original programming, as a distinctive feature of its cultural cachet, its quality brand label and (until recently) its leading market position. We do not wish to imply that these texts 'cause' controversy, but that, in analysing how its original programming is perceived and known, it is possible to discern the powers and practices at work within which controversy institutes and 'defines' an identity for the cable company in terms of cultural prestige, creative integrity, market influence and broadcast freedoms.

Power/Pleasure, Censoring Television and HBO

Forces at work in censoring American television culture, superficially at least, seek to regulate and restrict. Attempts to police broadcasting standards, to patrol television screens for obscenities, indecencies and profanities, incite a discourse of the illicit. The fact that America has experienced a seismic political and religious lurch to the right – shaped by the rise to prominence of the fundamentalist Christian right with its pro-life, pro-family, anti-gay agenda – means the sanctity of heterosexual sexual relations and moralistic conservative family values remain high on the political agenda as well as dominating the cultural public sphere. Traditional values coalitions, like Parents Television Council (PTC), American Decency Association, ACT Against Violence, Massachusetts Family Institute and American Family Association (AFA) (to name but a few), tirelessly campaign to track down, and take charge of, in fact, the illicit, and incite a discourse that lays bare a 'problem' and aims 'to allow it no obscurity, no respite' (Foucault 1998: 20). These groups hold that the illicit causes moral and social harm, and intensify people's awareness of it as a persistent danger warranting constant vigilance. Brent Bozell, founder and president of the PTC since 1995, writes thus: 'I represent the Parents Television Council's 850,000 members, along with untold millions of parents who, like me, are disgusted, revolted, fed up, horrified . . . by the raw sewage, ultra violence, graphic sex, and raunchy language that is flooding into our living rooms night and day' (2004). According to such views, morality is not about individual choice, but is rather a matter of public concern and should be subject to endless surveillance and regulation on the grounds that any breach of morality constitutes an offence against the community.

If, as Michel Foucault describes, knowing involves gaining mastery, then the attempt to make known transgressions is clearly an exercise of power. Public decency groups exercise power over the things they keep watch over, through unremitting observation and exhaustive inquisition, sensitive to any violation, drawing attention to peculiarities and describing them in intimate detail. Note, for example, how Bozell brings the illicit into discourse as he aims to intervene and censor: 'Sex on TV has become increasingly explicit, with children exposed to more direct references to genitalia, prostitution, pornography, oral sex, kinky practices, masturbation, and depictions of nudity during primetime viewing hours . . . Foul language during the family-viewing hour alone increased by 95% between 1998 and 2002' (2004). The attempt to expunge indecency from the airwaves justifies the exhaustive nature of the endeavour to monitor and keep the illicit in view. Prescribed areas of offence are thus established in the very act of observing, a point acknowledged by John Dicker in his assessment of the PTC's campaign against *Sex and the City*. 'To me the whole exercise is frightfully reminiscent of the dirty old priest clichés. You know, the padres who are only interested in a certain genre of confession' (2005).

Rather than concerning prohibition and silence, modern prudishness has intensified speech around profanity, sex and violence; 'an institutional incitement to speak about it, and to do so more and more; a determination on the part of the agencies of power to hear it spoken about, and to cause *it* to speak through explicit articulation and endlessly accumulated detail' (Foucault 1998: 18). James Poniewozik, reporting on how the PTC brings to light broadcasting transgressions, describes how PTC analysts explicitly speak about and incessantly accrue evidence of violations in decency guidelines. Taping all of primetime network television as well as hours of cable, they archive everything in the entertainment tracking system (ETS), which by 2006 contained more than 100,000 hours of programming. 'The ETS', writes Poniewozik, 'is thoroughly indexed by theme – "Threesome," "Masturbation," "Obscene Gesture". With it, the group can detect patterns of sleaze and curses and spotlight advertisers who buy on naughty shows. It is a meticulously compiled, cross-referenced, multimegabyte . . . library of smut' (2005). As if this is not enough, the PTC's website has posted transcripts as well as a visual archive of offending material. Labelled 'Warning: Graphic Content', extracts are made available under the guise of providing information to concerned parents. Making accessible what is limited by television scheduling and bringing it into the public realm means that the offence can be viewed at any time day or night. Nothing is meant to elude the moralistic dictum; instead, exhaustively searching out broadcasting indecencies, as a counter-effect, stimulates and proliferates an intensification of the illicit in speech and representation.

If, as Foucault contests, there is a pleasure that 'comes of exercising a power that questions, monitors, watches, spies, searches out . . . brings to light', then there is also 'the pleasure that kindles at having to evade this power' (1998: 45). Could it not be argued that part of the pleasure in HBO's original programming comes from how the institutional discourse works hard to tell us how the channel defies, resists and scandalises? Because HBO is free from commercials, advertisers threatening to pull lucrative dollars do not have to be placated. Even conservative campaign groups or those from the religious right remain reticent, accepting the fact that HBO is *only* available to those viewers willing to pay for the premium cable service. The station makes a virtue of its autonomy from the constraints and restrictions limiting network television. Institutional power comes from asserting pleasure in scandalising and flouting, from pushing the boundaries by broadcasting profanity, brutal violence and explicit sex scenes not seen (until recently) elsewhere. What is being suggested here is that HBO is caught up in *'perpetual spirals of power and pleasure'* (Foucault 1998: 45) along with the moral custodians, whereby each mutually reinforces the other.

In a country seemingly becoming ever more sensitive to moral violations, and a broadcast network increasingly subject to nervous censors, subscription channel HBO with its original programming (introduced in 1997 with *Oz*) has a licence to produce edgier drama. Doing things differently, setting itself against what is prohibited on network television, emerges as a crucial institutional strategy for HBO. Writers, producers and directors repeatedly talk about the creative freedoms enjoyed at the company. 'Primarily I wanted to do a comedy about sex, and I knew that couldn't happen on network television,' Darren Star, creator of *Sex and The City*, has said (quoted in Bradberry 2002: 8). 'On network TV it would have been substantially different,' says Scott Buck, writer for *Six Feet Under*, 'We couldn't show a dysfunctional family without trying to solve all their problems. Some episodes perhaps could play on the networks because they're not filled with "fucks" and such – *but that's not the difference really'* (ibid; emphasis ours). And veteran television writer David Chase, the maestro behind HBO phenomenon *The Sopranos*, never fails to vocalise his frustrations with the networks and underscore that the mobster hit series could have only achieved success on a channel like HBO: 'I had just had it up to here with all the niceties of network television . . . I don't mean language and I don't mean violence. I just mean storytelling, inventiveness, something that really could entertain and surprise people' (quoted in Longworth 2000: 34). This suggests that the freedom granted at HBO goes beyond writing brutal violence and lurid language. 'It [is]', says Chase, 'being able to tell the story in an unconventional way' (Monroe 1999: 3). Latitude to tell stories differently, creative personnel given the autonomy to work with minimal interference and without having to compromise have become the HBO trademark: how they endlessly speak about and sell themselves, how the media talk about them and how their customers have come to understand what they are paying for.

Yet this notion of autonomy is not random but about a continual struggle for institutional survival and market leadership. It is an unceasing interaction between cultural and commercial values; it is as much a systematic enterprise in defining broadcasting and creative freedoms as it is about producing a unique televisual product in the process of asserting a distinct brand identity and niche orientation. Contentious subject matter and edgy scripts containing adult themes are predicated on risk-taking that strains broadcasting limits. The perceived cachet of HBO as a haven for creative integrity is constantly being reasserted, through incessant self-promotion and brand equity, waged in aggressive marketing campaigns – and in particular through its original programming – initiating diversity and bucking convention that breaks the rules in terms of language, content and representation. Pushing the limits of respectability, of daring to say/do what cannot be said/done elsewhere on the networks, is entwined with being esoteric, groundbreaking and risk-taking. Assuming the mantle of industry pioneer and given latitude to think outside the box has led Chris Albrecht, former original programming president and until recently chairman and CEO of HBO, to go as far as to liken the company's position 'to the Medicis of Italy, the Renaissance patrons of the arts' (Johnson 2003: A6). Evoking the powerful and wealthy Florentine merchant family who sponsored a revolution in art is a bold statement indeed. It suggests nonetheless that HBO takes great care to be seen – but more importantly insists we never forget to think about the company – as benefactors of a television revolution that is experimental and searching out the new.

Risky Business: HBO's Original Programming, Controversy and the Quality Brand

Viewers and TV journalists have long come to expect controversial themes, provocative subject matter and thought-provoking television from HBO. Original programming like *The Sopranos, Sex and the City, Deadwood, Curb Your Enthusiasm* and *Six Feet Under* is not so much changing television as it is saying something important about how the institution of television has changed. The year 1996 saw the ratification of the Telecommunications Act in Congress. The legislation, according to Michele Hilmes, 'contained a curious mixture of industry deregulation and attempts to clamp down on media content, most of the latter obvious sops to the Christian right' (2003b: 66). HBO's original programming emerges at the very moment that the Act comes into effect: 'far from seeking to impose content restrictions, Congress intended to provide maximum economic and content freedoms for the broadcast industry' (Rowland 2003: 135). Increasingly, the television industry, supported by Washington, places emphasis on diversity, innovation and competitiveness, a change that makes visible the recent TVIII era driven by, among other things, consumer demand and customer satisfaction (Rogers, Epstein and Reeves 2002: 42–57; Epstein, Reeves and Rogers 2006: 15–25).

New broadcasting regulations, far from resolving the question of cable's status in the public sphere, in actual fact initiated a succession of struggles over precisely that question. Paradox (rooted in the legislation), as noted by Hilmes, has intensified since 1996 and the question of how cable television is classified, understood and in the final instance regulated stands at the heart of an array of discourses, practices and power participating in a mutual – but contentious and conflicted – project of what constitutes the medium. A great deal of uncertainty remains as to the future of cable, as seen by the 2006 Congress hearings on the Federal Communications Commission's (FCC) involvement in regulating pay-for-view channels. Straining the limits with its use of profane language, graphic representations of nudity and violence, HBO is embedded in and 'defines' the paradox involving industry protectionism and competition, broadcasting freedoms and regulation. Selling itself with the audacious tagline 'It's Not TV. It's HBO' seems in this context about more than just the company's intention to place itself in another league and say that HBO is different from anything else in the entire TV market, but as somehow making visible – and possibly redefining – what we mean by television in the post-1996 era.

'But HBO's best series weave sex and violence into the fabric of conflicts. The shows are hits because of the quality of the writing, acting and directing, which operate on a level that few series on other networks come close to' writes Jonathan Dempsey (2001: 75). Evoking ideas of quality in terms of creative risk-taking and artistic integrity are cited as a way of justifying the explicitness of what can be allowed. HBO takes control of the illicit and encloses it within its institutional discourse of quality. What is implied here is an original teleliterary product that places emphasis on smart writing, compelling stories told in an innovative way, high production values and a unique creative vision behind each project. HBO has not invented any new markers for defining quality, and it has doubtless not discovered any new taboos, but it has defined new rules for understanding the above. To this end HBO has spawned new forms of television culture and subjectivity, new opportunities for transformation in creative practices and business strategies. Yet, to pronounce the new is no easy matter; what HBO did with its original programming proved sufficiently groundbreaking that at first the cable network accounted for its existence and took charge of the illicit as something to be inserted into a system of values, institutionally managed and regulated.

Named the most profane Western in the history of the genre, *Deadwood* has become notorious for its unprecedented use of bad language. Several critics, including David Blum found the language 'distracting' and 'pointless' (2004: 16). He suggests that obscenity not only panders to the HBO crowd but is also gratuitous, deliberately included only because of the latitude enjoyed by those who have for years worked within the restrictions of broadcast network. Blum has a point. If the profane is 'condemned to prohibition, non-existence and silence' in our culture, 'then the mere fact that one is speaking about it has the appearance of a deliberate transgression' (Foucault 1998: 6). But with no commercials to interrupt speech, no FCC to censor language, and an institutional status that places the channel somehow beyond the reach of censorial power and industrial regulation, HBO stakes its reputation on consciously violating codes policing the illicit. The illicit is implanted in the original programming philosophy and made intelligible in each original series. So we find HBO, to a certain extent, disturbing established rules, mindful that the channel *knows* it is being subversive, while voicing its determination to change television fiction and how it is made.

Deadwood's creator David Milch cites 'scholarly fidelity' and 'historical rationale' as justifying the incessant cursing, 'a much closer approximation of the language of the real West' (Martel 2004: 34). Alluding every time to the meticulous research he undertook to realise the project, Milch constantly reasserts that 'the one thing upon which everyone agrees was that the profanity and obscenity was astounding' (Holston 2004: C19). Using the fact that this was the way Deadwood denizens actually spoke puts into discourse an alternative vernacular of the Old West, one that places emphasis on oral histories and living memory projects rather than official histories, the better known 'conventions of so-called high culture of that time [that] dictated a certain language' in print (Milch quoted in Holston 2004: C19) and, of course, entrenched generic media codes signifying the frontier. Whether or not the language is historically accurate (and several dispute Milch's claim) is less important than how it serves to support HBO's institutional policy for sponsoring original drama as well as how it functions as modern television dramaturgy. *Deadwood*'s linguistic use of the profane, the obscene, the indecent, emerges as a convention of teleliterary achievement; primitive expletives mixed with ornate rhetoric, 'often verging on Shakespearian verse or Victorian prose' (Millichap 2006: 106) and vulgarity spoken with poetic cadence or possibly as Jacobean oratory. Enclosing the profane in a discourse of historical verisimilitude, and saturating it in literary respectability and highly valued performative traditions, promises to liberate television fiction from the laws governing established creative practices and writing styles.

The solemnity with which HBO tells us about how it is challenging cultural taboos while asserting the importance of the creative contribution that it believes it is making to modern television drama is crucial. Take, for example, HBO's highest profile original drama *The Sopranos* and how the series raised the level of TV violence in an unprecedented way. A pilot script written by Chase without profanity, nudity and violence was initially developed at the Fox network. The network passed on making the series, as did CBS and ABC. HBO may have eventually taken the risk (taken a chance with his edgier script as well as given Chase the opportunity to direct the pilot), but what the cable company permits, and what would have been impossible on network, is made sense of by being inserted into a system of cultural value and managed accordingly.

Reliance on an original creative vision lying behind each project finds HBO placing a high premium on the kind of authorship associated with more traditional art forms (Lavery and Thompson 2002: 18–25). Violence is necessary to the verisimilitude that Chase demands for the show, and brutality and murder are spoken about in the context in which he and his regular team of writers (Robin Green, Mitchell Burgess and Terence Winter) and directors (Allen Coulter, John Patterson and Tim Van Patten) set about producing 'a powerful story told in an original way' (Monroe 1999: 3). Institutionalised notions of quality control are stimulated and provoked by a discourse concerned with the 'intensely personal vision' of Chase (Carter 2000: E1). Repeated apocryphal tales of his refusal to compromise or apologise 'for the way Tony's "violent line of work" is depicted' (Holston 2002: B10), the incessant emphasis placed on Chase's outsider status, his dislike of network television and admiration for independent filmmakers whom he credits with reinventing cinema, his personal control over script revisions and participation in the editing process, and HBO's willingness to wait patiently for him to deliver, all show an idea of authorship emerging as being about someone with vision enough to take risks and not afraid to buck convention. Freedom from the usual preoccupations engrossing broadcast networks, like ratings and advertising revenue, may explain why HBO can afford to be long suffering about the extended breaks between seasons (Grego 2002: A2), but it also institutionally justifies its decision in terms of allowing Chase time to develop his 'addictive storytelling' (James 2001a: E1). The cable network may have been nervous (or so it is reported) about the now-celebrated episode where, taking his daughter Meadow (Jamie-Lynn Sigler) to look at colleges in Maine, Tony Soprano (James Gandolfini) executes with his bare hands a loathed former colleague who turned state's evidence ('College', 1: 5), but authorial vision prevailed, and the episode eventually picked up the Emmy for Outstanding Writing for a Drama Series in 1999. Murder may be committed as a professional necessity in a business where those entering know the deadly (generic) rules, but how extreme violence crafts the morally complex and utterly compelling New Jersey mob boss Tony Soprano reveals how decisively those creative and institutional freedoms at HBO are used.

Named 'a contemporary American masterpiece' (Monroe 1999: 2) and cited as 'maybe the greatest work of American popular culture of the last quarter century' (Holden 1999: 23), *The Sopranos* is further enclosed in a sustained critical discourse ensuring the series is widely discussed and its bloodshed explained. Some of the most shocking violence committed by Tony may ambiguously weave unremorseful brutality with a strict moral code, but it is the role of the interpretative community to take charge of that meaning and make it acceptable that intrigues. Deciphering explicit violence as not merely some 'ratings stunt' but as 'the only way to remain true to the complex reality of Tony's life', Caryn James (2001b: E6) – along with other TV critics, cultural commentators and academics – legitimises graphic scenes and puts into discourse a cultural agenda for talking about such matters. James cites 'a piece of capicola as Tony's Proustian madeleine, evoking memories of his boyhood introduction to violence' (2001a: E1); and Stephen Holden describes the accumulated conflicts as having 'the force of Greek tragedy. Or is it a Chekhov comedy replayed in the profanity littered argot of New Jersey hoodlums?' (1999: 23). Claudia Rosett describes the 'intricately well-written . . . superbly acted . . . mobster story' as defying the usual television labels, likening it instead to 'a Greek drama adapted with all its gore and insight into the modern world – Oedipus with semi-automatics; the House of Atreus on Prozac' (2002: A13). Interpreting *The Sopranos* as using 'extreme violence to a profound artistic end' (James 2001b: E6) leads us to wonder whether evoking valorised literary and dramatic forms in order to give the violence respectable affiliations, and set it apart from the 'increased violence [that] has crept into network shows' (James 2001b: E6), does not bear traces of the same old snobbishness. It is as if those reputable associations are essential before a discourse of what constitutes originality in television drama can be articulated and/or accepted. HBO may tell us that *The Sopranos* is not TV but critical discourse classifies exactly what that might mean.

David Bianculli might say that 'HBO, more than any other cable network, has aggressively and intelligently pursued and developed original series capitalising on the censorial freedoms that the broadcast networks can't emulate' (1999: 116), but is not HBO victim of its own frankness? With so much censorial freedom it can be lax in representing nudity and sexual practices. Profanity can be uttered without undue reticence and extreme violence tolerated. Codes regulating the illicit allow for shamelessness and direct transgressions, but HBO seems far from at ease with its ability to redefine the rules governing the rude, the obscene and the lewd. For a company that prides itself on its original programmes, there is an awful lot of other television within its schedules that it seems reluctant to talk about. The presence of the *Real Sex* documentary series covering topics from Karma Sutra workshops to a penile puppet troupe, *Taxicab Confessions* and *G-String Divas*, for example, does not have the HBO team waxing lyrical in the same way as it does about its signature shows *Sex and the City*, *Six Feet Under* and *The Sopranos*. The channel's top-rated programmes may include boxing and the *Real Sex* documentaries, but as Tad Friend reports, 'nobody at HBO ever started a discussion with me about boxing or blowup dolls ... HBO executives would rather discuss its riskier, artier ventures, emphasizing just how different it is – some of the time anyway' (2001: 90). Discretion shrouds institutional practice; circumspection rules. Internal regulation is cautious in handling the salacious and gratuitous, and absorbs the illicit into the serious business of making original groundbreaking programmes.

This leads us finally to the audience. Brent Bozell might well sneer at HBO viewers, saying that '[it] never ceases to amaze [him that] people pay good money for this smelly garbage' (2006), but original programming has long been marketed at those who do not watch (regular) TV. The notion that this is television for those not interested in the medium gives additional meaning to their slogan 'It's Not TV. It's HBO'. Strategies for defining and regulating television have long been guided by assumptions about those who are imagined to be watching; HBO is no exception in making these assumptions, endlessly talking about (and, in turn, flattering) its audience for original programming as professional, college educated and discerning. 'In a recent *New York Times* feature', reports Grace Bradberry for the *Observer*, 'sophisticated New Yorkers boasted about how they packed the kids off to bed each Sunday night for a session of "guilt TV", this being the night when the channel shows its flagship programmes' (2002: 8). An obsessive preoccupation with an élite, intellectual niche audience with high expectations, willing to pay a premium price for the subscription service, has the effect, in fact, of shifting attention away from regulative activities onto sanctioning and protecting the right of HBO to take risks with the illicit in the first place. If, as noted above, traditional values coalition groups evoke fears about the exceptional vulnerability of certain television viewers to moral corruption, then HBO draws into this public debate another social grouping not so easily corruptible because, educated and sophisticated, they want something 'distinctive, high-quality [and] edgy' (Carter 2002b, E11), something challenging, different from the usual television fare, and are prepared to pay for it. Justifying the latitude granted him in terms of the viewers, David Chase talks of trusting the audience over the vicissitudes of broadcasting dictates: 'We all have the freedom to let the audience figure out what's going on rather than telling them what's going on' (quoted in Lavery 2005b: 5). The suggestion here is that the HBO audience authorise the illicit and safeguard institutional freedoms to defy established broadcasting regulations, lifting prohibitions and reinvigorating television fiction in the process.

Conclusion

Dealing explicitly with sex, brutal violence and profanity might well strain the limits of television representation for sure, but HBO's success with its original programmes (as well as miniseries) has had network executives striving to work out how to replicate the groundbreaking formula. For example, referring to the brutal beating of Tracee at the hands of Joe Pantaliano's character in *The Sopranos* cited in our introduction, John Dempsey reported that '[the] violence was so vivid that NBC chairman Bob Wright was moved to issue an internal memo – leaked to *The New York Times* – asking whether HBO had gone so far that NBC, to stay competitive, might be forced to ramp up the body count on its own primetime series' (2001: 75). That year NBC sold *Leap of Faith*, one of its new comedies for the 2001 season, as its version of *Sex and the City*, and its drama series *Kingpin*, which centred on a brutal drug-lord hero, unashamedly imitated *The Sopranos*. But cable-standard content does not necessarily translate well on broadcast network; NBC soon fell foul of FCC regulations and the compromises made between executives and programme makers, resulting in the cancellation of both shows after only one season. Even attempts to syndicate a series like *The Sopranos* on network met with resistance, this time from Brillstein-Grey Entertainment, which own the mob drama.

Despite receiving two lucrative offers, executive-in-charge Brad Grey turned both down on the grounds that he did not want 'to do anything . . . that would compromise its creative vision or put its reputation at risk' (Carter 2002a: C4). HBO original programmes might smack of revolt and force the industry to rethink what constitutes small-screen fiction, but the mere fact of trying to transform the breakthrough style into a discourse acceptable for broadcast network incites debate on how to manage the new, regulate it and make it useful to the future of the industry.

HBO has in recent times started to lose ground to other cable companies like FX who, absorbing the lessons, are producing dramas like *Nip/Tuck*, *The Shield*, *Rescue Me* and *!Huff*, which are as risqué and taboo busting as anything HBO can offer. The premium cable company itself has found it difficult to replicate the earlier success of signature shows like *The Sopranos*, *Sex and the City* and *Six Feet Under*, but what it has done with its original programming will be felt throughout the industry for some time to come. The point here is that HBO takes great pains to relate in endless detail how it purposefully uses the illicit to liberate television fiction from established rules and determine different industrial and creative approaches, how the illicit is essential to compelling story-telling, key to creating complex and morally ambivalent protagonists, vital to dramatic verisimilitude and elevating broadcasting standards. 'We've raised the bar', Chris Albrecht boldly claimed. 'We are vastly more vigilant in our standards as to what belongs to the network. We're also cognizant of the fact that the bar is set so high that we run the risk of becoming constrained in our decision-making. We must continue to take risks. We've built our success on risk' (Bart 2003: 8). HBO is conscious of defying television convention, adopting a tone with their original programming that makes it obvious that they know they are being openly transgressive. But their constant need to account for the illicit, to incessantly rationalise its use and to enfold subversion in respectability, betrays unease with articulating precisely what that might mean for defining originality. It finds HBO continually speculating about itself and seeking to rationalise what it does.

Such halting logic gives us insight into how HBO emerges as a chronicler of the modern illicit. Government may legislate for broadcast freedoms, and the industry might well initiate policies for encouraging diversity, innovation and competition, but freedom over what is permissible remains limited and requires careful coding. Modern prudishness demands that HBO take precautions; the subscription cable channel, in turn, seeks to manage the illicit through discrete spaces of distribution with limited availability. Reasoning itself as a place of intellectual, industrial and creative tolerance, HBO sanctions the obscene and coarse in language and deed, but only in and through circumscribed discourses that evoke 'quality' and respectability, as if such validation is necessary before what it does can be accepted and understood. HBO's original programming policy may well promise to liberate television fiction from the rules and broadcasting conventions in which it is embedded. But the struggle over how the distinctly new, the original, should be categorised, regulated (if at all) and valued in the public sphere remains subject to contestation and much intense speculation.

PART 2

. . . .

Defining Quality

Industry, Policy and
Competitive Markets

. . . .

6
Quality Control

The Daily Show, the Peabody and Brand
Discipline
Jimmie L. Reeves, Mark C. Rogers
and Michael M. Epstein

• •

Out of the convoluted sameness of media coverage of the last
presidential election sprang the irreverent and inventive *Daily Show*
with Jon Stewart: Indecision 2000. Offering biting political satire,
these scintillating segments had something droll and amusing to
say about almost everything and everyone associated with American
politics and the presidential election. The highly original pieces
covered the campaigns, conventions, election night and recounts
with flagging and with exceptional insight. Providing a bird's eye
view of an ever-expanding circus, *Daily Show* host Jon Stewart and
'Indecision 2000' lampooned politicians as well as reporters for taking
themselves too seriously . . .
    . . .
Through the momentous weeks of the 2004 Presidential Campaigns,
Jon Stewart and cohorts provided the kind of cathartic satire that
deflates pomposity on an equal opportunity basis. Somehow this
sharp commentary made the real issues more important than ever.
Much has been made of the fact that growing numbers of viewers, old
as well as young, turn to *The Daily Show* with Jon Stewart for 'news'.
Mr. Stewart, however, repeatedly reminds those viewers that his
program is 'fake news'. Nevertheless, the program applies its satirical,
sometimes caustic perspective on the issues of the day, on those
engaged with the issues, and on the everyday experiences that will be
affected by them. In the context of *The Daily Show* with Jon Stewart
serious, even-handed interviews with significant political figures

including many presidential candidates, commentators, reporters, and authors took on new significance and reached new audiences . . .
2004 Peabody Award Citation[1]

One anchor, five correspondents, zero credibility.

If you're tired of the stodginess of the evening newscasts, if you can't bear to sit through the spinmeisters and shills on the 24-hour cable news networks, don't miss *The Daily Show* with Jon Stewart, a nightly half-hour series unburdened by objectivity, journalistic integrity or even accuracy.

The Emmy and Peabody Award-winning *Daily Show* takes a reality-based look at news, trends, pop culture, current events, politics, sports and entertainment with an alternative point of view. In each show anchorman Jon Stewart and a team of correspondents, including Stephen Colbert, Robert Corddry, Ed Helms and Samantha Bee and Lewis Black, comment on the day's stories, employing actual news footage, taped field pieces, in-studio guests and on-the-spot coverage of important news events.

The Daily Show with Jon Stewart – it's even better than being informed.
Comedy Central, 'About the Show'[2]

Discourse on Quality

The accolades accorded *The Daily Show* from the Peabody selection committee and Comedy Central's own self-congratulatory website are examples of the honed double edge of public discourse on quality. For in celebrating the brilliant way in which Jon Stewart 'deflates pomposity on an equal opportunity basis', the praise also demonises 'the convoluted sameness' of 'the [presumably pompous] spinmeisters and shills on the 24-hour cable news networks'. The discourse on quality, then, is most properly understood as a disciplinary trophy/bludgeon – a kind of carrot–stick device in a system that offers rewards (and awards) at the same time that it metes out punishment for failure to obey certain 'standards'. Whether appearing as an aesthetic analysis published in this book or in a nostalgic lament by Bill O'Reilly (who falsely claimed to have won a Peabody), the discourse on quality is implicated in – and in dialogue with – other discourses on television that demonise, marginalise, normalise and even criminalise 'deviate' forms of television content. Furthermore, public discourse on quality television is rife with contradictions. Take, for instance,

The Simpsons and the Disney Channel. One has been celebrated for reinventing and reinvigorating the animated series – and condemned for being anti-family by aficionados of the Disney Channel. The other has been lauded for its line-up of 'quality' family-friendly programming – and also dismissed as bland drivel by fans of *The Simpsons*. The point is: the discourse on quality television is contested ideological terrain that includes not only the awarding of Emmies and Peabodies for off-beat election coverage, but also fines by the FCC (Federal Communications Commission) for wardrobe malfunctions or boycotts by O'Reilly-ites for stepping across moral/ideological lines.

The discourse on quality, then, is emphatically political. And yet, in using *The Daily Show* as a vehicle for exploring the commodification of quality television (and the exploitation of quality demographics), we still hope to avoid a disavowal that has plagued and impoverished traditional scholarship that appears under the banner of 'political economy'. This self-imposed blindness is none other than the denial of excellence. For us, recognising qualitative differences in television texts is not simply about appreciation and celebration; it is also central to grasping the political and economic ramifications of television in the age of digital reproduction. Indeed, we suggest that 'quality control', in its fullest sense, ranks as one of the organising principles in the logic of post–late capitalism. So, just as we believe the aesthetic analysis of television quality can be enhanced and enriched by attention to the text's dual status as communication and commodity, so too do we believe that the political-economic analysis of television can benefit from the recognition of qualitative differences driven by market forces. For instance, acknowledging the excellence of *The Daily Show* becomes the first step in understanding the economic incentives and enabling political conditions that make such a show possible. Of the many newspaper and magazine articles that have been written on *The Daily Show*, there seems to be a split between those critics who insist that it is a news programme and those who take Jon Stewart at his word when he says that the show is fake news. The reality is that *The Daily Show* is both; it is a postmodern hybrid (in both form and content) that operates more to reify the distinction between news and entertainment rather than blur that distinction. *The Daily Show* is really Comedy Central's news programme, a conceit that is made known by the stentorian announcer who date-stamps each new episode and makes reference to 'Comedy Central's World Headquarters in New York'. Or, as journalism critic Jon Katz might describe it, *The Daily Show* is an example of the 'new news' (1992).

The hybrid nature of the show is attributable to the hybrid nature of host Jon Stewart. As the anchor, Stewart processes and mediates the stories of the day, and in that sense he functions much as a journalist who selects and comments on news stories would. Stewart can roll his eyes in disgust over the news in Iraq or smile cynically at the arrogance of Donald Rumsfeld, and viewers, as well as the live audience, will acknowledge their position as his. By assuming this everyman role, Stewart earns the trust of his viewers, the same type of trust that older viewers may have once had in former CBS anchor Walter Cronkite. In the years since television news became ratings driven, such trust has proven elusive to today's journalists. But at the same time, Stewart also plays the role of comic foil to a cast of fake correspondents who report absurdly on news or personal interest stories, correspondents who essentially are simulacra of the self-important television journalist. In this role of comedic straight man, Stewart is once again positioned as rational and trustworthy, which serves to complement and reinforce his gravitas when he reports or comments on true news. Because he is 'straight' – that is candid and willing to expose absurdity – Stewart is believable as a journalist to his viewers and his guests. And since he plays it straight both in his engagement of the news – usually at the top of the show and occasionally during the interview segment – and in the fake correspondent segments, Stewart underscores for viewers that they should distrust and critique the absurdity of real newsmakers in the politico-media establishment, just as he playfully distrusts and critiques the absurdity of his faux reporters.

Stewart's profile as both media critic and media satirist became the subject of water-cooler conversation after his controversial 15 October 2004 appearance on CNN's *Crossfire*. Stewart showed disgust for *Crossfire*'s bombastic punditry, and accused hosts Paul Begala and Tucker Carlson of 'hurting America' by replacing reasoned political discourse with 'partisan hackery'. When the conservative Carlson criticised Stewart for asking presidential candidate John Kerry softball questions on *The Daily Show*, Stewart underscored his disgust by reminding the hosts – and the audience – that *Crossfire* purports to be a serious news programme while *The Daily Show* is on a channel that also shows puppets making crank phone calls. When Carlson told Stewart 'I do think you're more fun on your show. Just my opinion', Stewart shot back with, 'You know what's interesting, though? You're as big a dick on your show as you are on any show.' Though CNN cancelled *Crossfire* in January 2005, Stewart made his 'bones' as an angry everyman with that appearance. Like Peter Finch's disgusted anchorman in Paddy Chayefsky's film *Network*, Stewart's outburst on CNN gave him credentials with audiences as a truth seeker who is 'mad as hell, and not willing to take it anymore'.

For us, then, *The Daily Show*'s excellence is bound up in its hybridity, its place in the great Red-State/Blue-State polarities of contemporary American political discourse, and the extraordinary talents of host Jon Stewart. It is also a prime example of a programme that has helped build the brand of a basic cable network. In exploring *The Daily Show* as brand equity for Comedy Central we also hope to consider how quality television operates as an economic strategy in what we have termed TVIII. To make this discussion meaningful, we first briefly venture, once again, into history.

The Basic Cable Sector of American Commercial Television

In earlier collaborations, we have looked at programming originating on the broadcast and premium cable sectors of popular American television. Our work on *The X-Files* considered the emergence of cult culture in the TVII era. In our work on *The Sopranos* we explore how the first-order commodity relations of the premium cable sector make the production of such a quality television narrative possible. In many ways, Comedy Central and *The Daily Show* provide us with a 'missing link' that connects both of these analyses. For, though the basic cable sector was once described as 'fringe television', it is becoming more and more clear that the 1990s represented a period when the centre of gravity of American popular television shifted away from the broadcast networks and towards the basic cable sector. In other words, far from being fringe television, the basic cable sector now represents the heartland of the American television experience in the age of digital reproduction and brand marketing. This age, which we have called TVIII, is probably the final moment in the age of television. Though television will persist in the next great age of communication, just as radio and the movies have weathered the age of television, it is destined to be overshadowed by a converged set of interactive, virtual and mobile communication media that encompass the mobile phone, the iPod, the massively multiplayer on-line role-playing game (MMORPG), the X-Box 360 and eBay. Coming up with a name for this new period, though, is so confounding that we fear it will become another 'post' concept. The age of post-television? The age of post-mass-communication?

Although the cable television business has a history that reaches back to the late 1940s, it was little more than a common carrier until a series of regulatory and technological developments in the 1970s. In fact, what we recognise today as the basic cable sector of American commercial television is rooted in FCC rules approved in 1972. The most significant of these rules allowed cable operators to import distant signals. So the earliest manifestations of the basic cable sector would take shape as land-bound microwave services that brought the programming of independent UHF stations located in larger cities to rural communities with limited over-the-air viewing choices. One of the first and most successful of the pioneering broadcasters/cablecasters was a young entrepreneur from Atlanta named Ted Turner. Thanks to his partnership with TelePrompTer (at that time the largest multiple service operator in the USA), Turner was able to export the signal of his struggling UHF station broadcast on Channel 17 in Atlanta into Huntsville, Muscle Shoals and Tuscaloosa, Alabama. Turner's station at that time operated with the call letters WTCG. He also worked out other partnerships to distribute his signal along a string of expensive microwave towers to cable operators in the rural hill country of southern Georgia and northern Florida, expanding the audience for WTCG into Macon, Columbus and Tallahassee. In exploiting this new way to expand the audience for his small station, Turner had, in Porter Bibb's words, 'crossed the line from broadcaster to something else':

> Through the good offices of the FCC, Ted Turner had taken a dog-eared independent UHF and turned it, in less than thirty-six months, into an invaluable regional franchise, the first 'cable network' in television history. Perhaps more important, the signal he delivered proved uniquely popular with WTCG's newly expanded audience, which was in total sync with Turner's escapist programming (1993: 87–8).

And because of the success of this 'microwave network', Turner was uniquely positioned to capitalise on a new delivery system that would make it economically feasible for Atlanta's Channel 17 to be available to any North American cable system with a satellite-receiving dish.

In fact, we suggest that satellite-delivered cable television should celebrate two birthdays: one for the premium cable sector (30 September 1975), the other for the basic cable sector (17 December 1976). The 1975 date is, of course, the day of HBO's live satellite transmission from the Philippines of the Ali–Frazier heavyweight title bout that would go down in sports history as the 'Thrilla in Manila'. Though lauded as a watershed moment in the history of commercial American television, it is important to note that only two cable systems (one in Jackson, Mississippi, and the other in Fort Pierce–Vero Beach, Florida) were equipped to actually receive the fight live. The other birthday – 17 December 1976 – was the day that Turner's WTCG joined HBO on RCA's Satcom 1 to become the world's first superstation.

Both of these emergent programming sectors depart from the broadcasting paradigm of what we have termed TVI (or the network era). And the most significant departures, at least from a political-economy perspective, are in the area of commodity relations. As we noted in our 2002 discussion of *The Sopranos*, the so-called 'free TV' model of the network era was grounded on what Brian Jacob Nienhaus defines as *second-order commodity relations* – 'symbolic objects or flows producing aggregate individual time for sale to third parties' (1993: 309). The third parties in this arrangement are, of course, advertisers, who, in a strangely sinister sleight-of-hand, pay broadcasters for delivering audiences, in lots of a thousand, then turn around and pass the costs of this transaction back to those audiences in the form of higher prices for products and services. In other words, in the mystifications of second-order commodity relations, the costs to consumers of 'free television' are hidden in the profit margins of thousands of mundane transactions at the auto dealership, the supermarket, the fast-food restaurant and the mall. But, since broadcasters never sell directly to audiences, they are beholden to programme with the needs and desires of their 'sponsors' in mind. In the TVI era (roughly 1948 to 1975) these 'third parties' were largely mass marketers interested in sponsoring programming that attracted an undifferentiated mass audience.

The premium cable sector, as exemplified by HBO, embraces a set of commodity relations that stand in stark contrast to the broadcasting model. Put simply, 'It's Not (free) TV. It's HBO'. Or, using Nienhaus' distinction, the premium cable sector operates according to *first-order commodity* relations, which he defines as 'symbolic objects or flows actually exchanged for money or having prices attached' (1993: 309). In other words, unlike the broadcast networks, HBO performs a 'wholesaler function' for cable operations, who then operate as retail outlets that deal directly with cable subscribers. And, again, as we observed in our *Sopranos* article, first-order relations provide strong incentives for creating 'quality' television programmes – incentives that are not as relevant to the advertising-supported media. Permit us the indulgence of quoting our own work to drive this point home:

> Clearly, HBO deserves a prominent place in the annals of American media history for its pioneering efforts in introducing first-order commodity relations to the commercial television landscape. Programming free of commercial interruption and uncontaminated by the demands of advertisers – this has been the major selling point for HBO since its inception in 1972 (Rogers, Epstein and Reeves 2002: 46).

Where the broadcasting model is ratings driven, the HBO model is more concerned with 'monthly audience appeal' – with putting together a mixture of programmes that generate enough consumer satisfaction to justify writing the cheque to the cable company at the end of the billing cycle. The costs for subscribing to HBO, then, are not hidden in the nickels and dimes of thousands of consumer transactions.

This is not the case in the basic cable sector, however. Where premium cable operates according to the same commodity relations that govern the popular book publishing and motion picture industries, the basic cable sector, like the magazine and newspaper industries, embraces the political economy of *blended* first- and second-order commodity relations. In this system, the basic cable sector benefits from two major revenue rivers with several first-order tributaries and second-order streams. One major river, again like the magazine and newspaper industries, takes the form of subscription fees. Though much more modest than the fees charged by the premium cable services, basic cable services still charge cable operators a per-subscriber fee that is then passed on to consumers in the monthly charges for either a basic cable package or an add-on tier. The other major revenue river, of course, is advertising. Turner's superstation, with its mixture of what he termed 'good old days' programming – professional wrestling and baseball, classic Hollywood movies and serials, and off-network series (including *Star Trek*) – basically replicated the broadcast networks' Fordist strategy of scheduling a broad array of programming forms to build a demographically broad audience base (a strategy replicated again on cable by the USA Network in 1980). But by the end of the 1970s a wave of new basic cable networks would deploy a very different strategy. Rather than market to the masses, the new services would conform to the economic logic of post-Fordism – the logic of niche marketing.

In earlier collaborations, we have argued that this shift from mass marketing to niche marketing, in both the broadcast and basic cable sectors of the American television industry, represents nothing less than a new era television history – TVII (or the cable era). Just as TVI was one of the chief products and producers of Fordism, TVII exhibited a complicated product/producer relationship with post-Fordism's service economy. TVII's combination satellite and wire distribution system, augmented by remote controls, personal computers and videocassette recorders, was both source and outcome of what Mike Davis identifies as the 'overconsumptionism' of post-Fordism (1986: 156). In addition to expansions in the service sector (most notably, in the communication services industry), the new economic order was marked by acceleration in the pace of product innovations (and obsolescence), decline in the power of organised labour, reliance on part-time or temporary work arrangements, deregulation of most industries (chief among them the mass media) and, perhaps most important, explorations of highly specialised market niches. Though the broadcast networks would also shift from mass marketing to niche marketing in the 1970s and 1980s, it was the booming cable industry that became a veritable incubator for specialised programming services. In a five-year span beginning in 1979, cable's 'foundation' services would exploit many profitable programming niches: all-sports programming (claimed by ESPN in 1979), children's programming (claimed by Nickelodeon in 1979), educational programming (claimed by the Learning Channel in 1980), 24-hour news programming (claimed by Turner's CNN in

1980), popular music programming (claimed by MTV in 1981), weather reporting (claimed by the Weather Channel in 1982) and women's programming (claimed by Lifetime in 1984).

As exemplified by the 'I want my MTV' campaign, the blended commodity relations of these ad-supported basic cable services meant that these new programming services had both to promise consumer satisfaction *and* to cater to the needs of niche advertisers. Consequently, all of the new foundational services of this cable sector had both to enhance the monthly audience appeal of a cable operator's basic cable package *and* to demonstrate its viability to advertisers. Some, like the Weather Channel and CNN's Headline News, sold themselves to advertisers as 'cume services'. For instance, though the ratings for the Weather Channel in any given part of the day were minuscule, over the course of a 24-hour period a large portion of the cable audience would tune into the channel for at least a short period of time. But most of these services were attractive to advertisers because they delivered a narrowly defined demographic group that represented the target market for a niche product or service. Thus, toy manufacturers were attracted to Nickelodeon, brewing companies to ESPN, audio-system advertisers to MTV, and so on.

The cable boom of the 1980s, though, would be inhibited by a technological bottleneck – the limited channel capacity of coaxial cable. Because of this, these first entrants in the basic cable sector soon enjoyed a tremendous advantage over new entrants who, by the mid-1980s, found themselves in the unenviable position of convincing cable operators that had reached their channel capacity that the new service would generate enough monthly audience appeal to justify dropping an existing service. New technological developments associated with the age of digital reproduction would gradually eliminate these logjams and make it possible for new, even more specialised, programming services to find a place on the basic cable menu. This brings us finally to Comedy Central.

Comedy Central and Branded Television

Because the fog of history dissipates with time, we are now able to develop more refined accounts of the political economies of TVI and TVII than that of TVIII. Where HBO's satellite transmission of the 'Thrilla in Manilla' can now be seen as the watershed moment that marked the dawn of the cable era, the starting point of the digital era is, at this point, not entirely clear. Some possible landmark events include CERN's releasing of the World Wide Web in 1991, Marc Andreessen's introduction of Mosaic (the first web browser) in March 1993, the Clinton administration opening up the internet to commercial interest in 1993, AOL breaking the million-members mark in August 1994, the first banner ads appearing on hotwired. com in October 1994, Microsoft bundling its own browser (Internet Explorer) in Windows 1995 and the US Congress passing the 1996 Telecommunications Act. In earlier work we have suggested that TVIII begins in 1995, but we now believe that the transition from TVII to TVIII probably started as early as 1991, with the 1996 Telecommunication Act representing its moment of ascendancy. Using the vocabulary of the cinema, the transition from TVII to TVIII was more like a 'dissolve to' than a 'cut to'. But such is the case with most historical transformations.

So, for us, the founding of Comedy Central can be seen as an early event in the emergence of TVIII. For most of the 1990s, Comedy Central was the red-headed stepchild of the basic cable channels. The network was formed in 1991 by the merger of two competing channels owned by media giants Time-Warner and Viacom. During the growth of the cable industry in the late 1980s, comedy seemed like a good niche. In 1989, HBO, a Time-Warner subsidiary, founded the Comedy Channel. MTV, which had been purchased by Viacom in 1985, followed soon after with HA! Both fledgling networks struggled to get into cable systems. In 1990, the Comedy Channel had only 6.9 million subscribers and did not seem to be making progress towards its break-even point of 30 million homes; at 5.8 million homes, HA! was also struggling. The fact that neither channel was a runaway favourite made cable operators even less likely to commit to one or the other. The combined audience of the two channels was less than 25 per cent of the potential cable audience (Clash 1995).

Like many new cable outlets, both channels started off with a mix of inexpensive original programming and syndicated content. Other re-purposed content, such as brief film clips and taped excerpts from stand-up comedy shows, also played a prominent part. After the merger much of the original programming was cut, leaving the new network's schedule dominated by syndicated and re-purposed content. Programmes like *Stand Up, Stand Up* and *Short*

Attention Span Theater featured brief stand-up comedy bits. These shows were cheap; much of the content was taken from previously taped specials or earlier stand-up shows, and the cost of taping new comedians in clubs was relatively small. Both HA! and the Comedy Channel had been developed to take advantage of the popularity of stand-up comedy in the mid- to late 1980s, but the stand-up craze was already fading by the time of the merger.

One early original series was *Mystery Science Theater 3000*. The show was one of the few programmes from the Comedy Channel to survive the merger, and it continued on Comedy Central for five-and-a-half seasons (1991–6). The show, which featured a man and his robot friends riffing on old C-level movies, attracted a devoted and enthusiastic cult fan base, but *MST3K* (as it was known to fans) never really helped Comedy Central build their brand. The programme's dense intertextuality required a certain type of cultural capital to appreciate it; ultimately the show really had little to offer to those less steeped in the waters of popular culture, and was thus ill-suited to move beyond a cult hit to a mass success.[3]

By the mid-1990s, the merged network was doing better than its predecessors, reaching some 31 million homes by 1994, and 35 million by 1995, when it generated a small profit for the first time. But Comedy Central still had trouble establishing a clear brand identity to market to the cable system operators. Although subscriber numbers were growing, they were still about half of other cable networks like USA and TBS, which hampered the development of the network's original content. Furthermore, Comedy Central's most popular programming was mostly syndicated off network shows like *Saturday Night Live* and *Soap*. These attracted viewers and revenue, but did not generate loyalty among viewers, and did little to promote Comedy Central's original programming (Dempsey 1994; Clash 1995).

Three key developments in the late 1990s and early 2000s helped the network start to build its brand as the major comedy destination. First, the network began to develop irreverent programming based on politics and topical issues. In the summer of 1992, the channel announced that it would cover both the Republican and Democrat conventions, branding its election coverage as 'Indecision 92'. The network sent comedians to work the conventions as commentators. Most of the coverage focused on the absurdities of the political process, foreshadowing the approach of *The Daily Show with Jon*

Stewart. Comedy Central followed up in 1993 with *Politically Incorrect*, a late-night talk/public affairs show. Developed and hosted by comedian Bill Maher, the show presented a freewheeling discussion of the issues of the day by a panel of guests that usually mixed politicians, pundits and entertainers. The show was successful enough that it moved to ABC in 1997, where it ran until 2002.

The second important event was the development of Comedy Central's first major hit, the animated show *South Park*. The brainchild of Colorado filmmakers Trey Parker and Matt Stone, the show got its start as 'The Spirit of Christmas', a profane video Christmas card that had been commissioned by a Hollywood executive. Bootlegs of the cheaply animated card spread through Hollywood like wildfire, and it was an early viral video on the web. The exposure led to a development deal with Comedy Central for Stone and Parker, and *South Park* was the result. The card, which featured a battle between Jesus and Santa for the control of the holiday, set up the basic premise of the cartoon. It focuses on four young boys in a small Colorado town who swear like longshoremen. The show is filled with offbeat and irreverent pop culture references, scatological humour and pushes the limits of good taste.

South Park premiered in August 1997, and was an immediate hit for Comedy Central. By early 1998 the network had extended its original order of 13 episodes to include 20 additional episodes for a second season (Richmond 1998). Ratings continued to grow. When *South Park* returned for the February 1998 sweeps with its tenth episode 'Damien', in which Jesus fights Satan on pay-TV, it was the highest rated cable programme for the week, reaching three million homes. Because the ratings were based on Comedy Central's 46 million subscribers, other cable shows with lower ratings reached more households because they aired on networks like TNT and USA that reached 20–25 million more subscribers. Still, the show reached the fifth most viewers of any cable programme for the week, and remarkably its viewership among 18–49-year-olds, a key demographic, was higher than its total households, indicating that audiences were congregating to watch the show (Hettrick 1998).

More significant than immediate ratings, *South Park* brought new subscribers to Comedy Central and encouraged the network to build its brand by developing more original programming. The network's subscription base grew to 57 million in April 1999, and 70 million by March 2001 (Dempsey 1994; Time-Warner 2001).

Much of this growth was driven by the popularity of *South Park* as destination television.

Developing new programmes is always something of a crapshoot; the vast majority of television shows fail and Comedy Central's past is littered with failures like *The Upright Citizen's Brigade*, *CrossBalls* and *Kid Notorious*. But the success of *South Park* led Comedy Central's corporate parents to invest more money in original shows even as the mainstay of the network's schedule remained syndicated content. Through the late 1990s, Comedy Central's 8–10 pm slot during the week featured primarily syndicated programming (mostly movies), with original programmes beginning at 10 pm. Until 2002, when E! outbid Comedy Central for the rights, syndicated reruns of *Saturday Night Live* were some of the network's most profitable programming.

South Park also generated licensing income. By late 1998, Comedy Central had sold more than $150 million worth of t-shirts, dolls and other merchandise, and more than $500 million by 2000, when the network adopted a more aggressive merchandising plan (Johnson 1998; *PR Newswire* 2000). Merchandise sales are important for several reasons. Licensing revenue not only contributes to the bottom line profitability of a programme like *South Park*, but can also allow a network to enlist fans in the promotion and marketing of the programme itself. On some level, buying products is also likely to increase viewer loyalty; having already committed real capital to demonstrate their television preference, the audience is more likely to continue investing their time in watching the show.

South Park clearly was and is a great asset for Comedy Central. It brought new visibility and new subscribers to the network. In becoming appointment television, it gave Comedy Central a more significant role in the world of cable channels. But ultimately, the brand identity that *South Park* contributes the most to is *South Park* itself. The programme draws viewers to Comedy Central only when it is on. This becomes especially true now that a bowdlerised version of the series has been sold into syndication. Syndication, DVD and merchandise sales contribute revenue but do not build the Comedy Central brand.

The third and final significant event was Viacom's acquisition of Time-Warner's half of the cable network in April 2003. Although the network was already growing into a more valuable asset, many industry insiders felt that its status as a joint holding hindered

Comedy Central's growth potential. The evenly split ownership had both advantages and disadvantages for the network. Once it became profitable, both the media giants had largely left the network alone, leaving it free to develop offbeat programming like *South Park* and *The Man Show*. Although Comedy Central struggled to improve its ratings and to get into more households, neither parent was really willing to commit resources to improve the situation. At the same time, the network was profitable and the dominance of younger viewers in the audience made it attractive to advertisers. These factors meant that both Time-Warner and Viacom wanted to retain their interest. In 2003, however, Time-Warner was struggling with a massive amount of debt related to the company's disastrous 2000 merger with AOL. Viacom took this opportunity to purchase Time-Warner's 50 per cent interest in Comedy Central for $1.22 billion (Schneider 2003).

After the merger, Comedy Central became part of Viacom's MTV networks division under the supervision of Tom Freston, who had been one of Viacom's representatives on the network's board. Comedy Central's president Larry Divney, who retained his position after the merger, reflected on the changing situation. 'We've been the kids without parents. Viacom finally gave us the keys to the car. It will be terrific in terms of the resources we'll get. But we'll lose that independent stature of a stand-alone' (Schneider 2003). But the new structure, particularly the grouping with MTV, VH-1 and Nickelodeon, also provided opportunities for developing synergistic cross-promotions. Freston noted this clearly at the time: 'Being a standalone network is an increasing liability. Right now Comedy Central would benefit from much more ambitious and aggressive cross promotion. Now that it's fully in the family, all the other MTV networks can promote it and share a lot of the talent' (Schneider 2003).

The history of *The Daily Show*, though, pre-dates the Viacom takeover. In fact, *The Daily Show* started in 1996, even before *South Park*. It initially featured Craig Kilborn (previously an anchor on ESPN's *SportsCenter*) and was similar to most evening talk shows. It featured a monologue, some brief sketches or comedy bits, and an appearance from a guest, usually a minor celebrity promoting a project. In its early incarnation, it was more focused on the entertainment industry, though it did introduce some topical issues. In 1998, Kilborn left to host CBS's 12.30 am *Late Late Show*, taking with him the '5 questions' bit that had been a signature part of *The Daily Show*.

Kilborn was replaced by comedian Jon Stewart, who had been an early host of Comedy Central's *Short Attention Span Theater* and had hosted a talk show of his own, *The Jon Stewart Show*, which initially ran on MTV and later moved to first-run syndication. With Stewart as host, *The Daily Show* put more emphasis on the fake news programme as a source for humour and less on the celebrity interviews, which plays to Stewart's strengths.

Basic Cable, *The Daily Show* and Quality Television

Because of the basic cable sector's blended commodity relations, the ruling definitions of 'quality' embrace the old broadcasting model of creating texts that meet a 'third party's' advertising demands and also generate texts that produce brand equity for a network (the primary definition of quality in the premium sector). Producing quality programming in the basic cable sector, then, becomes a strategy for control in a multiple sense: (1) it allows basic cable networks to attract and commodify a 'quality demographic group' that represents the 'target market' for niche advertisers; (2) it allows basic cable networks to exercise some control in the ongoing challenge of forging a brand whose cultural currency can be converted to economic capital (especially in the age of ownership consolidation); and (3), at least in the case of *The Daily Show*, it allows basic cable networks control of the schedule and channels audience flow to other programmes.

The first definition of quality, then, deals with brute economics: ratings, revenue streams and quality demographics. No measure of a programme's quality means more to corporate parents than revenue. In the old network model that dominated TVI, more viewers automatically meant more advertising dollars. However, in the age of niche marketing, a larger audience is not necessarily a better audience. Advertisers either want 18–49-year-old viewers (the traditional 'quality demographic') or narrowly targeted niche audiences (such as the audiences of cooking or fishing shows). *The Daily Show*, broadcast in fringe time at 11 pm Eastern Standard Time (EST) where it competes mainly against local news and syndicated re-runs, delivers a regular audience of over one million viewers/consumers and is particularly strong in the 18–49-year-old demographic (Steinberg 2005).

The many other potential revenue streams for a programme, such as syndication, DVD sales and merchandising, also contribute to economic considerations of quality. Here *The Daily Show* has not been quite as successful. Though the show's publishing tie-in, 2004's *America: The Book* was a smash-hit bestseller, the topical nature of the show handicaps its shelf-life, making it tough to sell DVDs, and syndication for daily talk shows is unheard of. The show's first and only (to date) DVD, *The Daily Show with Jon Stewart – Indecision 2004*, which collects the show's 2004 election coverage, has not been a strong seller. Another big drawback of the show in this area relates to its limited relevance outside the US context. We would, for instance, not be surprised if most European readers had never heard of Jon Stewart – at least until he hosted the 2006 Academy Award Ceremony.

But *The Daily Show* makes up for these liabilities in the other two dimensions of quality. A programme that provides equity by generating the kind of cultural currency that is attached to critical acclaim, *The Daily Show* has bestowed the 'aura' of quality on the Comedy Central brand, an aura that did not exist before Jon Stewart's rise to prominence as a political/social observer and commentator. Winner of two Peabody and seven Emmy awards and lauded by critics, the show meets the traditional criteria of excellence. Beyond that, however, the show has a cultural reach that extends past its place on the cable schedule. Stewart hosted the 2006 Academy Awards, delivering a stronger than expected audience (particularly among 18–49-year-olds) in a year with no blockbuster nominees. Stewart has appeared on numerous magazine covers and the fact of his appearance on mainstream 'news' programmes is nearly as notable as his excoriation of *Crossfire*'s Tucker Carlson. Language from the show creeps into the American lexicon. All of this is evidence that the show has both critical acclaim and cultural power.

As we have discussed in our earlier pieces on *The Sopranos*, the ability of shows to generate buzz that builds the brand is an essential component of the digital era of TVIII. The fat pipes of today's fibre optic cable mean that competition for a position on the dial has been supplanted by a race for mind-share, a place in the cognitive structures of the audience. When we live in a world of countless television choices, networks and programmes must establish clear brands to attract and keep our attention. We can think of the process of constructing and maintaining brands as having two complementary modes, one that builds the identity of the network and one that builds the identity of the show. It is here that the quality of *The Daily Show* really shines for Comedy Central and its parent Viacom. The short shelf-life that hampers syndication and DVD sales becomes an asset in allowing the network to exert better control of audience flow. We live in the era of television de-scheduling. The technological Cerberus of file sharing, DVRs and DVD sales are creating an environment where viewers control the flow of television, making it more difficult to quantify and commodify the audience.

The Daily Show works against this trend. It is a prime example of a 'tent-pole' programme, in the sense that the show is designed mostly to build Comedy Central's brand, as opposed to building *The Daily Show* as a separate brand. This, of course, would differentiate it from shows like *Seinfeld*, *Star Trek*, *The Sopranos*, *Family Guy* and even *Chappelle's Show* and *South Park*, which primarily use (or used) their networks to build their brands, even as the networks try to capitalise on DVD or franchise popularity to attract viewers. Indeed, it is precisely because the 'fake news show' is really not fake, but a topical, playful and often subversive critique of the power of the political establishment and the daily hypocrisy of market-driven journalists, that the show does not play well in reruns and has not been syndicated. For shows like *Lost* or *The Sopranos*, sequence is the organising principle, and whole seasons can be collected and watched at the viewers' convenience. Jokes about Vice-President Dick Cheney and gun safety become stale if left unopened.

Because the programme is literally a daily show (Monday through Thursday at least), it also draws viewers to Comedy Central on an ongoing basis. The network has tried to use the programme to build the time slot around it, but struggled to find a suitable companion until 2004, when *The Daily Show* correspondent Stephen Colbert was spun onto his own programme, *The Colbert Report*. Doug Herzog, Comedy Central's president, calls the hour-long block '*The Daily Show* network', referring to its ability to draw viewers to the cable channel.

In the days before TiVo and appointment TV, programmers would schedule new programmes around the 'tent-pole' hit because of what was called the 'halo' effect. The notion of the aesthetic 'aura/halo' is, of course, something that many believe perished during the age of mechanical reproduction. While it may seem strange for analysis of the political economy of quality television to resurrect such an antiquated idea, we would suggest that the 'halo' effect is something that must be considered in any consideration of quality television. In fact, the network executives describe *The Daily Show* as Comedy Central's *SportsCenter*, meaning that it is the show that attracts quality demographics like moths to a flame on a habitual basis. Just as HBO trumpets its patronage of *The Sopranos* and not *G-String Divas* (though *Divas* attracts larger audiences), Comedy Central literally basks in the aura of *The Daily Show*. Though other programmes such as *South Park* or *Chapelle's Show* may attract more total viewers and sell more merchandise, their value is cash not cachet. As quality television, *The Daily Show* has not only made Jon Stewart a star, it has also put Comedy Central on the cultural map. Thus, at least in the basic cable sector, quality television figures prominently in the building of not only brand equity, but also the formation of a core, demographically exploitable viewer base.

7

Inside American Television Drama

Quality is Not What is Produced, But What it Produces

Peter Dunne

· ·

I have spent many years in the business of developing, writing and producing dramas for American network television. My experiences have ranged from glorious to regrettable; my accomplishments from worthy to worthless. The diversity of my career offers an insight into how things work. Through it all I have remained committed to quality work, although the American networks have not always remained committed to my need to express this commitment. My history is inextricably bound with that of the network; any discussion regarding quality in American television drama, therefore, must necessarily include a bit of historical review.

It is important as we look back, however, not to compare yesterday's programmes with today's as the basis for determining quality. Whether or not an older show's quality holds up when contrasted to current fare is a moot point. What is being produced today could not have been produced before today. And, more interestingly, what was produced two or three decades ago cannot be produced today. Progress brings both advancement and loss.

We look into history in order to study quality not in a vacuum, but rather in its context. The social, economic and political environments in which programmes are developed bring very real and often very disturbing influences with them. When we assess programmes within these climates, we recognise that their quality must be measured by their impact on, and contribution to, society. This judgement, then, is based on value rather than polish – by what a programme can provide, rather than what it can earn.

When American television drama works well, the writer is the king or queen. Everything begins with the writing. Period. We can look at the state-of-the-art technologies and the millions of dollars it takes to produce one episode of a primetime drama and base an opinion of quality on them, but nothing matters unless the writing is quality writing. It is American dramatic television writing that creates the best quality series in the world today.

The marriage of writer and producer is key in producing the one-hour drama. The most important person on a show is the 'show runner'; in the US, the show runner is almost always the person who created or co-created the show, and whose vision it is that must be produced consistently week in and week out. The reason American drama is so uniformly well done is because the writer is the final arbiter of what is to be filmed and how it will be filmed. This is absolutely necessary if creative quality is to be maintained over the long months of filming a series.

If the script isn't good, the film won't be good. The drama starts with the development of the story. The head writer and his team of writers work an obscene number of hours to develop the right balance of story and plot for each episode well in advance of filming. If anybody on the set starts fooling around with it, the house of cards collapses. An actor or director must always defer to the script, and stay with it.

In the mid-1990s I was invited to work on a British hour-long filmed television drama for Mentorn Studios and Jerry Anderson. There had been some difficulty getting the scripts into shape, and I was called by Jerry to get on a plane from Los Angeles and join the production group at the Pinewood Studios. I read a stack of their scripts on the flight over, and although they were not very strong, they were not awful either. I wondered if Jerry and Mentorn weren't overreacting. Once I arrived at the studio and observed filming for a few days, however, I saw two problems. First, the head writer-producer was not a writer. By his own admission he had never written any kind of teleplay or screenplay; so the person responsible for the content of the final draft of the shooting script was not qualified to do the job. Imagine, if you will, a parallel universe, say a surgical staff in a metropolitan hospital whose chief surgeon never operated on anyone before, and I think you'll see my point. Needless to say, the scripts that went forward to the stage to be filmed were a mess. The second problem, and to me one equally as shocking, was that once the script did go into production the director was free to change or ignore any parts of it he didn't like. Every episode felt as if it belonged in a different series. There was no consistency or continuity at all, because no one person acted as the show runner. In television, audiences are built on consistency. It is the number one rule in series TV. Mentorn broke the rule and the series died an agonising death.

In the USA, the majority of conversations within the production community – whether it's the day-to-day production meetings in the producer's office, or the more broadly addressed issues in network and studio development meetings – regard the technical and financial aspects of getting the work done on time and on budget. The technological advances in cinematography, special effects and editing have created the ability to produce extraordinary visual story telling for the small screen. The expectations at the networks for this kind of feature film quality have not only fostered a competition among programme suppliers and networks to produce more spectacular shows, they have also created a financial nightmare. The costs of producing this kind of 'quality' are rocketing out of control and very often surpass the advertising revenues that support them. Many shows have been cancelled not because the ratings were too low, but because the production costs were too high. Solving these problems in the writing stage before they become production problems is the only way to produce quality effectively.

As a writer and producer, I focus on a show's quality by constantly weighing the production costs against the story's value. Some things are worth going over-budget for, while others are not. For example, I love adding a rain effect to night work because it creates mystery and adds a special mood to the moment, but the costs of adding rain can be disproportionately expensive. A rainy night street scene may be more interesting cinematically, but if spending the money on special effects prevents me from hiring a more talented actor for the character playing the scene on the street I would be making a big mistake. It is a balancing act with quality always in mind. Keeping the show on budget is my responsibility to the studio and network. Maintaining the show's dramatic integrity is my responsibility to the idea and to the audience. More and more in recent years, though, the rain has been winning out. I remember fighting a losing battle with the executives on *CSI not* to build a US$20,000 hotel suite set just for one scene. It was an interrogation scene between a CSI investigator and a suspect and it could have played in any number of sets we owned or locations we already planned using. The hotel suite set had no impact on the content of the scene. It added nothing to the episode except $20,000 in costs we could ill-afford. Powerful people on hit shows often feel entitled to the excesses of fame, and these people were no exception. But I find that wasting other people's money, in this case the network's, is irresponsible, and certainly never a justification for quality. The writing did not need, and did not get better in, a hotel suite.

Unlike *CSI*, there was a particular quality in programming being produced two decades ago that cannot be duplicated in today's socio-economic environment. This is not to say that we aren't producing quality television today – we are – but we are producing a quality of a different nature. Relevance was the determining factor 20 years ago; technological excellence is the determining factor today. For this reason the dramatic dynamic has changed over that time from stories about people and purpose, to stories capitalising on visual feats. These new stories involve genres that can best show off technology. Series set in other dimensions, or outer space, or inner space such as *CSI* become the showcases. In many ways technology is the tail wagging the dog. *CSI* and its siblings, for example, are 'procedural' shows. The massive audiences that the special effects attract are seduced by the procedure of crime solving, not the characters who solve them. The terrible cost of this is not in dollars, it is in human value. Procedural shows focus on crime and the goriest details of them. It is shock television, not drama, the result of which fosters telling stories of horrible criminal behaviour, and the ice-cold, emotionless people who solve them. The lens is on the underbelly of humanity.

When other historical influences collide with this, the results can be catastrophic. If a political party immersed in a radical theology that corrupts the American values it pretends to honour rises to power at the same time that television entertainment is at its least educated, the citizenry is in deep trouble. Today's American population, already steeped in right-wing fear and evangelical fanaticism, succumbs easily to this verisimilitude of quality, and slips further into the negative culture in which television dramas that focus on the worst kinds of human behaviours are cultivated. This phenomenon will continue until politics or civil unrest forces change. We are already beginning to see change in the USA today as the voices of strong television writers and producers bring the issues into discussion on their shows. As quality series such as *Boston Legal*, *The Sopranos*, *Weeds* and so many others question the politics of extremism and the damage it is causing to humanity all over the world, human thought will again direct cultural advancement. And this advancement will include better television drama. And the dog will be wagging the tail once more.

Of course, as time passes and changes occur, not all of the changes will carry such advancements. Often American television drama is hailed around the world as the best of its kind, but this is a dangerously inclusive accolade. At its best, American television drama *can be* the best. But when American television drama is not at its best, it quickly becomes dreadful. There is no middle ground, it seems – which is, once again, a reflection of the political and social influences currently at work – because there is so little left of Middle America any more, as the war in Iraq and Hurricane Katrina have brought to light.

In American society there are the 'haves' and 'have nots'. And on American television there are the fine dramas and the awful excuses for dramas. The parallel is not coincidental. When the 'haves' provide the programming for the 'have nots', a great dumbing-down occurs. There is purpose behind the dumbing-down. There are goals and they are: do not sell enlightenment, do not sell principles, do not sow hope. For this is the business of peddling condoms and corn flakes, not thought. One only has to recall the 2005 season's 'up-front' sales meetings in New York, where the networks preview their new shows for the up-coming season to advertisers and the press, to hear the dreadful truth.

On 19 May 2005, standing before a packed house in a Manhattan ballroom, Leslie Moonves, chairman of CBS, defended replacing the critically acclaimed drama *Joan of Arcadia*, a show about an ordinary teenage girl's connection to her spiritual core, with a vapid melodrama starring the buxom Jennifer Love Hewitt, whose character chats with dead people, by chirping, 'I think talking to ghosts may skew younger than talking to God.' God, forgive us.

Thinking that lacks quality cannot produce quality programmes. When the industry's leaders declare that spirituality is too old for young people, the damage is done. There is nothing intellectually or morally relevant about this kind of decision making, and as we see, little good comes of it. The young audience that once watched a drama about someone like themselves struggle with questions of belief was left to stare in disbelief at Love Hewitt's bounty.

American television drama, by profit's design, has forfeited its right to illuminate thinking. It must pander instead, displacing thoughtful discourse through dramatic story telling with thoughtless titillation. This lack of enlightenment has created a unique escape mechanism, and a destructive one. Unlike in earlier years when television was considered informative as well as entertaining, the USA enters the twenty-first century seeking solace rather than Socrates. Network programmers have been quick to capitalise on this metamorphosis, and rightly concluded that change would work as long as the more things changed the more they stayed the same. Their choice to expand their quest for a larger audience rather than expand the thinking of the audience has altered contemporary culture profoundly and negatively. Homogenising dramatic ideas rather than deepening them has created a dangerous and irresponsible conceit that entertainment needn't have value. As this notion gained acceptance, quality was pulled up by its roots.

Network programmers knew something their audiences did not – that there is a difference between change and growth. Change is inevitable; growth is optional. Change can be derivative; growth cannot be. And, most importantly, it is only in growth where one finds quality. When a process relies on expansion without growth, that is to say on copying itself, that process is without quality. That a network can survive without quality reveals the economic basis for its existence in the first place. The American television network's job is not to provide programming, it is to provide advertising. Dramas are just a way to capture the viewer's attention long enough to sell him something. Drama is a sales tool.

Changes in programming and scheduling reflect changes in sales goals and network profits. The commerce of network television, the commercials and promos, take up to nearly one-third of every broadcast hour. Creative maturity has nothing to do with those programming changes. In fact, quality is neither something the networks court nor count on. This does not mean that quality and profits can't co-exist. They can. It's just harder to make happen, and the faster, easier way is most often the American way. In their arrogance or ignorance, depending on one's view, the major television networks continue to air programmes the dramatic quality of which compares to visual fast food. Aaron Spelling, the most prolific television producer in the history of the industry, admitted that his programmes were never meant to be thoughtful. Instead, he called his series such as *The Mod Squad, Charlie's Angels, Starsky and Hutch, Love Boat, Dynasty, Fantasy Island* and so many others, 'mind candy'. Critics had a less frothy simile, calling his product a sitz bath for the brain.

But Spelling succeeded where others did not. Spelling made money, lots of money. And the network's profits soared with his. So much were the networks regarded as money machines, that people and corporations with little or no show-business experience began to buy or construct their own networks. Fledgling webs sprang up almost overnight, hankering to get in on the riches. With more networks came the need for even more 'mind candy'. But producing simply more of the same candy wouldn't do. New types of shows, all derivative in some way, were developed in every genre. Drama was twisted and turned until it was barely recognisable. The massive appetite for programmes to fill all the broadcast hours created a business concerned with quantity over quality. Having to air *something* 24 hours a day, seven days a week, caused a migration of wealth seekers to California not seen since the 1849 Gold Rush. This was the new Gold Rush, and it did not take a love of show business to get in on it, it took a love of money.

Corporate America exhibited unbridled greed and bought into the show-business game. The immediate effect on the programme suppliers was confusion. One day they were selling to Universal, the next day to Seagrams. You may remember the buying spree. Sony bought Columbia-TriStar; General Electric bought NBC; Seagrams sold Universal to a Japanese conglomerate, who sold it to the French, who sold it back to NBC. Capital Cities bought ABC then sold it to the Walt Disney Company. Viacom (home of MTV networks and Nickelodeon) bought Paramount Studios and CBS. Time Inc. (part-owner of HBO) bought Warner Bros, which had already gobbled up the great and groundbreaking Turner Broadcasting Network (CNN being its crown jewel), all of which was merged with AOL.

Vertical integration was Hollywood's new mantra. A corporation could produce its own product and distribute it worldwide through a dozen of its subsidiaries. Make a product once and sell it over and over. Hollywood has always been intoxicating to those not in it, and it made the men on Wall Street, America's financial gurus, quiver with excitement. There was a caveat, however: in order to run an entertainment empire one needs to have an entertainer's gut. No one on Wall Street was a showman. Disaster loomed on the horizon.

As the studios bought the networks, the networks bought the off-network station groups in order to further own the points of sale along its distribution pipeline. They would now control syndication dollars because they would be selling to themselves. As a result, fewer media companies owned more media outlets. For dramatic television series, this spelled big trouble. A show now had to be written and produced to appeal to every conceivable audience along that corporate pipeline. Think of it. Viacom produces a show through its Paramount/CBS studios for primetime on the CBS network (which has the oldest skewing audience in primetime) and then distributes it, or parts of it, to its other outlets: UPN, Showtime and MTV (which has its youngest skewing audience). How would you like to be the writer/producer to create the show that makes everyone happy? I wouldn't either. It can't be done. And therein rests the Wall Street miscalculation. And this miscalculation cost everyone in the industry dearly. The networks rushed to fill the airwaves with junk until they could figure out a solution. It was a solution any showman could have told them. Profits do not create quality; quality creates profit. A multi-national media giant cannot be run like a department store, but that is how it was initially envisioned.

Investors suggested using Bloomingdale's or Harrods as examples. Different floors of the store, from bargain basement to penthouse salon, were their models for a network's 'day parts'. Early morning news and chat shows, soap operas, afternoon variety/talk shows, early evening entertainment gossip shows, primetime drama and comedy, late-night national news and late-night talk shows that take us right into the wee hours and the first of the morning shows again. Eventually networks were on the air 24 hours a day, seven days a week. They had added floors to their stores that would make Bloomingdale's shudder. They faced a monster with an appetite for programmes they could not feed. The financial weight of the real estate became overwhelming. With investors backing away, the economics of having to pay for all this programming forced the studios and networks to look for cheaper genres. Unable to come up with their own ideas, they looked to Great Britain and Germany, and the import of the decade – the universally despised 'reality show' – hammered quality drama into the ground. Some shows on the air were copies of copies.

With such a flood of look-alike junk clogging the airwaves, the networks scrambled to distinguish themselves from one another. 'Branding' became the buzzword and monikers such as the 'Must-See Network' and the 'Frog Network' were born. Yes, really, Warner Bros nicknamed its fledgling WB network the Frog Network. But no matter how hard the competing networks tried to differentiate themselves, their programmes belied them. Trends in programming based on a hit show's genetics were as prevalent as ever. If one 'procedural' show was good, then 10 were better; *Law & Order* and *CSI* became cottage industries. The trends created similarities among the networks rather than the differences they sought. And when the trend fell out of favour it created a collapse: instead of one show failing, suddenly the whole trend failed. Depending upon how trendy a network was, an entire schedule could implode. Without depth or distinction, then, the failure rate of new shows hit an all-time high, and fortunately for all of America, the Frog Network croaked.

As time passed, more influences entered the programmer's world. Discerning which of those influences – technological, theological and political – were worthy to embrace, and which were meant to be fought, depended on the creativity of the individual programmer. The greatest influence remained, of course, advertising revenue. With so many new networks and programmes to choose from, advertisers became selective, and broadcasters became worried. Business as usual would no longer suffice. Broadcast programming became bloated and redundant and something new was needed. While the traditional broadcast networks worked on solving *what* to produce, someone else was working on *how* to produce. Subscription-based cable networks arrived without the burden of advertising pressure, viewers subscribed based on the quality of programming. This simple notion changed the television landscape forever, suddenly 'quality' drama had a home again, and the quality shows began winning the vast majority of Writers' Guild, Directors' Guild, Screen Actors' Guild, and Emmy awards. It was a quality victory.

As a direct result of cable's success in capturing an ever-growing portion of all viewers, the broadcasting networks' advertising revenue began to shrink even further. To stem the loss the networks decided to fight fire with fire, and a little trickery too. First, they went after the quality producers and writers who were succeeding on cable to put quality dramas in development for themselves. Though a political move at first to quieten critics, this gesture would eventually save their collective asses. Second – and this is the trickery – as advertisers began questioning the Nielsen ratings system as a basis for pricing, the networks complicated the system instead of simplifying it. And the trick worked. Instead of an explanation, they devised a nuance that was inexplicable, and created a diversion by shifting focus from audience size to audience specificity. The illogical and unreliable '18–49' demographic was heralded as the 'key' demographic, and it just so happened that the network 'mind candy' was perfect programming for that group. The fiction here is, of course, that the 18–49-year-old demographic is not a group. Not in the least. The differences in the entertainment appetites of a 49-year-old mother coping with menopause and the cravings of her hormone-crazed teenager are huge. But it was, they insisted, this magical group that would spend the most money on the advertisers' products and stay the most 'brand loyal'. With no accurate research to back the claim, but with enough anxiety within the ad agency community on Madison Avenue for the networks to count on, a momentous change in broadcasting sales occurred. Every development exec had a new mandate. Hustle America's youth. Think young. Be young.

It was only a matter of time before young executives out of film schools and nightclubs, thought to have a better idea of what appealed to the 'key demo', were hired to develop and shepherd new programmes. This was more than another change without growth. In fact, it was a change of anti-growth. Young men and women who had no experience in life, much less experience in show business, were expected to know how to run a network. They failed miserably at developing original dramas of any quality, but they excelled at copying. Derivative programming consumed the airwaves because the only reference the new programmer had was what he had already seen, not what he could imagine. Originality, one of drama's key ingredients, was abandoned. Children of children were watching remakes of reruns.

The absolutism of the 18–49 key demographic backfired in the best of ways. Instead of minimising the audience migration to cable, the broadcasters' obsession for younger viewers maximised it. HBO, Showtime, TNT, Lifetime and numerous others saw their subscription numbers soar as they produced the highest-quality programming ever to a loyal and economically upwardly mobile audience. Instead of marginalising the competition, the broadcast networks had given cable centre stage. And television has never been better.

Cable dramas such as *The Sopranos, Six Feet Under, The Shield* and *Deadwood* to name but a few, raised primetime quality to a new level. Impossible as it was for the broadcast networks to ignore their audience erosion, it was also impossible to ignore cable's extraordinary accomplishments and the fact that intelligent viewers were paying good money for quality, adult drama. Fortunately for them, the same survival instincts that caused them reluctantly to open the doors to very talented writers and producers and give them creative control produced their own very fine dramatic hits. David E. Kelley, Steven Bochco, J.J. Abrams and many others whose voices are clear and rarely compromised breathed new hope into network television's future. They have the chance to become the Norman Lears and Grant Tinkers of their generation and they have already inspired writers and producers to be original and courageous. They have accepted the responsibility of challenging the odious political and religious pressures that corrupt television's freedoms and television viewers' rights. Clearly it is better to have this responsibility in their hands than the children who hired them.

Working in the industry for as long as I have has given me the chance to see how cyclical the business is. If I'm upset with the way things are going today, I know if I remain patient eventually things will change back to the way I like them. There is always a return to principles and standards, no matter how far afield some political parties and religious organisations have taken them. I first noticed this in 1974 after the Watergate scandal rocked our nation, Richard Nixon had resigned and Gerald Ford stepped into the White House promising a kinder, gentler presidency. The national sense of relief was palpable. Every one of us in programme development felt the compulsion to conceive shows that dealt honestly with social issues of the day. In 1980, when Ronald Reagan ascended to the presidency on a sabre-rattling, right-wing platform, programme development swung back to the less realistic dramas and the more superficial mind candy. Clinton's era 12 years later would see the return of social dramas. And so it went until the year 2000 when George W. Bush was appointed to the office of the president by the right-leaning Supreme Court following the worst case of voter fraud in US history. And, to no one's surprise, television drama was immediately under attack.

In the last six years, there has been a deeply disturbing expansion of influence given to the radical voices of the religious right. I say 'given' because that is exactly what the administration and the broadcast networks are guilty of having done. The radical evangelical influence on all broadcasting, television and radio alike, is a direct result of today's political climate. The public relations policies of the White House will always guide the business of the nation, and while Church and State are supposed to be kept separate according to our Constitution, business and State are not. And selling religion is the most profitable business in the world. So the *business of religion* and State are not kept separate. Then add this to the mix: evangelicals, the true believers of the radical right culture, are renowned brand loyalists. If the political-theological interests controlled broadcasting they would have a marriage made in heaven. As payback for their political support, they wrested control of the Federal Communications Commission (FCC), the regulatory body that oversees national broadcast standards, away from the politically moderate and highly experienced incumbent.

Inexperienced political appointees from the religious right now head up the FCC (as they do for Homeland Security, Federal Emergency Management Agency (FEMA), Department of Interior, and so on ad nauseam), and muscle their way into the boardrooms of networks and studios. Using threats of fines and suspended licences they are able to dictate programming models under the guise of modesty and fairness. I have personally seen networks and studios alter or toss out programmes in development for fear they might provoke the FCC.

Under these kinds of influences fewer dramatic shows will air controversial episodes. And – this is important to grasp – it is not because the religious right will find them offensive. It is because, acting as businessmen, not men of the church, they know that thought-provoking stories are not compatible with commercials. That's right, ideas and commercials are not compatible. Thinking audiences are harder to sell to; lulled viewers are more easily reached and persuaded, and persuasion is the Holy Grail of American broadcasting. The power to persuade rests not in lofty ideas but rather in broad, simple-minded entertainment. The network (and thus the advertiser) does not want its audience thinking about the programme, they want the audience thinking about the sales pitch in the commercial. 'Quality' programming, in the sense of thoughtful and thought-provoking dramatic material, inhibits commercial message reception. Thought-provoking drama can suppress emotion, even depress emotion. Suppressed or depressed emotions are the sales department's biggest worry because sad or contemplative viewers are not as easily influenced by commercials as happy viewers.

There is a saying in the music business that happy songs sell records and sad songs sell beer. In television I propose we have a saying that goes like this: silly shows stimulate sales and serious shows stimulate debate. Aaron would be proud of me.

So, just how bleak is the future of quality in American television drama? As far as I am concerned, the future is not bleak at all. As I write this the paradigms that drove vertical integration are collapsing. Larger corporations are selling off one division after another. Smaller creative shops are providing quality dramas once again. There is a tipping point in every process and presently we as a nation are reaching it together as our national hunger for peace and fairness brings with it a courage to voice dissent. A harbinger of that is already seen in the writing being done on current quality drama series. There is change in the wind, and, fortunately for all of us, there is growth in the change. Growth that brings quality not only to television drama, but more importantly to our experience as a nation among nations. Who knows, we may even start talking to God again.

8
Quality US TV

A Buyer's Perspective

Dermot Horan

. . . .

Since 1995, my responsibilities at RTÉ (the Irish public broadcaster) have included the acquisition of all non-Irish programming. This role followed more than 10 years' work in television production and direction, both in Ireland and the UK. This experience gives me a real insight into the way programming is bought, scheduled and marketed.

RTÉ, like most English-speaking territories, buys mainly English-language material. This is not only because English-speaking countries tend to be very lazy about learning other languages, but also because there is a common story-telling culture among the Anglo Saxon nations. Hence a 'cop show' in Australia, the UK, Ireland and the USA will tend to have a similar look, feel and pace. The budget may be bigger in the USA than Australia, but the premise will remain the same.

The Power of the US Majors

The USA is the biggest exporter of television and movies in the world. It controls over 70 per cent of the market. When you look closer the USA is actually made up of only six major companies: Warner Bros, Disney, NBC Universal, Sony, Twentieth Century Fox and CBS Paramount. These companies are familiar the world over. They produce the vast majority of the movies that go into your local multiplex; they own huge film libraries; they also produce the overwhelming bulk of US network and cable series.

Vertical integration in recent years has accelerated this dominance of the market. Of the five main US networks, CBS is owned by CBS Paramount (a Viacom company), ABC is owned by Disney, NBC is owned by NBC Universal (part of General Electric), Fox is of course owned by Twentieth Century Fox, and the CW Television Network is co-owned by Warner Bros and CBS. Similarly, these same media giants own the major cable broadcasters like HBO, TNT and Showtime. Other independent companies to be consumed over the last 10 years include Turner, New World, MTM, Rysher and Worldvision. This leaves the six 'majors' with huge leverage and the international buyer with very little choice as to where they will buy US products for their schedules.

Packaging

Television series are rarely bought as a one-off from these companies, except in very large territories. Latterly the UK broadcasters have been paying very large amounts for single series, on the basis of an auction or bidding process. This has come about mainly as a result of the recent successes of shows such as *Lost, Desperate Housewives* and the *CSI* franchise. However, in most territories, television series are 'packaged' with movies, which allows the distributor to 'move' as much product as possible. As studios can have good and bad movie years at the box office, so they can have similar fortunes with their television product. A 'package' can allow a major media company to sell a poor list of movies, because they are also selling a strong list of new television series, and vice-versa. Even the large movie and television series libraries can be 'forced' upon a luckless buyer, or they can prove good value and useful in a poor year.

From the buyer's point of view, there will be plenty of varying slots for acquired programming, some in-peak, but also many off-peak in daytime and late-night slots. There is little point in paying for blockbuster movies or highly successful television series for these off-peak slots, and thus a package that includes cheaper material, including classic older movies and TV series, can work for both parties. In short, 'packaging' involves heavy volumes, which means that smaller distributors, often with equally good product, have difficulties competing.

Television Tastes in the Early Twenty-First Century

In the 1970s television schedules across the world were filled with US television series – *Starsky and Hutch, Dallas, Dynasty, Knight Rider* and *The Six Million Dollar Man*. They featured in primetime and generated huge audiences. Now tastes have changed, particularly in Europe; the biggest channels in their given territories such as BBC One and ITV (UK), TF1 (France), RAI Uno (Italy) and RTÉ One (Ireland) have mainly local productions in their evening schedules, with the exception of movies.

There are a number of factors affecting this decline in US programming and the rise of local production among these bigger channels. The world is now a smaller place. In the 1970s a US cop show featuring glamorous cities like New York or San Francisco appeared very exotic; the cars were bigger, the cops brandished guns and the cast often had matinee-idol looks. Now Europeans spend weekends in New York and take their families to Florida in the summer; US cars are seen as old-fashioned gas-guzzlers. Local drama in Europe has cast indigenous actors, with less glamorous looks, leading to a view that the old US model harks back to a different time. Indeed, Americana and the Wild West are out of fashion: mainstream network shows like *Bonanza, The High Chaparral*, even *Dr. Quinn Medicine Woman* would not work outside the US market any longer. Dramas about astronauts and aliens are equally less successful outside the USA.

Local drama production is expensive but relevant. The larger European broadcasters can afford to make it and reap the rewards in ratings terms. The cheaper end of TV drama, the local soap opera, tops the ratings in most European territories. These soaps are rooted in a social realist tradition (unlike their glamorous US counterparts, designed only for daytime audiences) and feature storylines about issues happening in their respective countries.

Why Movies Still Work

Movies still work, however. Viewers can see these feature films at the cinema, rent or buy them on DVD, or access them on a pay movie channel. Nevertheless, movies play an important part in most broadcasters' schedules. They are produced with a budget that could never be countenanced by a television channel and often feature the best-known 'stars' in the world. A broadcaster could never afford to cast Tom Cruise or Mel Gibson in a drama made for the small screen, but they can show one of their movies.

Also, many television stations rely on advertising for their funding. Of all the demographics that the advertisers crave, the 15–34-year-olds are the most important. They are the people who haven't yet chosen their favourite brand of beer, bank or moisturising cream. Much of a broadcaster's primetime schedule, such as news and soaps, will not be particularly attractive to this age group. They do, however, watch movies in huge numbers. Movies are also long; if they generate an audience it can be kept to a high level for over two hours. In 'shoulder' (an industry term for the period immediately before and after a peak season) and off-peak seasons, such as the summer, movies can fill the schedule with attractive, cost-effective programming.

Where is the New Home for US Programming?

With the main terrestrial channels in Europe focusing on local production, there is another important market for the US distributors. In every country there are now several new commercial channels, some brand-new entities and some off-shoots of big media players. These smaller channels can afford to target smaller niche audiences. They are not looking to be number one in their territories, and US programming gives them volume at the right price. If the programme they are buying is critically praised, it can also give great kudos to the channel and help its branding. Within this context, the US distributors can still garner large amounts of foreign licensing dollars. These smaller commercial channels compete for share in the same way as the big boys; a strong US series, which lasts 22 weeks, can form the backbone of a schedule.

Below these smaller terrestrial broadcasters comes another level, the cable and satellite channels. Some of these will not be able to afford to compete for new US programming, but can acquire second or third runs of the product, to be shown well after the first broadcaster. This 'windowing' allows the distributor several sales of the same product over several years. In recent times, these cable broadcasters have also decided to pitch for brand new series from the USA, to give their network a signature show or two. They cannot afford the volume of the terrestrial commercial broadcasters, but still feel a loss leader show can bring to their channel an audience who in turn can be lured into watching other programmes on it.

Why Quality US TV Can Help Build a Brand

Whereas major terrestrial broadcasters rely on their own commissioned programmes to create their brand, smaller terrestrial and cable and satellite channels are reliant on acquired programmes to establish theirs. US series come in large batches and can remain in the same slot for almost six months, and this 'owning' of a particular slot can be marketed. Until recently this marketing was confined to on-air promotions, but now expensive 48-sheet poster campaigns, cinema ads and bus sides feature key acquired series. Channel 4 in the UK has admitted to spending over £1.5 million on the launch of *Lost*. Sky One, also in the UK, spent similar amounts on their exclusive UK screening of *24*.

Both these channels feature several US series in their primetime schedules. However, only a few shows get the big marketing treatment, and the priority is not necessarily given to those generating the largest audiences, but to those that give the channel an image of quality and of being ahead of the competition. Programmes like *Lost* and *24* tend to attract the 'early adopters' most coveted by advertisers, those who embrace a show early in its life and pass on the message to colleagues and peers that this is the 'hot' show to watch.

A few of these key series in a broadcaster's schedule can mask a multitude of more mediocre programming. The channel will gain and lose its reputation over a few key series, and long-running US series are among the most important.

Which US Series Have This Special Appeal?

Since I entered the acquisitions arena in 1995, the number of US series with the ability to enhance a broadcaster's brand has been very small. Every year the US networks commission over 40 new series. In some years not one of these shows would have the ability to be marketed as a core value of a channel. The successful series that immediately come to mind are *ER*, *Friends*, *The Simpsons*, *The Sopranos*, *Sex and the City*, *Six Feet Under*, *24*, *Desperate Housewives* and *Lost*.

Some of the above, such as *ER*, *Friends* and *Desperate Housewives*, have generated large audiences and given kudos to the broadcaster. Others, like *The Sopranos*, *24* and *Six Feet Under*, have been watched by small numbers but have made important statements about the ambitions of the channel. All of these series are sold for large amounts, or placed in large volume packages.

These shows are the lifeblood of the major US distributors. Every year in May, immediately following the announcements of the US network's autumn or fall schedules, about 1,500 international buyers arrive in Los Angeles to view those pilots that have been 'picked up' for the upcoming season. These screenings last a full week, and word soon gets out as to which are the hot shows among the pilots. It is a cyclical business among the distributors. Warner Bros were in the ascendancy in the late 1990s with their offerings of *ER*, *Friends*, *The Sopranos* and *Six Feet Under*. Disney, having had a poor selection of series for several years, launched *Desperate Housewives* and *Lost* in 2004. Both allowed Disney to negotiate long-term heavy volume deals in many territories.

What Makes These Shows Stand Out from the Crowd?

Why is it that just a few shows emerge to garner international success? Is it the theme? The casting? The timing? It is all of these things.

In 1994 Warner Bros launched *ER* in the same year as CBS offered their own medical series, *Chicago Hope*. Both were hospital based, both – ironically – set in Chicago, both had strong, well-produced pilots. However, *Chicago Hope* was produced in a traditional way, using camera techniques and pacing that could be found in countless other series. *ER*, on the other hand, brought emergency medicine into the living room, with an intensity and pace never seen before in a television drama. Dialogue was fast and furious; sometimes it was difficult to hear what the doctors were saying. This was deliberate. *Chicago Hope* lasted several seasons and was sold with some success internationally. *ER* was a global phenomenon. It broke records for the amount broadcasters would pay for it. It launched movie stars such as George Clooney, but the real star was the hospital and its emergency room. It has lasted for over 13 seasons.

Sex and the City was another show that broke new ground. Before, most half-hour series were situation comedies, shot in the studio with a live audience and with an enhanced laughter track added. Half-hour comedies were the fare of the big networks, not the cable stations. HBO broke the mould, firstly with an unsung hero of the genre, *The Larry Sanders Show*, and then more successfully, from a viewer numbers perspective with *Sex and the City*. Realising that their subscription numbers had reached a plateau, HBO thought it important to keep those subscribers happy, and if some did cancel their subscriptions, to make sure that others were recruited to replace them. Movies that had already been seen in the cinema and had been in video libraries for months were no longer the big draw they used to be. Thus, a new approach had to be found.

The new strategy involved the commissioning of brand new series, or what has become known as HBO original programming. Broadcast on cable, these shows were not subject to the same Federal Communications Commission (FCC) content rules as the free-to-air networks. Four-letter words, nudity and sexual content were introduced into the drama and comedy mix. Furthermore it introduced new aesthetic and production practices. For example, *Sex and the City* was shot on location in New York, a fact emphasised by the producers. There was no laughter track, no multi-camera studio scenes. It was shot like a movie using a single camera on 35mm.

More recently the networks have had more success with television drama. While they can never violate FCC regulations in the same way as cable, they have again begun to produce groundbreaking shows like *Lost, Desperate Housewives* and the *CSI* franchise. It shows that the audience wants something new, something different from the norm.

Quality US TV: The Future

As long as there are networks and cable stations, new, exciting product will be necessary to attract the audience and to sell advertising. Internationally, local production will continue to generate the largest audiences. However, the proliferation of digital channels means that there will always be a home for good international programming. Those series produced by the six US majors will be sold across the globe in bigger numbers than those from the smaller distributors.

The economics of running commercial channels ensures that programming that is attractive to an upscale audience with plenty of spending power will always be the most attractive option for a buyer. Thus, innovative, groundbreaking series from the USA will be seen in your living room for some time to come.

9

CSI: Crime Scene Investigation

Quality, the Fifth Channel and 'America's Finest'
Ian Goode

....

The arrival of Britain's fifth terrestrial channel came during the 1990s, when cultural debate often focused on the spectre of dumbing-down and when television was frequently blamed as both evidential symptom as well as a cause (Collini 2000). Talking about the early years, Dawn Airey, first joining Channel 5 as director of programmes before becoming chief executive in 2000, famously described its offering as 'football, films and fucking' (Wells 2003). However, after a rebranding exercise and adjustments to their programming policy, the identity of Channel 5 moved away from its earlier downmarket image to assume a more respectable position to now challenge Channel 4 in the area of quality drama.

Channel 5 has a relation with the very idea of quality television distinct to that of the other terrestrial channels that for a long time formed the duopoly of British television. Imported drama series purchased from the USA have been key to the development of the channel's identity and the most notable example of this relay across the Atlantic is *CSI: Crime Scene Investigation*. Indeed, it is the role of this series as a cornerstone of the crime dramas initially promoted as 'America's Finest' and more recently as 'Drama at 10' that I wish to examine here.

History and Quality

Following the 1990 Broadcasting Act the Independent Television Commission (ITC) was required to establish a fifth terrestrial channel in the UK by awarding the licence for the fifth channel, following a process of competitive tender. Seven years later, in 1997, Channel 5 was launched as the fifth and youngest terrestrial television channel in the UK and was initially owned by a combination of four media companies with RTL – Europe's largest commercial broadcaster – as the major shareholder. Christine Fanthome argues that in the early years the channel occupied a position where it was required to bridge the gap between public service expectations inherited from the past and the market realities arising from the increasingly competitive multi-channelled present (2003: 32). Under the licence granted by the ITC, Channel 5 was required to include a prescribed amount of programme diversity as well as attain a high level of quality (137).

Insistence upon diversity, a specified number of hours per genre and an ill-defined adherence to quality suggested that in the context of the fifth channel the meaning of the term 'quality' becomes more quantifiable and regulated by the provision of a prescribed level of scheduled choice and production requirements. This reflects a continuation of the uneasy balance between the legacy of public service broadcasting and the primacy of the market following the Peacock Report in 1986. There is a marked compromise here between the government, the regulatory body and the broadcasting company that reflects uncertainty over the meaning of quality. The public service broadcasting values of Reith's enlightenment ideal are compromised but not wholly abandoned by the commercial broadcasting company operating in the marketplace of the late 1990s. But, perhaps more importantly, the granting of the licence presents an understanding of quality that can be quantitatively monitored.

Christine Fanthome's research highlights how the channel failed to meet fully the requirements of the ITC review of the channel in 1998, which identified that 'the shortfall in original drama was a breach of the licence commitments' (167). This criticism brought the following response from David Elstein, the former chief executive of Channel 5: 'who doesn't want to increase the quality and widen the range of their programmes? We live in two realities . . . the economic one and the regulatory one . . . We aim for good quality and occasionally high quality . . . High quality on Channel 5 is relatively rare' (quoted in Fanthome 2003: 169). Elstein summarises the conflict between economics and regulation, and indicates how a more specific and graduated meaning of quality is necessary for a broadcasting company with the limited resources of the fifth channel.

Dawn Airey counters this assumption that quality is essentially production led, saying instead: 'quality doesn't necessarily equate to pounds spent on screen. It's relevance, it's how it achieves resonance with the audience through programming which is appropriate to the time – it's are you moving on genres, are you being intelligent in terms of your commissioning' (quoted in Fanthome 2003: 165–6). Airey questions the point at which the characteristics of quality are evident and attempts to shift the focus of the debate towards the audience the channel is trying to attract. At this point these responses to the regulatory pressure exerted by the ITC confirm how, during the early years, the fifth channel was still critically perceived as the home of cheap, low-quality programming epitomised by the scheduling of imported soft porn films late on in the weekend schedules; a practice that earned the channel the label of 'channel filth'. The evolution of the channel away from this impression began in 2001 with the arrival of Director of Programmes Kevin Lygo, who sought to review the identity of the channel. The schedule also began to reflect Airey's policy of intelligent commissioning along with delivering programming that achieved resonance with a core audience, which is aptly demonstrated by the purchase of generically innovative drama series from the USA.

The Rebranding of the Fifth Channel

The initial Channel 5 brand sought 'to cater for the modern mass audience whilst also focusing on the specific (younger) narrowcast demographic that is so keenly sought by advertisers' (Fanthome 2003: 38). The channel sold itself to advertisers on the basis of offering an alternative to ITV and reaching a younger more upmarket audience. It had partially succeeded in the early period in attracting a younger male audience than the general television audience, but suffered from a reputation for low quality. The Channel 5 schedule was underpinned by Hollywood movies scheduled at 9 pm each night of the week, but the Saturday night schedule was performing particularly badly. One solution to remedy this situation was the decision taken by Director of Acquisitions Jeff Ford to acquire *CSI* for the channel; he purchased the series through Alliance Atlantis – who co-produced the series with CBS and Bruckheimer Television – in 2001. As he points out, 'Channel 4 has been very lucky in that they had a long-term deal with Warner Brothers for *Friends* and *ER*, which gave them by default a number of other shows such as *The West Wing*. What we are trying to do is identify signature shows that will do well for us' (quoted in Wells 2003). Because *CSI* was a new series in the USA, the negotiations with Alliance Atlantis and CBS were not as difficult as they might have been if the series were already established through previous seasons. As a result, a bidding war, as seen between Channel 4 and Sky for *ER* and *Friends* in 2000, was avoided.

CSI offered something new to the heart of the Saturday evening schedule. The pilot screened as two back-to-back episodes with favourable ratings, delivering 2.3 million viewers, and this figure subsequently climbed to 3.7 million or 15 per cent of the audience in 2004 (Ford 2004). The decision to import *CSI* coincided with the rebranding of the channel following the appointment of Lygo from Channel 4 in 2001. Channel 5 became simply Five, and it commissioned art programmes and discontinued the type of programming that had tarnished the reputation of the channel with potential advertisers. As a result, the channel increased its share of advertisement revenue.

The introduction of *CSI* did as Ford hoped, and established a popular signature show for the channel. It also confirmed the identity of the channel as part of 'the modern mainstream' (Wells 2003). The recent history of the fifth channel shows how the introduction of *CSI* – and other series from the USA – has served to placate critics and deliver audience share during a period when the presence of selected drama series produced in the USA took increasing precedence over home-produced drama on the fourth and fifth channels (McCabe 2000). The recent addition of digital channels E4 and More4 to Channel 4 has created new space for home-produced drama, evident in the opening-night schedule of More4 in October 2005 with the one-off drama-documentary *A Very Social Secretary* alongside repeats of established American series such as *The West Wing, ER* and *The Sopranos*.

In most accounts of the performance of Five, *CSI* is mentioned positively (Chater 2004). The channel has since acquired more crime drama series from the USA in the shape of *Law & Order: Criminal Intent, Boomtown, The Shield* and the extensions of the *CSI* franchise *CSI: Miami* and *CSI: New York*. These series were promoted collectively and established by the channel as 'America's Finest'. This strategy has continued with the acquisition of *House* and *Prison Break* and the replacement of 'America's Finest' with the slogan 'Drama at 10', which functions to emphasise how the Five schedule now contains quality drama from the USA in this slot five days a week. The unity of this promotion and the expansion of acquisition enables the claim that Five is the home of America's finest drama and presents a schedule that is much less reliant upon Hollywood films. The high production values of these new crime dramas represent a means of branding imported quality for Britain's fifth terrestrial channel and competing more directly with Channel 4.

The Reception of *CSI*

The initial response to *CSI* by television critics in the UK confirms how the relationship between quality American drama and the fifth channel represents a different inflection from that initially associated with Channel 4 and drama series produced by HBO such as *The Sopranos* and *Six Feet Under*. Critics did not necessarily welcome the arrival of the slick and glossy surface of the new series without reservations. Andrew Billen wrote:

> when DNA analysis became common, some crime writers feared for the genre lest science made every case instantly open and shut replacing human drama with the drama of science works ... it is easily Channel 5's best import so far ... but never forget that it is a creature not of Steve Bochco's but of Jerry Bruckheimer's, the brilliant moron behind *Armageddon* and *Pearl Harbor* (2001).

David Chater also comments: 'the *CSI* gang is back to solve more far-fetched murders with its winning combination of high-tech equipment, deductive cool and lip gloss' (2004). Begrudging and sceptical as these comments are of the pedigree of *CSI*, their relatively elevated cultural sources function to confirm the position of the fifth channel as one of the mainstream. This is a location in the market-orientated spectrum of television drama where the high production values and spectacle of recent American drama enable the channel to meet its requirement to broadcast original drama.

Billen also wrote of his admiration of recent American television drama over British equivalents based on the claim that 'emotionally and intellectually the current batch of quality American imports provides all we need from television drama' (2002a). Though *CSI* appears in Billen's list, he lavishes most praise on *The Sopranos* and *Six Feet Under*. He suggests that 'the only difference between *The Sopranos* and *Goodfellas* or between *Six Feet Under* and *American Beauty* is that *The Sopranos* and *Six Feet Under* are the more sophisticated offerings' (ibid). Billen's argument is predicated on the cinematic antecedents of quality American drama produced by HBO and imported into the UK for the discerning audience of Channel 4. Five and *CSI* offer the possibility of a similar kind of valorisation but much less through the drama of human relationships and subjectivities that make up the Channel 4 series. *CSI* and the other constituents of 'America's Finest' offer the much more generic and episodic pleasures of crime drama that do crucial work for the brand identity of the channel. The recent expansion in the *CSI* franchise and the slate of American drama on Five means that this differentiation in the positioning of the channels vis-à-vis the perception of quality is less easily sustained. The recent acquisition of *Big Love* by Five and the increasing rivalry between the two channels where previously there was talk of a merger underlines this repositioning (Deans 2006).

The recent increase in the production of quality drama brought to the UK from the USA represents a continuation of the televisual style that John Caldwell describes as excessive, visually exhibitionist and cinematic (1995: 110). His argument can be recast and updated when reviewed in the context of a commercial British television channel required to find a balance between the realities of the market, the continued need to reach its core audience and the requirement to produce a prescribed amount of original drama by the ITC. The excessive televisuality of American drama serves as a marker of distinction when imported into a television ecology where drama is historically predicated on social realism. Since the fifth channel does not commission home-produced drama, except for its soap opera *Family Affairs*, the high production values and distinct style of *CSI* and other imported drama help to maintain the brand of the channel with its core audience at a time when Five is the only terrestrial channel just starting to exploit the possibilities of extra digital channels. (*CSI*, along with the others in the franchise, are key highlights of the new Five digital channel fiveUS.)

The distinctive style of *CSI* trades on the benefits of cinematic production and reveals a televisual quality that makes it difficult to make the straightforward allusion to cinema exhibited by the example of *Six Feet Under*. The concentration upon forensic investigation in *CSI* is not only generically innovative but consistently exploits the capacity of television to form relations of proximity to detailed procedures presented with unapologetically sleek style.

The Drama of Science

The work of *CSI* in making crime drama out of science functions by amending but not wholly dispensing with the generic terms of the investigation of crime. The application of the techniques of forensic science by the different members of the team at the various crime scenes in and around Las Vegas forms the basis for each episode. The characters that investigate the crime scene form a team of *criminalists* who work alongside a conventional detective. Elizabeth Devine, an executive story editor on *CSI*, formerly worked as a criminalist with the Los Angeles police department and she defines a criminalist as 'a scientist who uses scientific training in the different disciplines of science to analyse evidence and prepare for court' (quoted in LaTempa 2000). The criminalists specialise in investigating the evidence that is derived from the crime scenes that usually follow a murder. In the first episode there is a clear distinction made between cops and criminalists when the lead scientist, Gil Grissom (William L. Petersen), states, 'I don't chase criminals. . . . I just evaluate evidence'; he later says, 'We're not detectives, we're crime scene analysts, we're trained not to rely on verbal accounts, and rely instead on the evidence the scene sets before us.' The rational and detached disposition of the criminalists is tempered by their particular scientific enthusiasms and the occasional references to their personal lives. *CSI* shifts dramatic emphasis through the focus on a different means of investigation that reconstructs the crime through a forensic analysis of the crime scene. It is this dramatisation and fictionalisation of forensic science that creates the possibilities for the visual style of *CSI* and a new crime drama that has become a successful franchise of Alliance Atlantis with subsequent versions of *CSI* set in Miami and New York. The visual style is founded on closely scrutinising the surfaces at the crime scene using the optical technologies and other machinery of the forensic laboratory. This is demonstrated in two examples from season one: 'Blood Drops' (1: 7) and 'Sex, Lies and Larvae' (1: 10).

In the first example, forensic technology machinery is deployed to reveal the presence of blood drops on the surface of maple floorboards that had been lacquered to disguise a murder. Grissom deploys the optical tools of the chemical Luminol, which does not react with the surface, and then ALS (alternative light source), which pursues the protein molecules in blood to expose the evidence that is present on the surface of the floorboards but not visible to the human eye. The techniques of this exposure are used by Grissom to reconstruct the crime verbally, while the high-contrast flashback footage illustrates his interpretation of the evidence, which proves to be partially incorrect in the first instance. It is this search for and collection of evidence using an array of forensic techniques in conjunction with DNA and fingerprint matching to detect, collect and process evidence that creates the style and drama of *CSI*. Such scenes, where evidence is collected and processed, usually to selective accompanying music, typify the work of the *CSI* team and the style of the signature show. The detection and collection of evidence combines the related senses of smell, touch, hearing and vision. This process is conveyed to the viewer visually, and *CSI* televisually intensifies the act and scope of looking and seeing in crime drama through such set pieces of forensic work. In this way the use of forensic science in the process of detection functions to displace the singular figure of the detective and its attendant repertoire of generic elements such as the trailing and interrogation of witnesses and suspects (Brunsdon 1998: 224).

Despite the hi-tech gadgetry of *CSI*, the figure at the head of the forensic team is the older, single and cerebral figure of Grissom, who is clearly invested in the enlightenment and the history of knowledge. The scientific hermeneutic of *CSI* drives a narrative of cognition where the technologies of forensic analysis, in combination with the individual specialisms of the *CSI* team, still offer the satisfaction of a desire to reveal the truth through evidence. Unlike other recent dramas such as *The X-Files* with its self-consciously postmodern epistemology, *CSI* represents episodic drama with definite narrative closure.

A key element of the generic iconography of the forensic drama is the autopsy of the dead and disfigured body. In 'Sex Lies and Larvae' an unidentified woman is found dead in the mountains, having been shot in the head. The autopsy room is dedicated to the examination and study of the dead body, and the coroner is rarely seen outside this venue. The gaze at the body on the slab is a clinical and investigative one involving Dr Al Robbins (Robert David Hall), Grissom and Sara Sidle (Jorja Fox) as the cause of death is identified and partially reconstructed. As Dr Robbins reports on the causes of death based on his examination of the body, the insertion of a visual effect into the current dramatic scene restages the moment of death by showing the penetration of the flesh by a bullet from a gun. This device forms part of a larger narrative scheme that frequently draws on the flashback to shift perspective back to the crime, as it is being investigated and reconstructed, and underlines the necessity of forensic science as a means of solving crime.

The visual effect begins with a close-up of the side of the victim's head and then shifts to a macro-photographic close-up shot of a bullet leaving the barrel of a gun and hitting and piercing the flesh. At this point the head is a prosthetic model used to simulate the action of the murder and the kinetic effect compensates for the spatial shift and the disjunction between the real and the simulated. The spectacle of microscopic and magnified visual effects suspends the temporalities of classical editing and reanimates the moment of death and the crime that is being investigated. These inserts have come to be known as 'the *CSI* shot' and serve an expositional function accompanying dialogue within the investigation as well as helping to maintain the pace of the narrative (Hamit 2002). It is through the process of fictionalising science and the representation of the body that the forensic television drama can be related to science fiction. This has less to do with the futures imagined through science and more to do with the corporeal imaging of bodily interiors and genetic structures such as DNA. The increasing visualisation of the body confirms Warren Buckland's suggestion that visual effects can be used to represent '*possible worlds* – that exist between science fact and science fiction' (1999).

The next shots of the autopsy scene show how the forensic gaze at and into the body functions to exhibit the different specialities of the team. Close shots of Sara looking at the body lead to her observation that the proximity of gun barrel to scalp confirms that 'this was an intimate killing', and the facial fractures revealed by X-rays suggest 'a long-term abusive relationship'. Grissom's knowledge of entomology transforms the presence of an insect on the body into potential evidence that will reveal the time of death. In *CSI* the body becomes a site for the dramatic anatomisation of crime using the techniques of forensic science.

The autopsy room typifies the cinematic look and style of *CSI*. The use of light hitting the metallic surface of the autopsy room and the extensive manipulation of contrast through post-production techniques have the effect of highlighting the surface and texture of the skin of the faces in shot to the extent that the face becomes another surface that is probed by the forensic look of *CSI* (Bankston 2001). The televisual qualities of *CSI* are located in the techniques that enlarge, magnify, manipulate and expose the depths and details of the surface to create a spectacle of the surface. The production draws upon the resources and technical craft of film-industry professionals but produces a different optical scale to that which is usually associated with cinema spectacle (Lury 2005). One of the consequences of this emphasis upon the surface of detail is to limit the degree of social context given to the violent crimes of Las Vegas.

A slightly later addition to the stable of 'America's Finest', *The Shield*, is a more naturalistic drama from Fox Television that gives a larger and ongoing context to crime by continuously problematising the separation between the criminals and the corruptibility of the officers and detectives of the Farmington district of the LAPD who pursue them. Whilst both dramas belong to the stable of 'America's Finest', the differences between them also help to promote the uniqueness of the dramas over their derivativeness.

The arrival of *CSI* on to Five in 2001 introduced a popular and innovative series to the UK audience. The dramatic possibilities of the crime genre were extended by exploiting forensic science as a means of investigating crime on television. The high production values of drama from the USA function to represent a differentiated quality for the fifth channel and its core audience. *CSI* comes out of a period of American television that Caldwell associates with excessive style, but such excess becomes revised and critically desired when viewed in the context of British television and the new fifth channel hitherto associated with a much lower quality of production but now in a position to challenge Channel 4, despite not being able to call upon extra digital channels.

This exchange reflects a period of British television drama in the late 1990s and beyond where, despite the cultural pessimism of some critics, the symbiotic relation between the issue of quality and cross-Atlantic exchanges of television production now warrants comparative rather than oppositional attention (Cooke 2005). Meanwhile, commercial channels such as Five are likely to continue to depend upon the acquisition and promotion of US quality drama series such as *CSI* over series produced in the UK in order to maintain their brand identity.

10

The Problem of Quality Television

Television Schedules, Audience Demographics
and Cultural Policy in New Zealand
Geoff Lealand

• •

Quality of life [we] understand; quality of television is a mystery
Les Brown, American television critic
(quoted in Lealand and Martin 2001: 216)

When I last wrote at length about quality television in New
Zealand, in 'Searching for Quality Television in New Zealand:
Hunting the Moa?' (2001), I suggested that debates about 'quality'
had been 'under-articulated and impoverished, with the default
meaning implying middle brow and conventional taste formations'
(448). I also pointed to examples of New Zealand-produced youth
programming that were, without attracting attention, fulfilling
the expectations of Marion Hobbs, then-minister of broadcasting,
that quality television ought to have the ability of taking viewers
'outside their comfort zone', whilst avoiding being 'diverted into
questions of personal taste' (ibid).

Some six years on, in 2006, the Labour government is in its third
consecutive term in power, there is a new minister of broadcasting
(Steve Maharey), but arguments about quality television have not
greatly advanced. A new set of considerations has emerged, with
significant shifts in television at both the policy and structural
levels. Debates about 'quality' are still very much on the agenda and,
indeed, have become central to current efforts to shift the dominant

state-owned broadcaster – Television New Zealand – towards a more openly public service television role. In all these endeavours, which will be described shortly, considerations of 'quality' are both implicit and explicit.

Occasional disputes, or murmuring of discontent, about the value of television as a 'quality' medium and its appropriate ranking in the canons of cultural value are sometimes still heard across the land, but the bulk of New Zealand viewers do not appear to be greatly engaged with this particular issue. Disquiet about this aspect of television remains the preserve of small lobby groups such as the right-wing Voters for Television Excellence Inc, in snide comments expressed on rival media (especially state-owned National Radio), or smug pronouncements in Letters to the Editor. The last group of opinions usually take the discursive lines of 'we don't have TV and my children are so creative!' or hark back to an imagined Golden Age of Before-Television.

Television has been part of life in New Zealand since its beginnings in 1960, and, 47 years on, retains its central place in the social, political, economic and symbolic life of the nation. In over four-and-a-half decades, television has been in a continuous state of flux. Indeed, it has been variously characterised as 'a menace to mankind' (L.D. Austin, quoted in Lealand and Martin 2001: 246), a 'political football' (Lealand and Martin 2001: 22), and a 'cash cow' (Alley 2003: A7). For more than four decades, successive governments have taken on television as a project to be restructured, deregulated and re-regulated.

In the most recent manifestation of change, the Labour government (led by Prime Minister Helen Clark) has turned to the state-owned network of Television New Zealand (TVNZ) for another significant round of restructuring of television in this South Pacific nation. Having inherited 10 long years of free market ideology and government policy that placed minimal restraints on commercial imperatives, the network prioritised ratings-led programming, increased domination by imported programming in the schedules and actively encouraged the sale of New Zealand-owned broadcasting assets to overseas interests. Indeed, by the mid-1990s it could be claimed that the deregulation of the New Zealand television system was 'probably without peer in the rest of the world' (Lealand 2000: 78).

Labour swept into office in November 1998 promising, amongst other things, to reverse the direction television had been taking for 10 or 15 years. There was widespread agreement among the newly appointed politicians and various opinion makers that the prevailing purely commercial broadcasting was inadequate to fulfil cultural and democratic functions. Through the 1990s, as a state-owned enterprise, TVNZ had been obliged to maximise profits for government coffers. Residual public service roles had become the responsibility of the funding agency New Zealand On Air, which commissioned New Zealand-made programming from revenue from the Public Broadcasting Fee (abolished in 1998 and replaced by a direct government grant), and some light regulation through the Broadcasting Standards Authority.

Inheriting years of free-market policy from the previous National government, there was little Labour could do about controlling privately owned free-to-air channels TV3 and C4 (owned by Canadian-based Canwest Global Communications) and Prime and Sky TV owned by Sky Network Television. Nevertheless, Labour intervened by funding the setting-up and ongoing costs of the Maori Television Service, to fulfil cultural objectives (Maori is the second official language) and obligations under the Treaty of Waitangi, which shapes bi-cultural relationships in New Zealand. It also turned its attention to TVNZ, the state-owned television system that continued to dominate the television landscape (with 65 to 70 per cent audience share), whilst returning considerable profits to the state (over $NZ250 million in dividends between 1989 and 1999). During the 1990s, the National government had been positioning TVNZ for privatisation (most probably through sale to overseas interests).

Labour had no such plans, but instead set out to retrieve ownership of state-owned television and set out to reshape TVNZ in its own image. To this end, it created the Television New Zealand 'Charter' to steer the broadcaster in new directions, instructing it to,

- strive always to maintain the highest standards of programme quality and editorial integrity;
- feature programming across the full range of genres that informs, entertains and educates New Zealand audiences;
- play a leading role in New Zealand television by setting standards of programme quality and encouraging creative risk-taking (Television New Zealand 'Charter' 2003).

Even as it continued to derive considerable dividends from TVNZ (most recently $NZ38 million for the period June 2003 to June 2004, with $NZ11 million of this returned to TVNZ after top-level protests), the Labour government was providing the broadcaster with substantial funding to pay for Charter objectives ($NZ16 million in 2004, with a further $NZ17 million in 2005). The ambiguity of these transactions (taking away with one hand and giving back with the other) is seldom commented on, but it can be seen as another manifestation of the tension that has long been a characteristic of television in New Zealand, which makes it a fascinating object of study.

It is not just a question of finance and funding: there are the continuing expectations of TVNZ (a state-owned broadcaster shaped by the competing objectives of commercial viability and public service requirements) to sustain such mixed objectives. Together with the repositioning of competing channels, the new regime at TVNZ has implications for notions of quality broadcasting and quality programming. Unlike television systems in other countries (the BBC, with its public service remit, for example) TVNZ has to satisfy different kinds of 'quality' to

- commission and produce quality programming that will fulfil Charter guidelines;
- generate considerable output in quality genres (drama, news and current affairs, children's programming);
- provide quality viewing options, across two channels, through a mix of locally produced and imported programming, across broad audiences;
- deliver quality audiences to advertisers, to sustain audience share and advertising revenue;
- provide quality alternatives to other television suppliers (private free-to-air channels and pay TV), and other competing attractions (such as the internet); and
- satisfy competing expectations of 'quality television'.

As might be expected, there are significant (possibly irreconcilable) tensions in this set of mixed objectives, as Peter A. Thompson points out, 'TVNZ's dual imperative to fulfil a broad range of Charter functions while maintaining its commercial performance has so far inhibited radical change' (2005b: 44). One rather ludicrous outcome of the changed television environment was the emergence, in May 2005, of three personality-led current affairs programmes (*Close Up@7* on TV One, *Holmes* on Prime, *Campbell Live* on TV3) competing head-to-head in the 7–7.30 pm time-slot. This happened when TVNZ's star performer Paul Holmes, who had fronted the top-rating *Holmes* on TV One for 16 years, defected to the Australian-owned network, to set up an equivalent current affairs programme. After failing to make a dent in the ratings of *Close Up@7* (TV One), Prime shifted Holmes to the earlier 6 pm slot, to compete directly with TV One and TV3 evening news bulletins, before eventually dumping him.

The details of these complicated scheduling rearrangements by the main free-to-air channels is less important than the fact that they demonstrate how competition, audience share and ratings continue to dominate the television discourse in New Zealand. There is fierce competition between the free-to-air channels but also from pay TV, with the dominant provider Sky Network Television (43 per cent owned by Rupert Murdoch's News Corporation) supplying more than 80 pay channels to more than 600,000 subscribers (41 per cent of New Zealand households) in May 2005.

A Quality Soap Opera

The sudden appearance of three near-identical programmes in the same time-slot across three leading channels is one manifestation of a competitive environment that won't go away. In May 2004, the only alternative to personality-led current affairs programming on free-to-air television, in the prime viewing slot of 7–7.30 pm, was the local medical soap opera *Shortland Street* (South Pacific Pictures). First launched in May 1992 on TVNZ's Channel 2, this long-running soap opera continues its run every week night (Monday to Friday) throughout the year (with only a short break around Christmas and the summer holidays). After 15 years it continues to attract a loyal and substantial audience, regularly winning over half of the viewing audience. Ratings for all viewers aged five and over have often been in the 20s; even in June 2005 when it was registering ratings of 13 to 14 per cent, it continued to take a place in the weekly top 10 programmes. *Shortland Street* is also a rare example of a New Zealand television export to the UK and other territories.

Examples of such stripped (Monday to Friday) serial dramas are rare across the globe. *Shortland Street* continues to occupy a vitally important place in the Channel 2 schedule, seeing off competitors and returning healthy advertising revenue to TVNZ. This is despite the tremendous task of introducing, extending and resolving storylines within the context of a fictional private medical facility with an extraordinary ability to churn through stories, situations and characters. It is also distinguished by its willingness to include content that is not the norm for early evening television – with recurring storylines about race relations, gay relationships (male and female), infidelity and divorce, drug and alcohol abuse, crime and criminal manipulation, out-of-control teens, medical misadventure – as well as the usual births, deaths and marriages. Bi-culturalism and multiculturalism have become commonplace with a wide range of characters who reflect the contemporary make-up of New Zealand society (Maori, Pakeha, Chinese, Tongan, Indian, Samoan). There is also a matter-of-fact approach to sexual diversity with a popular lesbian couple being married in a civil union ceremony on the Valentine's Day 2006 episode and their looking to produce children. This storyline has been seen as another example of the uncanny ability of *Shortland Street* writers to anticipate external events and the social concerns of New Zealanders in the storylines they develop months before events unfold, with this fictional storyline coinciding with the passing, against considerable opposition, of the 2005 Civil Union Bill, which sanctions non-traditional forms of marriage. All this happens within a non-didactic, funny and well-produced stripped local serial that continues to occupy a central place in New Zealand life. It has been praised by commentators and reviewers: 'Soap opera is well suited to develop issues that are genuinely divisive within a society, since soap operas are successful only if they grab the audience's attention. Effective soap operas cut to the underlying angst of a society' (Slade 2002: 86). 'The reasons for *Shortland Street*'s success have been widely rehearsed. It is dramatic and well paced. Longevity helps: people know it is around. The characters are recognizable archetypes. Humour abounds, a particularly New Zealand ha-ha, delivered with a straight face. There is controversy and a moral sub-text' (Wilson 1999: 72).

Whether *Shortland Street* should be considered quality television or, more specifically, 'quality New Zealand television drama' is an open question. Because it has been a staple in the TV2 evening schedule for so long (a very long time in New Zealand television terms) and because it is often referred to as 'a national institution', familiarity can breed contempt, or levels of indifference. Certainly *Shortland Street* no longer draws the levels of over-heated media attention and fan activity it generated in its first few years, when it often seemed like a national obsession. The stars still pop up on the covers of women's magazines and are part of a circulating body of 'celebrities', but many have disappeared or turn up in new guises (in supporting roles in *The Lord of the Rings* film trilogy, for example).

Nevertheless, even before it went to air, *Shortland Street* was embroiled in debates about 'quality' television. The serial was financed by a partnership of NZOA (New Zealand On Air) and TVNZ, and produced by South Pacific Pictures in conjunction with Grundy Television (Australia). NZOA first floated the idea of such a soap opera as a vehicle for fulfilling its cultural brief of reflecting New Zealand life on television and raising the profile of local television drama. Their rationale was that a primetime soap would be the most effective genre to invest in, reaching a broad cross-section of viewers, in a spirit of maximising returns to those who were paying for it, through the Public Broadcasting Fee that funded all NZOA activities.

In 1992, in a television environment dominated by commercial imperatives and free market ideology, NZOA was responsible for the residual public service obligations of television. It was the guardian of public service ideals with a particular responsibility for providing for minority and specialist audiences (women, children, ethnic groupings). As a consequence, its championing of serial drama (soap opera) was regarded by numerous commentators as being at odds with this brief, especially when *Shortland Street* faltered in the ratings in its early months; '... how on earth a soap that is sub-*Neighbours* and that at five days a week aims for quantity over quality, could ever be called better than anything else, is mind-boggling' (Kan 1993: 22). And: '"TVNZ foots it with the worst" thundered critics appalled at the "preoccupation with trivia and vapid content" of New Zealand's first five-nights-a-week sudser' (Grant 1997: B8). *The Evening Post*, demonstrating typical gracelessness, pronounced: 'It's a disgrace and an insult to ordinary New Zealanders to waste limited finance on such rubbish' (Wilson 1999: 72).

In his feature on the seventh anniversary of *Shortland Street*, Tim Wilson explains why NZOA was involved in its early years, despite the barrage of criticism it attracted,

The commercial reality at the outset ... was that *Shortland Street* needed state money to become viable. During the credits that roll at the end of each show, you can still see the thank-you note to New Zealand On Air (NZOA). The programme, which began development in 1991, was a three-way split between NZOA, South Pacific and Australian production house Grundys. Each pitched in about three million dollars. Over the following four years the NZOA contribution declined to nothing. The total investment came to $8.9 million dollars (1999: 72).

Four years earlier, the chair of NZOA had similarly argued, 'Without our initial support, *Shortland Street* would not have been made' (Norrish 1995: C5). The eventual success of the serial with New Zealand viewers has mitigated or diluted criticisms of NZOA's early involvement, and after 15 years in the schedule it probably has passed the quality threshold test for a substantial number of young, female viewers. Nevertheless, there are probably just as many (male, older viewers?) who cannot conceive of including soap opera in their canon of 'quality', and are even less likely to consider that it should receive public funding at any stage of its development.

Public Money and NZ Idol

In 2004, a similar debate emerged over the funding of the New Zealand version of the talent quest *NZ Idol*, based on the Freemantle Media-owned format, and produced in New Zealand by South Pacific Pictures. NZOA contributed $NZ450,000 to the production costs of this short-term series, which proved to be highly popular with viewers, recording the highest ratings (24 per cent) as the most-watched programme on New Zealand television in 2004. In its 2003–4 Annual Report, NZOA congratulated itself for its participation in this popular success: '*NZ Idol* created a shared experience for the whole country and gave ordinary New Zealanders an opportunity to show that they were capable of extraordinary things' (New Zealand On Air 2004: 8).

Other commentators, variously motivated by political opportunism and another opportunity to criticise NZOA's cultural agendas, lambasted the funding agency for its involvement: '. . . the Broadcasting Minister was pressured to explain why taxpayers' money had gone into the first [*NZ Idol*]. Steve Maharey insisted *NZ Idol* was an outstanding – and he echoed *Idol* winner Bem Lummis when he said critics of the funding "can't take that away" from the show' (Mediawatch 2004). TVNZ responded to such criticisms by arguing that the high cost of making local versions ('versioning') of such international formats required a subsidy injection from NZOA.

Television Formats, Schedules and Quality

In a world where the trade in television formats and local 'versioning' of proven formats is becoming ever more important than the longer-established international trade in television programmes (the traditional flows from the USA and UK to the rest of the world), there are new changes to conventional notions of 'quality' in television. When she writes about the spread of formats across Europe, Jeanette Steemers pretty much describes the New Zealand situation as well:

> Faced with an expansion of transmission time and the loss to pay television of key sporting events, entertainment formats provide a more cost-effective way of filling schedules with local productions than locally originated drama. For channels trying to stand out in a crowded marketplace, locally produced formats have greater appeal to audiences than cheaper imports. Tried and tested in other markets, risk is reduced, there are savings on development costs, and seriality provides opportunities to build audiences (2004: 74).

Steemers in addition cites Australian Albert Moran's suggestion that format adaptation also has political benefits in environments where local production is fragile, in that such programmes are invariably classed as domestically produced rather than as imports. This is very much the case in New Zealand, where a high level of locally versioned formats (home and personal 'make-over' programmes, job-swapping scenarios, ordinary-people-in-extraordinary-circumstances, the New Zealand version of the UK *Strictly Come Dancing*) are found across all the leading channels. Many of these attract healthy ratings and contribute hours of programming to local content tallies, which have always been far fewer than hours of imported television. In 2004, for example, New Zealand-produced programming occupied 32.6 per cent of 6 am to midnight schedules on TV One, TV2 and TV3.

Nevertheless, local versions of imported formats are carefully placed across such schedules. TV One, as TVNZ's flagship channel for news and current affairs, has long occupied the position as the more 'serious' partner in the TVNZ two-channel service. It dominates the television landscape, dictating weekly ratings and audience share, and offering a staple diet of nightly news, current affairs, national sport (except for rugby, which migrated to pay TV years ago), British drama (serials such as *Coronation Street* and series such as *Cold Feet*) and New Zealand documentaries. TVNZ promotes its leading channel thus: 'TV One is primarily targeted at a more mature audience', whilst its partner 'TV2 caters primarily to a young and family oriented audience, with an emphasis on providing entertainment and information to the young and young at heart' (Television New Zealand Charter 2005).

Television ratings regularly reflect this division of the audience and TV One's domination, as in the following typical list of top 10 programmes, all of which screened on this channel.

Top Ten Programmes. June 12–19 2005 (all viewers 5+)

		rating
1.	*Dancing with the Stars* (NZ-produced, UK format)	22
2.	*Sunday* (NZ current affairs)	20
3.	*Off the Rails* (NZ, documentary series)	20
4.	*ONE News* (NZ, 6 pm news)	19
5.	*Coronation Street* (UK, soap)	17
6.	*Border Patrol* (NZ, customs reality)	16
7.	*Piha Rescue* (NZ, surf rescue reality)	15
8.	*Close Up* (NZ, current affairs)	14
9.	*Fair Go* (NZ, consumer affairs)	14
10.	*Little Angels* (UK, documentary series)	13

(Source: AGB Nielsen NZ Media Research)

The above ratings are very typical of weekly performance, wherein such measurements are consistently dominated by the viewing choices of the older and predictable audience profile of TV One. The other leading channels (TV2 and TV3) usually begin to make an appearance lower in such lists; in the week above, *Shortland Street* (TV2) appears at number 11 and the US drama series *Lost* at number 16, and the first TV3 programme (the US drama series *Medical Investigation*) appears at number 22.

In the full list of the top 50 programmes for this particular week in June 2005, TV One occupied nearly half (23) of these top slots, with a mixture of New Zealand and British television programmes.

There were no American programmes in this list, reflecting their rare appearance in the schedules of this dominant channel. In this week in June 2005, there were four American television dramas: a late-night (11 pm) repeat of *Six Feet Under*, Showtime's *!Huff* screening at 9.30 pm on Tuesday, preceded by the forensic drama series *Cold Case* at 8.30 pm, and a late screening (11.05 pm) of the cult series *Carnivàle* on Friday night. None of these programme made much of an appearance in the weekly ratings.

The favoured viewing of TV One viewers, as regularly recorded by the mechanics of ratings, ranges across locally produced news and current affairs, reality television series and British drama series. It is important to point out that the reality programmes on TV One are either British or based on British formats. All formats from elsewhere (especially the USA) – and the local versions of these – appear on TV2 or TV3. Formats too expensive to produce locally are imported from the closest source; for example, the first two series of *Big Brother* were imported directly from Australia with some local phone-in add-ons.

The New Zealand television audience has been long polarised by scheduling practice, wherein TV One viewers regularly encounter a narrow band of 'quality' television defined by the following well-rehearsed imperatives:

- public service ideals;
- high professional and production standards;
- a consistently serious tone;
- engagement with age-appropriate audience expectations;
- popular, rather than populist, programming and scheduling; and
- British and local (New Zealand) programming rather than American or Australian programming.

In addition to the markedly different styles of programming across TV One and TV2, there is another point of distinction in the sources (country-of-origin) of television drama. TV One viewers have been long accustomed to British drama (series and serials) and seem disinclined to watch much US television drama. Indeed, such American television programmes are frequently in contravention of the New Zealand viewers' notion of 'quality'. Such attitudes are a reflection of wider cultural rankings and taste formation, most usually determined by age and generation gaps: the lingering prejudice I identified nearly 20 years ago, whereby older viewers 'dismiss American television because it is American' (Lealand 1988: 51).

When programming from American sources appears in TV One schedules, it is usually within the HBO mode of quality television, that is *The Sopranos* and *Six Feet Under*, or HBO's close relative Showtime. In June 2005, for example, *!Huff* was being promoted on TV One (quoting *Slate* magazine) as 'Television's gold standard', and it seems to fit this criteria, as Jane Feuer argues, '. . . a series that was promoted in *TV Guide* as a "little bit *Six Feet Under*, a little bit *thirtysomething*." and thus a perfect candidate for quality drama status' (2005).

What is particularly interesting about the scheduling of *Six Feet Under*, and other similar series, in New Zealand is that such programmes appear on free-to-air television, in direct contrast to their first outing on subscription television in the USA. New Zealand viewers have been long accustomed to – and accepting of – a high threshold of adult themes, sexual content and strong language. Content standards echo those of British or Australian television, and there is certainly a much greater freedom than that provided to American free-to-air viewers. In July 2005, for example, the New Zealand-produced drama series *Outrageous Fortune* was being promoted (along with the promise of bare breasts on screen) in the following terms: 'TV3 is hoping sex and crime do pay for its new local drama . . . The crime is petty and there's sex a-plenty' (Wicks 2005: 3).

Television in New Zealand abides with a voluntary watershed, which begins at 8.30 pm and allows for more adult content to be screened after this time, even though adult themes can often sneak in earlier in the evening especially in *Shortland Street*. There are occasional complaints to the Broadcasting Standards Authority, the sole regulatory body – and sporadic campaigns by fundamentalist Christian groups – but, on the whole, New Zealand viewers appear to be comfortable with a regular diet of sex, nudity and swearing and strong themes as part of their primetime television entertainment.

Finding Quality on New Zealand Television

In his 1996 investigation 'Quality in Television: the Views of Professionals', Timothy Leggatt cites 'clarity of purpose' as a primary 'programme maker characteristic'. Such an objective is difficult to sustain in New Zealand television given the competing objectives and mixed economy described above. It is certainly easier to attain and sustain in television environments where state-funded or cross-subsidised public service channels persist (such as the ABC in Australia, the BBC in the UK, YLE in Finland), and public service objectives or directives remain the top priority. The BBC, for example, faces new political and structural challenges, and it can no longer claim exclusive rights to being the voice of the nation. Nevertheless, the BBC remains confident about state funding, which, together with programme and format sales, ensures its continuing viability and centrality in the British broadcasting environment.

The role of television in the social, cultural and political lives of New Zealanders is considerably more ambiguous, and a continuing arena for competing interests. Television New Zealand, for example, now must work to public service objectives, even though the ratings discourse continues to dominate measurement of success. In the absence of a clear consensus various *default* notions of quality prevail. Ratings success remains the primary indicator of popularity, and thus quality, for many in the television industry – both for private broadcasters and state-owned TVNZ. For New Zealand On Air and other cultural commentators, local content (New Zealand-initiated and produced programming) equates to quality, irrespective of genre, originality or production values, as Thompson points out, 'Amidst the continuing confusion about how to evaluate public broadcasting initiatives, local content may seem like a relatively unambiguous quantitative measure which permits easy comparisons over time' (2005a: 3).

Other commentators point to the presence or absence of prestigious genres (news, current affairs, documentaries) as a marker of quality. For some technocrats, quality television implies technical matters of transmission and reception (especially in respect of the long-delayed move to free-to-air digital television) with programme quality a secondary consideration.

Quite what the average New Zealand viewer thinks of 'quality' is less clear, except when it is displayed in the viewing choices of TV One viewers (alluded to above). Nevertheless, if you ask any New Zealand viewer about their perceptions of quality on television, there will be three likely outcomes: everyone will be confident that there is not enough of it; everyone knows it when they see it; and, across the range of opinions, there will be little agreement on what it is or should be.

PART 3

Defining Quality
Aesthetics, Form, Content

11
HBO and the Concept of Quality TV
Jane Feuer

• •

In his foreword to *Reading Six Feet Under*, British television journalist
Mark Lawson writes: 'So what is most notable about *Six Feet Under* is
not only that it is bold and original within the context of television
schedules but also that it has no clear ancestry in any area of culture'
(2005: xix).

The goal of this paper is to refute this statement utterly. I believe
that *Six Feet Under* not only has a clear ancestry within art cinema
but also that the series bears a significant debt to a tradition that I
am going to call 'quality television'. Like Alan Ball's *American Beauty*
(1999), surely the most art-cinema derivative film ever to win an
Academy Award, *Six Feet Under* reeks of a European art cinema
heritage in combination with a more televisual tradition of quality
lifted from the miniseries of Dennis Potter and also from the more
serialised tradition of American quality television that I will outline
below.

The judgement of quality is always situated. That is to say,
somebody makes the judgement from some aesthetic or political or
moral position. If I had had the language of reception aesthetics at
my command in the early 1980s when I first used the term quality
TV, I could have said that the decision as to which TV shows, if
any, to name as *quality* TV comes from within what Stanley Fish
calls an *interpretive community*, that is, a professional community
whose norms, ideals and methods determine an interpretation's
validity (2005). Tony Bennett politicises this concept when he calls
the interpretive community a *reading formation* (2003). (That is,

situating readers within institutional structures determining what counts as a text or a context, and what distinguishes literary from non-literary concerns.) Reception theory teaches us that there can never be a judgement of quality in an absolute sense but that there are always judgements of quality relative to one's interpretive community or reading formation. That is why the term quality TV has to be used *descriptively* if one wants to understand how it operates discursively. Politically, of course, one always has an agenda and mine has been and will be to deflate some of the more pretentious claims by which intellectuals and the *culturati* use cinema and theatre to denigrate TV. I will not have time here to trace the total history of an opposition between quality TV and 'trash' TV (Feuer 2003: 98). Let me just say that such an opposition goes back to the very beginning of US television programming, when a sharp contrast existed between live anthology drama and the emerging forms of series TV.

Even before a normative notion of 'everyday television' had solidified, the idea of 'quality drama' existed in the form of the live 'anthology' teleplays of the 1950s. Written by New York playwrights, appealing to an élite audience and financed by individual corporate sponsors as prestige productions, these live TV dramas carried the cachet of the 'legitimate' theatre. In their minimal use of film techniques as well as the excitement of their live broadcasts these 'single play' dramas exhibited a pattern that would remain important to future generations of quality drama. On the one hand, they defined themselves as quality because they exploited an essential characteristic of their medium: the ability of television to broadcast live in a way films could not. On the other hand, their prestige came from an association with a 'higher' form of art: theatre, a form that at this time was widely acknowledged by intellectuals as superior to the film medium as well. Thus when, as sometimes happened, one of these anthology dramas was adapted into a movie (for example, *Marty* in 1955; and *Days of Wine and Roses* and *Requiem for a Heavyweight* in 1962), it underwent an odd transformation in cultural prestige. No matter how prestigious the film version, the television version has come to be seen as of lasting quality, because of its exploitation of the essence of the medium (liveness) and because it was thus closer to the theatrical. The film adaptations of these teleplays remain obscure, but the live dramas are still admired and studied even in the technically crude kinescope versions of them that remain. The Golden Age of Live TV achieves its aura in both directions: technologically it was experimental, and structurally it was 'theatre' and (like the future HBO) 'Not TV'.

To the US television industry – defined as a community of profit-minded capitalists interested in 'delivering' audiences and not texts – the term quality describes the demographics of the audience. Delivering a quality audience means delivering whatever demographic advertisers seek, or in the case of premium cable, attracting an audience with enough disposable income to pay extra for TV. Although excellent articles on the political economy of the shift to cable have already been written (Jaramillo 2002: 59–75), I would like to stress here the continuity in audience quality between the networks and cable services. The shift of 'quality drama' from the networks to pay cable does not alter this; in fact it intensifies it. Although a cable service such as HBO has a very small audience of subscribers, much smaller than the equivalent audience for network quality drama, they happen to be the very upscale demographic willing to pay extra for more specialised and more highbrow fare. Pay cable services value Nielsen ratings as well as subscriber numbers. Compare these judgements of value made in 2002 for *Six Feet Under* and *The West Wing*, respectively:

> [From *Variety*] . . . the hoped-for audience bounce for the final hour of *Six Feet Under* on June 3 at 9pm never materialized, but the episode still delivered a 10.7 rating in cable homes. That's almost exactly on par with the 11.0 that the series averaged over the previous 12 weeks of original episodes (Dempsey 2002).

and

> [from *USA Today* discussing a decline in ratings for *The West Wing*] . . . yet NBC argues that *West Wing* is still extremely valuable because it reaches a high concentration of wealthy viewers – it's the only prime-time series whose viewers ages 18–49 have a median income of more than $75,000 a year . . . it remains the series that attracts the most upscale demo on television, and it's arguably in the most competitive time slot [against *The Bachelor*] according to Warner Bros. TV president Peter Roth (Levin 2002).

But most other interpretive communities do not define quality by economic criteria alone. The Christian right defines it by adherence to their own sense of religious values. Others such as the now-defunct activist group Viewers for Quality Television tend to value programmes that convey a morally and politically positive message from a more liberal perspective. For most journalistic reviewers, quality is an aesthetic choice of a particular kind defined by a consensus among programme creators and liberal intellectuals (more about this later). And for academic television studies, 'quality' is a descriptive term that identifies a television genre called quality drama. By the 1990s, Robert J. Thompson was able to argue that, 'quality [drama] has become a genre in itself, complete with its own set of formulaic characteristics' (1996: 16).

Thus there can be a serious conflict of interest among interpretive communities making judgements of quality regarding the same television programme. In order to illustrate the rhetoric of what appear to be primarily aesthetic judgements of quality, I would like to present an extended comparison between two more or less contemporary examples of shows I have already identified as possessing a quality audience: NBC's *The West Wing* and HBO's *Six Feet Under*. Contemporaneous with each other and often in close competition for the prestigious Emmy Awards (in 2003, for example, *Six Feet Under* received 16 nominations; *The West Wing* had 15), these programmes lay claim to defining quality drama today. As always with claims to 'quality', the discourse surrounding these shows contradicts an analysis of their structure. *The West Wing* almost perfectly conforms to Thompson's model for quality TV defined as a genre of television. Yet the discourse surrounding it works to separate it out from the rest of television. *Six Feet Under*, by contrast, conforms to the HBO model of being 'not TV'. It does this in the same way as other HBO dramas and in a way similar to the most famous network yuppie demographic 1980s show, *thirtysomething*. The claim to being 'not TV' is made by claiming to be something else: namely, art cinema or modernist theatre.

The West Wing adheres so closely to television's mainstream of quality drama from the 1980s and 1990s that I consider it almost a textbook case. The fact that the show claims to be totally unique and original only reinforces my point; quality drama always claims to be original in relation to the regular TV norms of its era. Yet generically speaking, an analysis of the first four episodes of the show reveals just about every 'formulaic characteristic' developed by quality drama in the 1980s and 1990s.

First of all, it is serialised (this always links quality drama to a potentially negative comparison to soap opera, as we shall see when we look at the reception context). Like all quality TV drama, *The West Wing* is a soap opera in terms of narrative structure although not in terms of melodramatic style. Like other quality dramas (and as sometimes happens on daytime and primetime soaps), it does not simply break down each segment into a standard number of separate storylines, but rather it attempts to juxtapose, interweave and orchestrate the plot threads together in a quasi-musical fashion. Aaron Sorkin has been praised for his ability to juxtapose storylines and vary levels of seriousness, sometimes through a startling juxtaposition, other times by a theme and variations rhythmic mingling of the different threads. For example, 'In Proportional Response' (1: 3) begins by picking up two major storylines from the end of 'Post Hoc, Ergo Propter Hoc' (1: 2), the death of Morris Tolliver (Ruben Santiago-Hudson) and the Sam Seaborn (Rob Lowe) call-girl incident, both of which have to be 'managed' by the White House. After the credits, a new thread, the hiring of Charlie Young (Dulé Hill) to be personal aide to the president is woven into a scene about the military response to Syria's downing of a military plane on which Tolliver was a passenger. However, *West Wing* executive producer John Wells had already employed these techniques on *China Beach* 10 years previously, even though he never gets mentioned as a *creative* contributor to *The West Wing*.

The West Wing uses a large ensemble cast who function as a family of co-workers, indeed – as was true of *Hill Street Blues* and *St. Elsewhere* – it is a supremely patriarchal family. The emphasis on bringing domesticity into the workplace does not distinguish this show from quality medical or cop shows; it is the type of work they do that differs, a distinction of subject matter rather than genre or structure.

In the quality tradition, *The West Wing* juxtaposes moments of comedy with scenes of high seriousness, often ending on an elegiac note. The first three episodes conclude with a 'presidential moment' in the oval office. Like *Hill Street Blues* and *thirtysomething*, the scripts employ elevated language and overlapping dialogue with many quick clever exchanges of wit. Certain recurring 'stock' scenes punctuate the episodes and give them regularity: for example, C.J. Cregg's (played by Alison Janney) press briefings echo the roll call scenes in *Hill Street Blues*.

The HBO 'not TV' series take a different stance towards the US network quality drama tradition. Following a less well-trodden path, these dramas want to avoid being associated with the quality drama genre. Tracking a minority tradition within quality drama but one identifiable from *Twin Peaks* and *thirtysomething*, *The Sopranos* and *Six Feet Under* rely on media other than television for their structure, even though both contain obvious elements of serialised narrative. David Chase originally wanted *The Sopranos* to be sold as a film and he considers each episode to be 'a little movie' (Longworth 2000). *Six Feet Under* is highly serialised, uses multiple storylines and an ensemble cast, but it too identifies stylistically with the non-televisual genre of European art cinema. This greater structural reliance on cinema is obvious from the opening credits. The imagistic *Six Feet Under* title sequence (by Digital Kitchen) is like a little art movie in itself and even merits a featurette on the US DVD release. The musical theme by second-generation Hollywood film composer Thomas Newman bears no resemblance to classic TV drama theme music. According to an internet source, 'Newman often utilizes a set of unusual and rare instruments alongside a standard symphony orchestra to create an enigmatic and highly unique sound that is both lush and pastoral, but infused with the rhythms and textures of world music' (Newman 2003). The sound of the *Six Feet Under* title theme is primarily comprised of a combination of piano and synthesised strings. The pizzicato-style strings come from a live orchestra. Viola and violin weave throughout and the melodic theme is performed by an 'evi' (electronic valve instrument), which sounds like a soprano clarinet. The instrumentation is said to sound 'African' (Newman 2005) *The West Wing*, on the other hand, follows in a tradition of television quality drama theme music, composed by W.G. 'Snuffy' Walden, known for his themes for such TV series as *thirtysomething, I'll Fly Away* and *My So-Called Life*, and *Once and Again* (i.e. the Zwick-Herskovitz franchise but also *Roseanne*). The featurette on the first season DVD describes how Walden composed the theme on guitar and then synthesised it for full orchestra to give it a more 'presidential' sound.

Six Feet Under's ancestry in television drama could not be clearer than in the little homage to television auteur Dennis Potter in 'The Foot' (1: 3).[1] In this sequence, Claire Fisher (Lauren Ambrose) walks into a realistic scene in the family kitchen and immediately goes into a musical number that might have been a direct quotation from *Pennies from Heaven*. In 'The New Person' (1: 10), David Fisher (Michael C. Hall) does the little Bob Fosse number, 'Got a Lot of Living To Do', like a number from *All That Jazz*, a film that tried to blend the dream sequences of a Fellini movie with a more native American show-business tradition – in form if not in content not unlike *American Beauty*. Not surprisingly, the actors who play Claire and David are accomplished musical comedy performers.

The use of paradigmatic narrative derived from TV soap opera, as opposed to the more linear narrative of the typical 'classical Hollywood film', structures *Six Feet Under* in a tradition of American television drama. The show's reliance on alternating storylines portrayed by a large ensemble cast was never clearer than in 'That's My Dog' (4: 5), when the writers attempted a more cinematic and linear mode of narration. David's abduction by a hitchhiker turns the multiple storyline format into a suspense thriller as the single narrative thread takes over the episode. Subsequent episodes detail the aftermath of David's attack and his post-traumatic stress, isolating his storyline from others in the ongoing family saga. Without the paradigmatic structure, David's storyline descends into a second-rate Hollywood thriller, but the writers must have felt that rendering the narrative more linear would make it more 'cinematic' and thus 'not TV', forgetting that quality drama was always 'not TV' but rather a peculiar elevation of soap opera narrative structure.

Beyond its avant-garde music, *Six Feet Under* reaches out to an entire tradition in modernist cinema that thematises life and death, dream and reality: the cinema of Federico Fellini, Ingmar Bergman and Alain Resnais, to name a few of its godfathers. In the second season premiere, Nate Fisher (Peter Krause) enters into a fantasy that his father is playing Chinese checkers with a man and a woman, who turn out of be Death (Stanley Kamel) and Life (Cleo King). This thinly veiled allusion to Antonius Block (Max von Sydow) playing chess with Death (Bengt Ekerot) in Bergman's *The Seventh Seal* (1955) serves to remind us that *Six Feet Under* shares the thematic materials of films that have been certified as serious art. But now the strained seriousness of the original film text is subject to postmodern parody as Life and Death attempt to hump each other. This use of dream diegesis has become a staple of art cinema. In *Seeing through the Eighties*, I traced the curious evolution by which the dream sequence – a staple of popular entertainment forms such as Hollywood musicals and soap operas – evolves via *thirtysomething* into the *dream diegesis*, a much more art cinematic confusion of levels between dream and reality (Feuer 1995: 86–92). Dream diegesis becomes a structural lynchpin of *Six Feet Under* in which the issue of dream or reality can be easily linked to the issue of dead or alive. Ghosts populate this show, with the father (Richard Jenkins) who died in the first episode appearing constantly in a nether status between dream and symbolism. The dead bodies that populate the show reappear as ghosts, most notably when the apparition of a dead gay boy (Marc Foster, played by Brian Poth) appears to David at the end of the first season in 'A Private Life' (1: 12) and spurs him to action in his coming-out dispute with the Episcopal Church.

Throughout its first season, *Six Feet Under* frequently relies upon a fantasy trope often used by Potter and also common to a long tradition of US quality drama. In these subjective wish-fulfilment point-of-view shots, characters see not reality but rather their desires. In 'An Open Book' (1: 5) and 'Knock, Knock' (1: 13), David's discomfort with his gayness in his role as a church deacon is expressed first by a point-of-view shot from the pulpit in which he imagines a congregation full of naked men, and later by a fantasy that the actual congregation applauds when he comes out to them. But David is not the only character to undergo subjectively portrayed wishes. Claire expresses her dissatisfaction with high school by making her math teacher's head explode and by imagining the popular girls reciting narratives about their futures ('Brotherhood', 1: 7). When Ruth Fisher (Frances Conroy) accidentally takes Ecstasy, she enters a desaturated, blue-filtered dream world complete with an appearance by the late Nate Sr ('Life's Too Short', 1: 9). Even without drug enhancement, Ruth fantasises that her Russian florist boyfriend (Ed O'Ross) appears in a military uniform when she is supposed to be on a date with Hiram Gunderson (Ed Begley Jr). In 'The Trip' (1: 11), her consciously avowed tolerance of David's homosexuality is belied by an image of her son having sadomasochistic sex with another man; in the fantasy she responds by squirting them with a very phallic garden hose.

In yet another manifestation of dream diegesis, dead characters or characters' past selves appear and interact in the present with live characters in a manner reminiscent of modernist theatre. Most notably, Nate Sr appears frequently throughout the show as a subjective memory image for other family members. Claire, for example, dreams that she is watching TV with him, she converses with her dad at Federico Diaz's (played by Freddy Rodriguez) son's christening party and imagines that her father is taking home movies of her ('Knock, Knock', 1: 13). Throughout season one Mark Foster haunts David, aiding him in his coming-out process, and Brenda repeatedly has flashes to scenes from the book her therapist wrote about her as a child, *Charlotte Light and Dark*.

Surely, though, the most extended use of dream diegesis occurs in the third season premiere ('Perfect Circles', 3: 1) in the form of Nate's 'dream' while undergoing brain surgery. Both this sequence and the less extensive Chinese checkers match that opens season two were directed by Rodrigo García, who is the son of Nobel Prize winner for Literature Gabriel García Márquez, a writer associated with the 'magical realist' style of twentieth-century fiction that David Lavery argues exerts a powerful influence on both *American Beauty* and *Six Feet Under* (2005a: 27–32). Some of the series' most surrealistic moments were his. Although, as Rodrigo García puts it in his DVD commentary for the season two premiere, Alan Ball 'moves in and out of reality and fantasy seamlessly', this effect is just as easily attributed to García's own direction of the show's most 'magical' dream diegeses. As Lavery puts it, 'When critics identified *American Beauty* as "magic realism", the plastic bag scene being key to the designation, and when *Six Feet Under* is similarly identified, is it not because of its comparable recognition – sometimes grotesque, sometimes fantastic – of "this entire life behind things"?' (27). He continues that 'Latin American authors such as Gabriel García Márquez, Julio Cortazar, Isabel Allende and Jorge Luis Borges have made "magic realism" a literary household phrase' (ibid), yet I would argue that it is a phrase that, to the American television viewing public, would still be considered a manifestation of high culture.

I am not going to analyse this sequence (as Lavery offers an extensive account as cited above) in the sense of trying to interpret what it means because structured ambiguity is always built into such sequences in art cinema. Suffice it to say that it used a *mise-en-abyme* structure, at first implying to the audience that Nate has died but then revealing the dream diegesis to have its origins in Nate's unconscious state. I would identify this sequence as the most drastic example of *Six Feet Under*'s self-identification with modernist art cinema. Not only does *Six Feet Under* reference art cinema, the show also interprets itself as art cinema. It does this through self-promotion on HBO, through supplementary materials included on the DVD release and by encouraging critics such as Lavery to offer readings of it.

HBO has for a while used the clever technique of inter-diegetically connecting its Sunday night shows in its promotions into a single, unified world. In its promotions, HBO shows us how savvy it is and how postmodern in that it interprets its own texts. Realising the pretentiousness of its claim to being 'Not TV', HBO has already parodied itself in the form of the water-cooler promos that claim that 'It's Not TV. It's H2O'. Allow me to quote from the self-promotional materials put out by the company that made the water-cooler ad:

> HBO recently called upon Wonderland Productions' editorial, music, sound design and audio post services to help them create the critically acclaimed promo, 'Watercooler'. This deadpan, mockumentary-style campaign credits the cable network's stellar line up of shows with bringing back banter around the office water cooler, and saving the US water cooler industry from oblivion.
>
> Since producer/editor/composer Bill McCullough launched Wonderland in 2001, HBO has called upon him to execute the creative vision of promo campaigns through the post production process for a prestigious line up of shows, including *Six Feet Under*, *Def Poetry* and *Angels in America*. 'Watercooler' is the most recent HBO project to take advantage of the Soho-based boutique's collaborative, full-service approach to post production (*New York, NY*, 25 March 2004).

As a savvy postmodern cable service, HBO is always one step ahead of critics who think that HBO doesn't know how obvious its 'not TV' campaign really was.

Moreover, just in case you miss the promos, creator Alan Ball's commentary on the DVD interprets the show for you as you watch it. It's like getting a little critic/auteur in the handsomely packaged DVD box. In his commentary on the first season finale, Ball points out some of his favourite symbolic shots. He informs us that a shot looking down a road echoes another 'tunnel' shot in the pilot and that this was a 'conscious choice' to symbolise the journey to death. He explains that the ghosts are not ghosts per se but rather 'a dramatic technique we use to portray the internal dialogue of the character'. For instance, Mark Foster's ghost 'articulates David's internal homophobia and self-loathing'.

So, HBO is a full-service cable service. It gives us texts that are not TV. It interprets them for us. It promotes them as art cinema. It punctures its own promotions to show how postmodern it is. It praises its promo spots as art cinema. It completely eliminates the need for this book. What is left for us critics to write about?

We might want to ask: how can a show so obviously making use of serialisation be 'not TV'? HBO might answer: because it uses serial form so clumsily and takes pride and brand recognition from its status as art cinema. That is exactly what *thirtysomething* did for the 1980s and exactly what placed that show outside the conventions of the quality television genre. What places *The West Wing* firmly in the centre of the quality TV genre is its smooth orchestration of storylines.

Yet interviews in the trade and popular press given by the creators of HBO drama make every attempt to reinforce the claim that their shows are *theatre* not TV. An August 2002 article in *Variety* quotes Alan Ball saying that writers like him, who come out of the theatre 'tend to have a more grounded understanding of structure and storytelling that's outside the standard TV paradigm' (Hofler 2002). Craig Wright, story editor for HBO, who had a new play *Water Flower Water* at the summer 2003 Contemporary American Theater Festival says that 'unlike other TV shows, which might be more explicitly plot-driven, a huge focus of *Six Feet Under* is to show the complexity of the people. That's what feels theatrical about the show to me' (quoted in Hofler 2002). Jill Soloway continues: 'As opposed to quick TV moments, the human conflicts are played out over time. We have those slower moments that you often see in a play' (ibid).

In case you were thinking of a few examples of those slower, more character-driven moments from quality dramas of the last 20 or so years, I should like to point out that the claim to theatricality is achieved through the erasure of a long tradition of quality TV drama that *is* TV. My point is borne out by an astonishing story in *USA Today* right after Sorkin left *The West Wing* (Bianco 2003). The article claims that 'the thrill is gone' for having allowed hack TV people like John Wells and John Sacret Young to take over from Sorkin. I am not going to cast my vote as to whether the thrill was gone before or after Sorkin left. I just want to point out that two of the prime architects of quality drama responsible for the last season of *China Beach* and the first season of *ER* have been relegated to the status of game-show producers, while Sorkin replaces them rhetorically as a unique authorial voice.

Although *The West Wing* follows the tradition of a serialised orchestration of quality drama perhaps to the same level as had *China Beach* and *ER*, rhetorically – in competition with *The Bachelor* – it still gets to be 'not TV'. If reality TV is said to be 'unscripted', *The West Wing* achieves its reputation by being perhaps the most 'scripted' text to appear on turn of the century network television. This comes from the stature given to Aaron Sorkin as a TV-outsider auteur. For instance, when *The West Wing* was taking its lumps from the press for losing its prized 18–34-year-old female viewers to *The Bachelor* in the fall of 2002, Aaron Sorkin gave a tongue-in-cheek interview to *Newsweek* saying he TiVos his own show but he *watches The Bachelor*. Sorkin then confesses, of course, that he's never really seen the reality show but 'we understand that some of the younger women have gone to *The Bachelor* so instead of starting our episodes with a recap, what we'll be doing is having Janel Moloney marry a millionaire celebrity boxer. There's gonna be a quick ceremony. Then they're gonna eat worms' (Anon 2002). Obviously he has never watched *The Bachelor* because he has confused it with stereotypes from other reality shows. But then there is no cultural capital for Sorkin in knowing the nuances of reality TV. In fact he knows that his cultural capital lies in not knowing anything about reality TV.

Reality TV is the great other to quality drama. Yet discursively, reality TV can also be authored, as proven by the well-known branding of producer Mark Burnett's franchise on *Survivor* and now on *The Apprentice*. Read this from Burnett's bio on the NBC website:

> One of the driving forces behind reality television and a true visionary, Mark Burnett has a long history of executive producing Emmy Award-winning television in international locations. Burnett's entrepreneurial spirit pioneered the success of the reality 'unscripted' drama series, garnered skyrocketing ratings and introduced millions of Americans to an entirely new television genre (NBC website).

Since reality TV is arguably no more or less 'original' than HBO drama and since both genres have their authors and geniuses, why should one form have so much more artistic status than the other? Both are what Todd Gitlin (2000) called 'recombined' forms of television. The reality show merges certain forms of documentary with the game show and the soap opera. Quality drama merged soap opera with an established genre such as the cop show or the medical series. HBO drama merges series or serialised TV with postmodern theatre or art cinema. And there's the rub. To the interpretive community that *writes* about TV, and who share a field of reference with those who create quality TV but not reality TV, only certain re-combinations matter.

I believe I have demonstrated that there is nothing 'new' or 'original' generically between HBO drama and the television tradition of quality drama that cannot be ascribed to an equally generic tradition of art cinema. Thus we can locate a gap – I am even tempted to call it a contradiction – between the textual analysis of quality drama and its discursive context.

12
Seeing and Knowing

Reflexivity and Quality

Jonathan Bignell

. . . .

The critical evaluation of quality in television takes many forms, but it depends on attributing value either by claiming that quality television attains this status because it matches what the medium is or does, or because bringing into television an aesthetic from outside redresses an inherent predisposition for the medium to be of low quality. The influential US television theorist Horace Newcomb (1974) argued that the primary attributes of broadcast television are intimacy, continuity and immediacy, and his establishment of these criteria led him to claim that the medium is most suited to working on contemporary social anxieties through narrative forms characterised by verisimilitude and involvement with character and story. He associated visual stylishness, on the other hand, with cinema rather than television, and this distinction between media on the basis of their supposed specificities has dogged critical work ever since. In the British context especially, television has been considered a writer's medium, setting up an opposition between an aesthetically conservative essence of television as driven by dialogue and character and a more adventurous interest in style and narrative form in cinema. As contemporary Hollywood cinema has invested in films that base their appeal on spectacle, effects and distinctive directorial intervention in *mise-en-scène*, this supposed distinction between television and film has gained greater purchase

(McLoone 1997). The result has been a relative neglect of television style, especially where style is significant to popular and generic programmes. Furthermore, the interest in British academic work on forms of television realism has focused attention on the paradoxical cultivation of apparent zero-degree style in British television drama, a style that effaces itself in order to witness character and environment rather than to draw attention to the mediation of narrative by specific audio-visual forms. This separates quality in British television from its US counterparts, including those US programmes shown in Britain.

Theories of television viewership interact with these conceptions of the specificity of the medium. Assumptions about the ways television is watched justify conceptions of the medium as intimate, continuous and immediate, and conversely, such conceptions of television justify models of the viewer as someone 'casting a lazy eye over the proceedings, keeping an eye on events, or, as the slightly archaic designation had it, "looking in"' (Ellis 1983: 137). If audiences watch sporadically, inattentively and continually, then the attractions of self-consciously wrought *mise-en-scène* are largely wasted on them and would not be of economic value to producers or broadcasters. This chapter argues that contemporary US police/investigation series have been one of the locations where television style has in fact become a key component of their textual form and their appeal to audiences.

The analysis focuses on US programmes screened in Britain, and after a brief discussion of industrial and institutional factors that are part of this change in television aesthetics, it demonstrates how reflexive emphasis on *mise-en-scène* relates to the generic components of police drama and more broadly to the understanding of quality in television drama. In keeping with the primary focus of this book on contemporary US television drama, this chapter discusses the series *CSI: Crime Scene Investigation* in most detail, a series featuring the forensic team examining evidence from Las Vegas homicides and fatal accidents. But because this series is a filmed production with a complex aesthetic of reflexivity about seeing, I contextualise it with a brief account of some previous filmed US series in the police/investigation procedural tradition from the 1980s onwards (see Rixon 2003; Bignell forthcoming). This leads to a brief concluding argument that quality and medium specificity are linked by the significance of reflexivity, and that together these characteristics negotiate a shifting understanding of what television looks like and how its identity as a medium can be known. The police series is a programme type that necessarily addresses the meanings of seeing and knowing, and is especially prone to metacommentary on what television can be.

Industry, Technology and Televisuality

US network television underwent considerable change during the 1980s and 1990s, and this led to a reconfiguration of the aesthetic criteria through which television quality was understood. Series were designed to reward sustained viewing and involvement, through the creation of distinctive visual styles, serial character and storyline development, and generic hybridity such as blending the fantastic with the hermeneutic puzzles of detection in the crime series (Curtin 2003). This questions the continued purchase of the concepts of the glance and flow for describing television viewership, and also emphasises visual brands or signature styles in combination with, for example, a continued emphasis on star performers that characterised earlier phases of production and marketing of television.

Each of the series discussed in this chapter was shot on film, following the long history of series production for television based in Hollywood and using the resources of studios and personnel originally established for cinema early in the era of US dominance of the film business and its institutional mode of production. While made for television, the emphasis on *mise-en-scène* associated with the greater depth of colour, contrastive lighting and more elaborate camera movement of production on film is responsible for much of the aesthetic quality attributed to these programmes. By shooting using single cameras, with film stock used for both interior and exterior sequences, planned and consistent visual signatures are made possible for these series. Thus programme 'brands' are set in place as much by visual style as by the consistent planning of narrative arcs across episodes in a series, the continuities of settings and character that are conventionally determined by a series 'bible', along with a continuing author-producer's management of the production process. Because of the production system using single cameras, each shot can be individually lit and its camera positions planned to exploit point of view as much as possible. Post-production of the film footage can harmonise aesthetic patterns of colour and contrast through grading processes, producing further opportunities for creative intervention after the period of shooting itself.

However, the institutional mode of production of filmed series does not necessarily lend itself to aesthetic consistency, richness or experimentation. Many US-filmed drama productions, especially in genre series such as sitcom but also in police/investigation series where the emphasis is on physical action or star performance, lay down a much more conventionalised *mise-en-scène*. The demands of the production schedule for television series can give little time for directorial finesse and experimentation, especially since different directors are hired for a few or single episodes, and therefore stylistic continuity will be assured by providing a template for those new arrivals to follow. The result may leave little leeway for direction that does not match the standard conventions of using wide shots and two-shots of main characters, alternating with close-up in a very conventionalised system for quickly obtaining shots for either coverage or dramatic emphasis. This was particularly the case in long-running police/investigation series of the 1970s where programmes were built around performers, and storylines tended to emphasise characteristic moments of performance and the props, costumes and catchphrases supporting them. While there are occasional examples of interesting *mise-en-scène* in *Columbo*, *The Rockford Files* or *Quincy M.E.*, for example, these series do not exploit the aesthetic of filmed drama in the ways that *CSI* and some predecessor series have done. In series where visual style is offered as one of the principal attractions of the programme, however, the directorial contribution within the established aesthetic offers series producers opportunities to exploit auteurism at the same time as an established stylistic brand. When film director Quentin Tarantino wrote and directed the season five finale of *CSI* in 2005 ('Grave Danger: Parts 1 and 2', 5: 24–25), the episode garnered an audience of 30 million (McLean 2005). It encouraged the identification of a directorial 'signature' by including sequences of body trauma that reference both his film work and also the established series trademarks of visceral CGI sequences reconstructing injury that are discussed below.

In the US context, Robert J. Thompson (1996) regards quality as an exception to the industrial production of most programming, mentioning writer-producer-led or creator-led series such as *Hill Street Blues* and *ER* that were made after the loosening of power held by the big three US networks in the 1980s. As work by Simon Frith (2000a) and Jane Feuer (2003) has shown, discussing UK and US television respectively, contemporary quality television is simultaneously defined in relation to its aesthetics, mode of production and audiences. Quality television drama means an aesthetically ambitious programme type with the literary values of creative imagination, authenticity and relevance. As a mode of production, it is where writing and *mise-en-scène* are prioritised. Quality television is also valuable television in that it is what valuable viewers (relatively wealthy and educated ABC1 social groups) enjoy and, perhaps more significantly, what they will pay for through subscription to paid channels in both the UK and USA.

In relation to US programmes that were acquired for UK terrestrial broadcast, like those discussed here, the assumption that quality television is not commercially produced (as most US-acquired programmes are) was reflected in the stipulation in the 1990 Broadcasting Act that the Independent Television Commission (ITC) must apply a 'quality threshold' when it awarded ITV franchises in 1992. Companies had to demonstrate a commitment to quality programming associated with high culture rather than commercial culture, thus implicitly denigrating US television acquired for the UK. However, inasmuch as programmes are televisual or televiterate, they exhibit quality because they stand in opposition to the mass-audience popular forms such as soap opera and sitcom that are said to characterise the medium. I argue here that televisuality can be a criterion for quality in US programmes, in a way that deconstructs this opposition.

The mantle of 'quality' police drama has been inherited by *CSI*, which has been the tent-pole programme in the CBS network's Thursday schedule, the most significant weekday evening in the USA. In its second year (2001–2), *CSI* achieved the second-best ratings of any programme and in the following year was top-rated. By the fifth season in 2005, the franchise had spawned spin-off series *CSI: Miami* and *CSI: New York*. The original *CSI* continues to be shown in syndication and sold to overseas broadcasters. The scheduling of *CSI* and its spin-offs contributed significantly to the profile and audiences for Five in the UK. Shown in evening primetime as part of a strip of acquired US police series including

Law & Order, for example, the *CSI* franchise contributed to Five's repositioning in the mid-2000s. From a beginning in which the channel attempted to peel away audiences from Britain's main commercial terrestrial broadcaster ITV by offering what its first chief executive, Dawn Airey, called 'films, fucking and football', Five subsequently sought a reputation for quality by changing its mix of genres in evening programming and heavily marketing a small clutch of acquired US programmes in the established genre of the police procedural. Naming this strip of programmes as 'America's Finest' references not only the slang designation of the police force, but also the claim that these programmes represent the highest quality primetime imports.

CSI was created by Anthony E. Zuiker, and is jointly produced by the Hollywood film production company, Jerry Bruckheimer Productions, run by Bruckheimer – whose films (*Top Gun, Days of Thunder, Black Hawk Down*) share some of its interest in 'cool' masculinity. Though the series develops a sense of a community among its ensemble of lead characters, *CSI* is primarily structured through paired buddy teams and dual storylines in each episode. In common with *Homicide: Life on the Street,* it is much less about the commission of crimes than the process of solving them. While questions of narrative structure and character identification are significant, the relationship between visual style and the body is *CSI*'s greatest innovation. The use of rapid zooms towards and inside body parts or items of evidence (often at extreme magnification) shows how the integration of computer-generated imagery 'demonstrating' aspects of a crime develops the notion of vision as an evidential-investigative-conclusive activity in the police genre (see Lury 2005: 44–56). There is a strongly apparent physical agency of the detective's and the camera's look in identifying, understanding and proving.

Quality and *Mise-en-Scène* in *CSI*

CSI is distinctive in its use of long takes showing the processes of autopsy and the scientific analysis of fragments from bodies or crime scenes. Fluid but very slow camera movements track around the dimly lit spaces of the crime labs while the characters conduct procedures such as examining clothing fibres or skin cells through microscopes, or painstakingly arranging the fragments of an object on a light-table so they can identify how they were broken. Pace is created in these long takes by the addition of non-diegetic music and the camera's elegant dancing motion. The emphasis in these sequences is on the concentration of the investigators and their systematic absorption in their work, connoting their professionalism and efficiency. These uses of the long take match the shot type's aesthetic histories in US cinema, in the films directed by Max Ophuls, for example, and more recently by Martin Scorsese. Long takes produce the impression of temporal continuity, and allow the camera to follow characters in a space that they interact with to reveal themselves and the relationships between character and environment.

The long take suggests a generosity with time in which there is the opportunity to consider what can be seen, thus handing interpretive authority to the audience. The continual extended look at the character places pressure on them, by enforcing the viewer's concentration on the detail of how the protagonist acts and reacts across a sustained passage of action. At the same time, the use of long shot within a long take to show the character moving in space permits the camera to have a physical and emotional distance from them, so that an analytical and critical understanding of the person can be gained by revealing movements of the body, gesture or costume, and embedding action in a represented world that contextualises and reflects on it.

Space shown by the long take dramatically determines characters and shapes them in counterpoint with it. This is a distinctly different visual system from the rapid alternations of shot-reverse-shot and close-up, which segment the human body and the relationships between characters and space, and determine how the viewer can perceive action and character differently. The selection and segmentation of rapid cutting and extensive close-up can be analytical, presenting directorial interpretations of character and action, but the long take allows the viewer to make sense of space and character in a different way, close to the Brechtian notion that viewers are empowered to choose where to look and must work to bring frameworks of interpretation to the images. The long take empowers the audience in this way by offering interpretive agency, and setting up levels of significance, parallels, contrasts and contexts. The long take draws on the theatrical set-up of a space for action that privileges performance, whereas segmented shooting and close-up leave no 'dead space' that can open up additional meanings. The camera in *CSI* seems to force objects to reveal their secrets, paralleling the agency of the forensic investigators with the agency of the camera. The camera not only matches the investigators' look, but it also supplements it, explains it and concretises its activity of gathering knowledge. So one of the functions of the close-up, and especially the zoom into an object or body in *CSI*, is to link the camera as narrating agency with the agency of the human characters. In fact, the relative paucity of conventional physical action in the series is chiasmatically related to this. The stillness and reticence of the characters are parallel and opposite to the fluidity and revelation given to the camera and its narrative agency. This also sets up a relationship between present and past. The present is characterised by its stillness, seen especially in the criminalists' absorption in their work and the literal stillness of dead bodies or evidential objects. But this stillness is made to reveal movement and passion that happened in the past. From the evidence they gather, the team reconstruct a crime that is then either restaged in the manner of a conventional flashback, or an injury to the victim's body is analytically re-enacted by means of CGI, prosthetics and models so that the causal processes that gave rise to physical effects on the body become knowable. In doing justice to the evidence, the forensic reconstruction of the process of the crime gives a body or object back its story. The present is therefore known by restoring a past that leads to it, and what is seen in the here-and-now is explained by another form of seeing that projects a history onto it.

This foregrounding of how seeing leads to knowing, and presents are given meaning by the restaging of pasts, has important effects on the significance of performance in *CSI* – and thus further distances the series from the potentially action-driven melodrama of the police procedural genre. Referring to critical reaction to the series' beginning, and the principal characters of its Las Vegas, Miami and New York incarnations, *CSI*'s executive producer Carol Mendelsohn explains that 'because *CSI* was very black and white – the evidence never lies – it was comforting in a grey world. There is comfort when Gil Grissom or Horatio Caine or Mac Taylor are on the case. There aren't many people you can trust in the world today' (McLean 2005). However, there is little character development in *CSI*, and only fragments of the characters' domestic lives or past experiences are revealed. These people who might be trusted are almost unknown except in their roles as professional investigators who see scientifically and know because of how they see. This connects the camera as agency of seeing to the characters as agents of knowledge acquisition, and to the camera as a supplement that shows the audience what the characters have found out or think they have found out. However, the characters' reconstructions of events are hypotheses, and are sometimes wrong. Events in the past are reconstructed fragmentarily, sometimes repeated differently as more facts become clear, and attention is drawn to the processes of investigation. The investigative look is presented as a process of seeing that emphasises the linkage, whether easy or difficult, with knowing. The looks of the camera, characters and the audience are made surprisingly active, and the role of the look as an action or performance becomes significant in itself. What this leads towards is the conditional nature of seeing and the provisional nature of knowledge. *Mise-en-scène* and the foregrounding of visual style are not only markers of quality in terms of production value, but also perform seeing and knowing as meaning-making activities carried out for and in television.

A Lineage of Provisional Knowledge

The conditionality of seeing and the provisional nature of knowledge in *CSI* are by no means new. *Hill Street Blues*, for example, was a late-evening precinct drama following an ensemble of uniformed police and detectives. Created and executive produced by Steven Bochco and Michael Kozoll, it was the first in the long run of successes that established Bochco's reputation as a television auteur. *Hill Street Blues* developed complex character drama with both serial and series storylines woven around an ensemble of about a dozen recurring characters, yet also claimed a level of 'realism' that was groundbreaking back in 1981 and depended significantly on stylistic cues drawn from US direct cinema documentary (especially PBS's *The Police Tapes* in 1977). The colour palettes of the episodes, and the use of sound montages and apparent 'wildtrack' background sound textures, for example, work in parallel with an emphasis on visual style. Camera movement and unstable framing and composition support the structuring of sequences by parallel montage between storylines, and the often complex partial closure achieved at the ends of episodes. The series' reputation for innovative visual style, structure, political slant and authorial quality depend on forms of television aesthetic that emphasise unsteady, fractured and multiple points of view.

This self-consciousness of medium is not dependent on a specific television form, but rather on formalism itself as a key signifier of quality, as a brief reference to a stylistically quite different series shows. *Miami Vice* is widely regarded by academic critics and television aficionados as one of the most innovative television series of its time. Centring on vice-squad detectives Sonny Crockett (Don Johnson) and Ricardo Tubbs (Philip Michael Thomas) and their undercover investigations of drug, prostitution and firearms crime, it pays more attention to design and production values than storylines. Contemporary (men's) fashion was selected to match a consistent colour palette for sets, architectural backgrounds and props, and rock-based pop music was laid under a greater proportion of action sequences than was usual in filmed US police drama. There has been some significant critical writing about *Miami Vice* that uses the series as evidence of how postmodern themes are expressed in popular culture (Wang 1988; King 1990), but the aesthetic of the series is constituted by *mise-en-scène* as much as by the manipulation of conventions of genre and format. The series was apparently created when an NBC executive sent executive producer Anthony Yerkovich a memo that read simply 'MTV cops', and Yerkovich and fellow executive producer Michael Mann created *Miami Vice* to fit this brief. Its episodes include many examples of slow motion, thematic colour contrast, specially written music, repeating shot compositions that emphasise surfaces and visual appearances (for example by prominently featuring props and costumes such as sports cars and sunglasses) and referencing characters' construction of an undercover persona and consequent questions of authenticity and deception by metaphorical sequences using mirrors or water.

Homicide: Life on the Street took on the aesthetic of hand-held documentary filming that was used in *Hill Street Blues*, but also some of the self-conscious dramatic stylisation of *Miami Vice*. David Simon, who spent a year with the Baltimore police's homicide unit, based the series on the book *Homicide: A Year on the Killing Streets*. The documentary-like authenticity deriving from this source is supported by the specificity of place that one of *Homicide*'s executive producers, Barry Levinson, brought to the *mise-en-scène* as a native of

Baltimore who wrote and directed the Baltimore-based films *Diner*, *Tin Men* and *Avalon*. The use of hand-held cameras on location in Fells Point, Baltimore worked together with an emphasis on the process of detection rather than the witnessing of crimes themselves, and the arrival at a crime scene usually opened each narrative strand. Place and evidence became more important than physical action, and character interaction was sometimes so foregrounded that the tone of dramatic performance became reflexive and almost parodic. *Homicide* therefore marked an interesting development of *Hill Street Blues*'s realist aesthetic, together with some of *Miami Vice*'s self-consciousness of style and performance, and this was also evident in the prominence of music accompanying the narrative from the second season onwards.

NYPD Blue is another of Steven Bochco's productions (co-created by him and David Milch), and developed authored quality in police drama by building on some of the successful elements of *Hill Street Blues*. The series aimed to maintain the urban texture of Bochco's earlier work with the use of hand-held camera. But this realist aesthetic was a convention that signified aestheticisation, together with slow motion and prominent music to underscore emotional tone. These distinctly different markers of quality combine with an emphasis on performance by the lead actors, especially Dennis Franz as Lt Andy Sipowicz, and a commitment to represent challengingly 'adult' sexuality (in US terms). This 'seriousness' and quality earned the series 80 Emmy award nominations, of which Franz had eight (and won four). Franz, along with the other lead actors (David Caruso, James McDaniel, Jimmy Smits, Kim Delaney), appeared in other Bochco productions, and perpetuated a performance style that contrasts with both *Miami Vice* and *CSI*. The 'signature' stylistic elements included moving camera and fluid shot composition, percussive and pervasive music tracks, and interesting use of different depths of field and slow motion. The decision to wound one of the leading characters in the opening episode, apparently fatally, and to include a lengthy sex scene, drew attention to the style and structure of the programme and announced it as an innovation in the police series genre while also connecting it to the heritage of quality work associated particularly with Bochco.

Boomtown was created by the writer Graham Yost and director Jon Avnet, and each episode centred on a crime seen from the different points of view of the people it affects, including the central team of detectives but also uniformed police, paramedics, reporters and the district attorney. This produced moves back and forth in space between these characters as well as shifts in time. The premise for this format derived from Yost's experience in shooting interviews with Second World War veterans to appear as framing sequences in HBO's *Band of Brothers*: 'I thought, what if I told one person's point of view of their whole experience of the battle, and then you see someone else's experience of the battle, and let the audience take these real and subjective viewpoints and put them all together?' (Bianco 2002: D9). Arriving at this idea from watching the film *Rashômon* (1950), he reported that NBC was willing to risk it, having used temporal and spatial shifts in *The West Wing* and fractured point of view in the 2001 season's opening episode of *ER*. *Boomtown's* shifts in point of view are used to provide new story or character information, rather than simply to offer a replay of the same scene from another viewpoint. The shifts are signalled by a fade in which the image's colour is bleached out to suggest a subjective or hallucinatory quality. Despite the unusual and relatively innovative visual aesthetic, *Boomtown* storylines were self-contained rather than serially linked, thus adopting an older form compared to series-serial hybrids such as *Law & Order: Criminal Intent*, which *Boomtown* followed in NBC's Sunday schedule.

As this brief backstory to the arguments about *CSI* shows, the effect of a combination of the regularities of format with the exploitation of *mise-en-scène* and film style has given the police and detective genre new ways of making narratives visually distinctive. These include punctual moments that foreground spectacular effects, rapidly cut sequences underscored by music, or long takes that develop the analytical possibilities of temporal extension. Developing a distinctive aesthetic in niche programmes was not very significant in the USA's period of network dominance and the policy of 'least objectionable programming' when three US networks provided a restricted diet of programming for mass audiences. But from the 1980s onwards the emergence of a culture of niche programmes, repeated viewing, programme-related merchandise and exploitation of franchised formats was significantly dependent on the visual and aural aesthetic developed in the specifically televisual form of the long-running police procedural/investigation series. 'Quality' refers not only to character, dramatic logic and thematic complexity, but also to the distinctive use of visual and aural resources. The provisionality of knowledge and the link between seeing and knowing as a conditional and often fragile relationship are crucial to this.

Popular television series rely on recurrent narrative patterns where, as Umberto Eco (1990) argued, formulas produce pleasure for the viewer by rewarding predictive activity. So the pleasures of a specific narrative, such as setting up an enigma that will subsequently be resolved, produce a second kind of pleasure at the level of the series as a whole through repetition of narrative patterns and the programme's conformity to viewer expectations. Those US series considered quality television work with an economy comprising generic verisimilitude's adaptation of programmes to audience expectation, and also play with verisimilitude and genre by means of visual pleasure and spectacle. A reflexive awareness that these programmes are television is crucial to their play with contrasts between excessive or unconventional *mise-en-scène* and generic narrative, characterisation and dialogue. They are series television but cinematically rich in visual terms. They are writer-producer led but exploit directorial control over camerawork and shot composition. They establish the specificities of US settings and use the resources of Hollywood's filmed television production system but are also recognised by British audiences, critics and broadcasters as quality television.

Acknowledgement

This chapter is one of the outcomes of the research project 'British TV Drama and Acquired US Programmes, 1970–2000', funded by the Arts and Humanities Research Council and based at the University of Reading. Jonathan Bignell leads the project, working with a postdoctoral researcher in the Centre for Television Drama Studies.

13
Quality and Creativity in TV

The Work of Television Storytellers

Máire Messenger Davies

> The 'Powers of production' are essentially products of the human mind as well as gifts of nature . . . the measure of the relative values of commodities is to be found in the amounts of labour incorporated in them.
>
> G.D.H. Cole, introduction to *Capital* (1946: xvii)

This chapter raises issues of authorship, value and the nature of creativity in an industrially mass-produced medium – television – with particular reference to the contributions of writers. The term 'quality' in television has a number of connotations. A major one is institutional, as in the criteria for public service broadcasters such as the BBC, in which the word tends to be equated with 'unpopular' and applied to genres such as documentary, and religious and educational programming that public service broadcasters are required to supply because they are 'good' for us. This discourse was evident in the March 2006 government White Paper on the future of the BBC. The minority PBS channel in the USA also invokes the quality label in this sense. Series that received mass audiences in the UK (such as *Upstairs Downstairs*, produced by the commercial London Weekend Television in the 1980s) were coded 'quality' merely by being broadcast on the less-popular PBS, and by being labelled as 'Masterpiece Theatre' and framed in a set of heritage-style images, including a teacherly introduction by Alastair Cooke (see Jarvik 1999).

Institutional criteria for this kind of quality (associated with tradition, education, literariness and upward social mobility) can also be found in US commercial television discourses. Jane Feuer's book on MTM (1984), the production company that produced many 'socially relevant' (another quality criterion – see Gitlin 1983) drama series, such as *The Mary Tyler Moore Show* and *Lou Grant*, introduces the term 'quality demographics'. Commercial network shows such as these recognised the existence in the mass television audience of upwardly mobile young professionals, particularly women, and the shows were tailored to attract both them and, more importantly, the advertisers to whom they were desirable.

Other discourses of quality derive from discussions of genre, particularly the genre of costume drama, associated with history, aristocracy, canonical literature and expensive production values (see Brunsdon 1997) and, of course, from personal opinion and taste – a neglected area of academic discourse, because many scholars seem to be nervous of saying that they think something is 'good', as Jason Mittell (2005) recently pointed out. I would like to follow the Mittell argument and address the question of what is 'good' because I agree with him that film and television scholars have avoided this question for too long and have left passionate and pleasurable analyses of 'great telly' or 'terrific movie-making' to journalistic critics, fans and ordinary viewers. But, in the context of this chapter, my main reason for addressing this question of 'the good' is that it is a crucially necessary one for those who actually produce the texts. How can, and do, producers (whether writers, directors, editors, sound, music, costume, makeup artists) decide and determine the quality of their own work? If we are seriously interested in how television works and how cultural and other values are arrived at, these are voices that need to be heard.

So I want to question the ('low quality') notion of mass production as applied to TV and to give a voice in this debate to the people who do the work. Although some television scholars do draw attention to the industrial and structural role of labour in the film and television industry (see, for example, Toby Miller et al 2004: 119), the opinions and value judgements of the workers, as distinct from their economic status, are seldom heard in intellectual debates about quality and cultural value.

Focusing on the Writer

Because of the centrality of the writer in determining everything else (including there being a text of any kind at all for subsequent scholarship to argue about), I particularly want to focus on the role of the writer. I will use examples from an ongoing research project that Roberta Pearson of Nottingham University and I have been working on for the last five years: a study of American television, using *Star Trek* as a case study. I argue that the writer is crucial to any discussion of production quality because the script is the one irreducible currency of value (both commercial and aesthetic) in film and television production. The executive producer of *Star Trek*, Rick Berman, when asked what would be the biggest problem he could face in keeping the show going, put it most succinctly:

> The biggest problem that we have is writers. It is very, very difficult to write *Star Trek*. You can get writers to come in here who are top writers of television, top writers of feature films, playwrights. And the odds are one in 20 of them will be able to write this show . . . We're always getting new writers and most of them don't make up (interview January 2002).

At that stage, the last of the *Star Trek* TV series, *Enterprise*, was in the first stages of its production, and optimism about its future was still apparent. However, with hindsight, Berman's words have proved all too gloomily true; the writer problem on *Enterprise* was never really solved (although there were other pressures on the show, including structural and technological changes in the industry and the advance of the internet), and the series steadily lost viewing figures until it was cancelled in 2005.

I will quote material mainly drawn from interviews with two of the writers we met at Paramount in January 2002, when we were able to talk to 25 people working on the series, from set dressers to executive producers. The first writer is the late Michael Piller, who sadly died in November 2005. When we interviewed him in January 2002 he was no longer working at Paramount. Piller worked primarily on *Star Trek: The Next Generation*, *Deep Space Nine* and some of *Voyager*. The other writer is Brannon Braga, who was a co-executive producer on *Enterprise* at the time of interview. Braga, too, was a veteran of the other post-1987 series.

In using their accounts to address the theme of storytelling, I am proposing that their stories – their personal accounts of how they worked – have a value for us as scholars. Not only are they witnesses to the historical conditions of production at the time they were working, but these accounts also give revealing insights into how to read the texts, the stories we see on screen. I also suggest that one possible reason for the relative failure of *Enterprise* (among many others, including a change in the climate of both film and television, in which fantasy replaced science fiction as a dominant genre) could be the different ways in which these two writers worked. In his interview, Piller stressed the importance of working cooperatively, as a team leader and negotiator. Braga was, and is, a brilliant individualist, more like a literary auteur, in the literary sense of having a recognisable personal style. A Braga script usually reveals an interest in formal experimentation, and in extreme mental and physical disintegration; because of this he has been called 'The David Cronenberg of *Star Trek*' (Reeves-Stevens 1997: 158). In their role as writer-producers if not full-scale managerial hyphenates, Piller and Braga had to be responsible for other writers as well as themselves, and to collaborate closely with other production departments. In this role, Piller seems to have been more comfortable; however, it may be that the Braga scripts will endure in any future study of the series as televisual text. This, of course, raises not only the question of authorship but also the question of cultural value and permanence.

Who is the Author of *Star Trek*?

In 2005, I had the opportunity for another valuable first-person insight into television production. I was able to interview Herb Solow, the executive producer at Desilu (the production studio run by Lucille Ball and her husband Desi Arnaz) who sold *Star Trek: The Original Series* (*TOS*) to NBC in 1966 and thus was instrumental in launching the whole phenomenon. For most people who have heard of *Star Trek*, and that is probably most people, Gene Roddenberry is the recognisable authorial name. Solow made some uncomplimentary remarks about Roddenberry's self-promotion and his exploitation of fans to make himself 'the Great Bird of the Galaxy'. As the author, with Robert Justman (whom we also interviewed in Hollywood), of a major source of information about the original series, *Inside Star Trek: The Real Story* (1999), Solow is a key contributor to a further branch of TV storytelling: the backstage production narrative. There are a number of alternative versions of how *Star Trek* came to be the phenomenon it was, but in all of them Gene Roddenberry is the central figure. A major organising narrative of the *Star Trek* myth, if I can call it that in the proper sense, is a series of different narrative points of view about the character and actions of Roddenberry. Solow belittled Roddenberry, as did William Shatner (Captain Kirk). Others we spoke to, such as Herman Zimmerman, the production designer for the post-*TOS* series and films, praised him. But in the story of the story, whether he be good guy or bad guy, Roddenberry remains the central protagonist.

In the actual making of the series, as distinct from the *accounts* of the making of the series, it was a different story. One remark Solow made to me was particularly illuminating. He said, 'If you're doing a TV series or anything creative, you can't have competition within the production. You have to have cooperation. Gene promoted himself, not the show' (interview April 2005).

Mass Culture or Handcrafting?

As mentioned, our interviews with individuals raised the methodological question of how to include the contribution of creative production workers to debates about culture and value, as initiated by Pierre Bourdieu (1986), for instance. The debate about mass culture and its degeneracy previously launched by the Frankfurt School in the 1930s, in its focus on consumption and the 'problem' of mass audiences, tended to underestimate a key Marxist component of value: the contributions of labour. Our book – and briefly this chapter – gives an account of the social relations of production, the ways in which those who make cultural artefacts operate professionally to produce the value of those artefacts. If television *is* to be treated as an economic commodity, any analysis of its use value, of its exchange value, of its absolute value, or of its surplus value (in Marxist terms) has to incorporate the contributions of the workforce. Labour in cultural production not only includes material, physical activity (as in the case of craft workers and set builders, what Miller et al [2005] call 'below the line' workers), it also includes less tangible sources of value such as workers' creativity, their judgements about the quality of their work, and that of their fellow-workers, concepts more usually associated with what Miller et al (ibid) call 'above the line' – that is, concepts that are usually attributed to directors and high-profile stars.

TV storytelling comes to us via mass distribution; that is, TV is a technology that delivers messages into millions of homes simultaneously. But TV storytelling is *not* a form of mass production, whatever else it is. Hand-crafting and traditional forms of labour organisation remain crucial determinants of the quality – however defined – of the finished product.[1] In American episodic television, with its pressurised, industrialised production lines producing a show a week, the contributions of the regular workforce are central to its successful operation. This pressurised production schedule is a major difference between episodic television and feature film, and has been a source of denigration of the television medium (although it does have similarities to the pre-Second World War Hollywood studio system). Our (Pearson and Davies') research with Hollywood craft workers suggests that industrial pressures should also be seen as a source of value. This was particularly evident in the ingenuity with which creative people, such as Dan Curry, the visual effects producer, responded to time and resource pressures, leading to memorable images and effects, many of which, as in the case of Curry's design for the Klingon weapon, the ba'atleth, became iconic and a source of the product's surplus cultural and economic value.[2]

The Importance of Writers in Television: Two Key Writers

Television episodic drama running for 26 weeks of the year is a form that devours ideas. A sellable concept for a series is the first, and toughest, form of idea to produce; most fail, as has been pointed out by many people, such as James Twitchell (1992). The originator of the idea of *Star Trek* is still universally acknowledged to be Gene Roddenberry, although he wrote comparatively little of it. Of the 79 episodes of the original series, he had 22 story ideas, and only 15 of them were used (Gerrold 1973: 180). But he was responsible for the *Star Trek* 'bible', and Gene's creation is acknowledged by everyone associated with the series who has ever spoken or written about it, including those who are known to have disagreed with him, such as Herb Solow. 'Gene's vision', however this might be defined (and it has been extensively documented in accounts by both production insiders like that of Solow and his colleague Robert Justman in *Inside Star Trek* [1999], and by academic critics), continued to shape the way writers worked, and this, we have come to believe, is also a crucial component in writing a successful series: even where the vision may be challenged in the writing process, and even where it becomes mythologised into something grander than it really was (as Solow told us had happened with Roddenberry's contributions), it is still a necessary ingredient. Michael Piller's comments below give an example of how this writerly negotiation around a contested version of the 'vision' worked in practice.

As Rick Berman points out, his biggest problem as the executive producer with overall responsibility for 'everything' was finding writers; this was the one currency, or source of value, that the production could not afford to be without. In literary culture, the writer is a traditionally respected figure, and one that fits an auteurist model of individual creativity, but in Hollywood this is much less so. Screenwriting, according to William Goldman, 'is shitwork' (1983: 78) and Goldman spent much of his celebrated work, *Adventures in the Screen Trade*, vigorously debunking any model of screen production that elevates individuals – including directors – to auteurist status. But he ends his book by ultimately privileging the writer: 'we're the ones who first get to make the movie' (403).

Whatever the status of screenwriting in movies, it could be argued that this status is even more lowly in the less culturally prestigious medium of television. However, because TV writers have to keep writing every day, week in, week out, the relatively leisurely processes of adaptation, destruction and reconstruction of movie screenwriting, as described by Goldman, are less applicable in television. The production line has to be kept going and there is little time for frequent false starts and revisions. In television, the writer, or more accurately in American television the team of writers, is the crucial and precious, because constantly necessary, source of raw material: the major source of value. I suggest that this industrialised process of production does not detract from the cultural and aesthetic value of the output; it is, on the contrary, a primary source of it.

Writers Speaking

In the rest of this chapter I will draw on interviews with two key *Star Trek* writers, Michael Piller and Brannon Braga (both interviewed in January 2002), to illustrate this point further. Piller left the series after the third season of *Voyager*. Braga became joint executive producer with Rick Berman on the fifth, and relatively short-lived, series *Star Trek: Enterprise*. Michael Piller ran his own company, Piller Squared, which produced *The Dead Zone*. He was one of a group of writer/producers whose creative contribution was not only writing some of the outstanding episodes of the *Next Generation* series (*TNG*), including the third/fourth season cliffhanger, 'The Best of Both Worlds: Parts 1 and 2' (3: 26; 4: 1), which helped to launch the series into mass popularity, but particularly in reorganising the way in which the series functioned. Piller, like Berman, recognised the centrality of writers in generating overall quality and consistency for the series, and he set up what seems to have been an effective, if unorthodox, system for making sure he found them. Above all, he went against standard industry practice by accepting unsolicited scripts. He pointed out to us that:

> My fundamental responsibility . . . was to ensure that every story in every script was as good as it could possibly be, every week and it was a full-time job and I worked with a staff of writers – five or six writers at a time on *TNG* . . . and we hired people and took pitches from independent writers and read material from freelancers and even amateurs, I just needed ideas, I needed to be to be bombarded with ideas for shows, which I would then buy and work with the writers to develop.

Piller had to deal with a lot of problems on the new series when he took over – problems well documented in the authorised insider accounts and corroborated by what he told us:

> It was not a nice place to work for the first year. I came in the third episode of the third season and had a very angry and disenchanted writing staff that were all furious with Gene because he wouldn't let them do what they wanted to do. His rules were very strict and he was very adamant about keeping them. And I just felt that it wasn't my job to change the show and battle with Gene. I figured if this franchise had lasted 30 years, Gene must have been doing something right, so rather than be intransigent, I listened, and tried to figure out what it was. And it took a few tries.

The following account from Piller enumerates his version of the key ingredients in a successful script: the individual bright idea (in this case from a novice who was to become a star writer of the series, Ron Moore); the importance of consistency to the central vision; the importance of developing and sustaining both the new and the traditional; the painstaking negotiation with colleagues:

> The very first show I developed, there were no scripts in development, and I had to get something ready for the next week and I said I want to see every piece of material there is in this building, anything that's been abandoned and rejected. Someone gave me a script by a young kid about to go into the navy, Ron Moore. It was 'The Bonding' [3: 5, written by Ronald D. Moore, directed by Winrich Kolbe]. I looked at it and it had a great idea about a kid whose mother was killed on a ship, she was a crew member, and the kid is terribly overwrought with sadness and the aliens, seeing this, basically provide a substitute mother, the image of a mother, just a replica . . . I took it to Gene . . . and he said, 'it doesn't work, death is a part of life in the twenty-fourth century; no one grieves when somebody dies, children accept death as a way of life, the kid won't be unhappy that his mother has died.'
>
> And I said to myself 'OK' and I went back to the writers' room and said to the guys what Gene said. And I said, all right, look, that's about the freakiest thing I've ever heard, that a kid's not going to cry when his mother dies but that's what Gene says it is . . . So that's what we start with – the freakiest thing you've ever seen, a kid who doesn't cry when his mother dies . . . Troi, who was a very underdeveloped character in the third season – we bring Troi forward and she basically says the only way we can get rid of this replica mother is if the kid absolutely strips away at levels of civilisation and lowers to feel the true emotions that this loss represents. And ultimately that's the way we went and it was a far more interesting story than if the kid was whining for two acts.
>
> That taught me that ultimately Gene had these rules for a purpose and I used to call it 'Roddenberry's box' and I liked the restrictions of the box. A lot of writers didn't, but I did. It forced us to be more creative and forced us to find new ways of telling stories . . . and as time went on I became . . . among the writers at least, the defender of the box, so it ultimately turned into Piller's box . . . I take a great deal of pride over helping to direct the show in a way that Gene Roddenberry really cared for.

I have left these lengthy quotations as they were transcribed because they are a good illustration of the writer's storytelling styles. Piller, from his own account, and also from those of others, does appear to have been a good team manager, able to gather and motivate teams of writers, able to go along with the apparent straitjacket of 'the

Roddenberry box', and creatively and shrewdly adapt it to his own authorial ends. The above quote is a well-crafted account of events, with a narrative problem, a sense of suspense, and a moral at the end: it is a good story. Piller was also one of our interviewees who spoke most openly about his own personal feelings about the show and how they had influenced his work on it. With Piller's account of the writing process, explanatory concepts such as 'inspiration' began to seem appropriate, as did the insight that the experiences of the writers *as writers* were being fed into storylines and character development.

We asked him, as we did everyone, what he thought his own personal contribution had been: did he have a personal style, a recognisable Piller script? He deflected the question by suggesting that the auteur role didn't belong to writers, it belonged to directors (something our director interviewees were to dispute). But he then went on to describe his own approach to script construction – strongly influenced by the book he believes every writer should read, Goldman's *Adventures in the Screen Trade* – and how he worked his own emotional experiences into this.

> It's almost always to find a character, some character with a very high personal stake. People remember 'The Best of Both Worlds' and say, 'Oh yes – the BORG!' But the truth is that story is really about Riker and whether he's big enough to sit in the big chair. If you look at that particular story . . . in that third season you can learn a lot about me. That story is about 'what have I lost?' . . . He's trying to decide whether he should stay on the Enterprise, and that was happening to me, deciding whether I was going to leave *Star Trek* or not . . . What I brought to that show was an inner life that came straight from my own inner experience.

Brannon Braga: 'The David Cronenberg of *Star Trek*'

Brannon Braga, unlike Piller, was a writer-producer still working on the television series, in this case *Enterprise*, at the time we interviewed him. He had also graduated to the role of co-executive producer, alongside Rick Berman. He had moved from being 'the bad boy' of the script-writing team, the 'David Cronenberg' who liked to explore mental and physical disintegration, as Reeves-Stevens described him (1997: 158), to having major executive responsibility. Braga wrote some of the more experimental episodes of the series, specialising in stories in which characters are pushed to the limit, such as 'Frame of

Mind' (6: 21), from *The Next Generation*, in which the usually stolid Commander Riker (Jonathan Frakes) is subjected to a series of mind-breaking experiences where neither he, nor we, know exactly what is 'real' and what is delusion.[3] The episode examines this question by framing the story of Riker's disintegration within a theatre set. 'Frame of Mind' (like Pirandello's 1921 *Six Characters in Search of an Author*, to borrow a 'quality' comparison from avant-garde theatre) is a reflection on the nature of performance and pretence; it is one of many episodes in which the *Star Trek* writers reflect dramatically on the often-disturbing nature – 'the struggling and fighting' as another writer, Ron Moore, put it – of their own work.[4] I would argue that the use of such innovative narrative techniques, activating intertextual comparisons with writers such as Pirandello is a 'quality' marker, to the extent that it derives from the – again – culturally respectable discourse of literary criticism. To adopt the Mittell position ('why can't we say something is good?' [2005]), I don't see why I should have to borrow the respectability of literary criticism to justify my enthusiasm for the writing of this episode. However, the fact that I have done so is an indication of how debates about television quality are often constructed: a text is 'good' by virtue of comparison with some supposedly higher cultural form.

In our interview with him, we began by asking Braga the same question we had asked Michael Piller: how would anyone know what a Brannon Braga script is? His answer revealed how his role had changed from being the 'bad boy' writer, to being a man with major responsibility for the whole product:

> I don't know ... I could have answered this question a few years ago, when I was doing certain kinds of episodes ... the more high-concept, science-fictiony episodes, or the offbeat darker episodes. On *Next Generation* and in early *Voyager*, I did a lot of dreams and screwing around with reality. I did virtually all of the time travel episodes. But now ... I've written so many episodes, more than any of the writers, I don't know what are mine. I don't even know what I'm doing ... I've done everything ... And with *Enterprise* I'm trying to do something completely different. I'm trying to do a show that isn't grounded in high concept science fiction – that is more grounded in the characters.

Braga's take on the process of production reveals the writer's eye and ear, and a certain impatience with the kinds of decisions that are handed down from on high – decisions that he told us he did not feel he had much influence over (surprisingly, given his co-executive position).

> We have two production meetings on every script with all the department heads, and we discuss it scene by scene by scene – it's very tedious . . . The schedule is that the scripts are usually written right up to the last minute, like I'm writing a show right now . . . [We] start shooting on Tuesday, and I'm half-way done, so I'll get this one done and get on with the next and it's been that way for 20 in a row . . . We have six more to do. It's quite a lot . . . There's seven to eight days for shooting, which is ludicrously short for a show of this magnitude, and then we have quite a long post-production time . . . for editing and visual effects and sound effects, they'll have anywhere from four to eight weeks to get that done. We have a very big lead time, because they need a lot of time for the effects . . . When they [the actors] rehearse it, they're rehearsing it right before the scene is shot. It's intensely high pressure. It's non-stop.

Braga pointed out the extra pressures under which *Star Trek* production workers operate, compared to other sorts of series television:

> We can't go out into Los Angeles and shoot on location in restaurants and in the streets. We have to create brand-new worlds every single week. And our episodes are, I think, much more ambitious than most television in terms of their production value. And we have a shorter shooting schedule than a lot of shows, nine days. And we do 26 episodes, whereas most shows do 22, and that extra four, are a killer.

Enterprise, in contrast to *TOS*, with its $33,000 per episode budget, and *The Next Generation* with its $1.2 rising to $2 million budget, had a budget of around $3 million per episode, which could still, according to Braga, be a problem, but, he said gloomily, as he had to leave us for yet another meeting: 'My number one enemy is that calendar right there, which I stare at.'

Braga's account was rather like one of his scripts: sounding like a man under extreme pressure, with disjointed phrases, emphasising stress, tension and the pace at which he and his colleagues were required to work. It was evidently different from Piller's way of talking, quoted above. Of course they were interviewed under different conditions: Piller recollecting his time on *Star Trek* in the relative tranquillity of his new production offices at Piller Squared, Braga right in the thick of a tight schedule, still at Paramount.

Nevertheless, these accounts can be compared and corroborated with other interview material produced by these and their fellow writers that exists in the public domain. There have been many fan conversations and journalistic interviews with *Star Trek* creatives on both official and unofficial websites, and in magazines, and, as we have said, we believe that these kinds of discourses can provide revealing insights into the texts produced by these writers' labours – what we see on the screen.

Team interdependence is a constant theme in the stories told in the show: the survival of the various *Enterprises* always depends on the crew working together, and the standard plotline for many episodes is that of survival being put at risk either by somebody breaking ranks and letting down the team, or by outside interventions and accidents that threaten the completion of the ongoing mission. As mentioned above, a frequent mechanism for introducing these tensions is a breakdown in the integrity of the series' regular characters, and we can speculate, as Michael Piller pointed out, that the stories told in *Star Trek* often reflected what was going on in the writers' own lives. Braga's account illustrates the point that the central and most pressurised activity of all TV writers' lives is the weekly meetings in which the team has to produce scripts or not have a show to transmit.

I want to end by referring specifically to *Star Trek: Voyager*, interestingly, with its woman captain and several female senior officers, the most consistently cooperative of all the series in its storytelling. There were behind-the-scenes problems with its production, some of which resulted in Piller's departure. Many storylines in *Voyager* sound like a desperate appeal for everybody to get along. The recurring theme of the reconciliation of the rights of individuals with the needs of the collective was put particularly succinctly by Captain Janeway (Kate Mulgrew) in a fourth season *Voyager* cliffhanger, 'Year of Hell: Part 1' (4: 8) (which at times felt like a particularly problematic writers' meeting): 'The moment we split apart we lose the ability to pool our talents . . . One ship, one family'. Or, to put it another way – 'from each according to his abilities, to each according to his needs'.

The extent to which themes, dialogue and situations in a TV series invoke these kinds of ideological intertexts is another measure of the potential quality of a television drama. It is an aspect that cannot be dealt with in depth here. But certainly where *Star Trek* is concerned (as well as many other series, such as *Buffy the Vampire Slayer*) the ideological subtexts of the creative material produced by television writers continue to provide a flow of secondary writing from us in the academy. Whether all this writing is of high quality or not is certainly as much a question worth asking of ourselves, as it is of the TV professionals.

Part of this chapter first appeared in a paper given at the conference on 'The Work of Stories', Massachussetts Institute of Technology, 6–8 May 2005.

14
Mark Lawson Talks to David Chase

Mark Lawson

• •

It's a common fantasy of television viewers to imagine ourselves as part of the programme being shown. Children dream of assisting Dr Who in his Tardis, adults about breakfasting with the Ewings at Southfork or drinking in the Rovers Return. But, with the new wave of American television dramas, the interactive fantasy is potentially dangerous. Unless we choose our role carefully, taking part in *Six Feet Under*, *Nip/Tuck* or *The Sopranos* could leave us damaged or dead.

So, finding myself sitting in the consulting rooms of the therapist Dr Jennifer Melfi in the summer of 2005, I was relieved to be in one of the safer subplots of *The Sopranos*, although even Dr Melfi has suffered serious violence since the mobster series began on HBO on 10 January 1999. Most viewer projections involving Dr Melfi will have involved becoming her patient, but I was in her chair. The couch was empty, although on another chair beside it sat David Chase, creator of *The Sopranos*. This was not a dream but a television programme: an interview for the series *Mark Lawson Talks to . . .*, which runs on the British television network BBC4. The location was the set of the New York studio where Chase was preparing to shoot the episodes that will conclude the story of Tony Soprano and his clan in spring 2007, completing a sequence of 78 episodes over eight years.

Chase had initially been reluctant to agree to the conversation. After watching a DVD of a Terry Gilliam encounter from the same series, he had telephoned the director, Clayton Smith, to say:

'You don't want me for this. Gilliam's made all those movies. I've only ever done one thing.' We eventually convinced him that *The Sopranos* was a singular achievement in more than the numerical sense, and that there might be some interest in how a man with a career of impressive but low-profile work on *The Rockford Files*, *Almost Grown* and *I'll Fly Away* had peaked, in his mid-50s, with a show widely considered to be one of the great achievements of TV.

A fit, slight man of 61, Chase seemed wary during the early part of the interview, explaining later that it had felt like a form of therapy (a key subject in both his private and professional life) that was taking place with people watching. As he relaxed, though, his delight in language and grim comedy – vital qualities of his writing – came through.

In preparing the transcript for publication, I have removed obvious false starts or mis-statements, in the same way that a television editing process would. However, I have retained many qualifications and rephrasings because the conversation of a writer frequently reveals the template for their dialogue and this is certainly the case with Chase.

Mark Lawson, November 2006

ML: Given the career you went on to have, an obvious place to start is the first television you watched in America.

DC: We got our set late. My father didn't let me watch the TV. Probably *Howdy Doody* and a show called *Winky Dink and You*, which was – you got a piece of plastic that you put on your TV screen. And they would draw in the studio and you would draw along with them. It was kind of neat. You'd follow their pencil on the thing. You draw your own Winky Dink cartoon. And also there was a show called *Andy's Gang*, which was Andy Devine. I don't know how they did this show. It was a Saturday morning kind of variety show. It was Andy Devine and a bunch of strange talking animals. Midnight the Cat and Froggie the Gremlin. I don't know if you're familiar with the show at all.

ML: I've read about it. Never seen it.

DC: And there seemed to be a live audience but probably it wasn't. It was probably like stock footage of kids jumping up and down. And so they intersperse these routines that Andy would do with these strange characters. And then they'd have old serials like *Sabu* and stuff like that cut into it. That was the first stuff I remember.

ML: You were born in 1945, just after the end of the Second World War. You lived in New York and then New Jersey. What kind of childhood do you remember?

DC: It's an interesting thing because if you watch the show, obviously there's a big psychiatric component. So I went through a lot. I did a lot of therapy and it's probably been written that the character of Livia's kind of based on my mother. But lately either it's some sort of historical revisionism, or I don't know what's going on. But I've begun to realise I had a really happy childhood. I think I was anxious a lot of the time. My mother made everybody anxious. (Laughs) But I think I was anxious and scared fairly often.

Living like in Jersey in those days, there were woods you could go to play. You disappeared all day long. Go and play in the woods and live out these Davy Crockett fantasies and my mother worked so I was sort of on my own after school. Kind of running wild. And I had a really good time.

ML: And what was your mother's job?

DC: My mother was a proofreader for the telephone company. She proofread the phone directory. That was her job. She didn't work when I was from like zero to five. She didn't work at all. Or six. And then my father changed professions and she went to work, I guess as a bookkeeper, or something for a steel company. And then later on she worked as a proofreader for the phone books.

ML: It would be fantastic in a drama. It's an amazing job to have had. And maybe that's why she was so difficult. She just sat there going down lists of names day after day.

DC: This is pre-computers, you know? Yeah. She would just read pages and compare it to some master list, I guess. Mark Lawson (Laughs) 15 Evergreen Road. Mark Lawson . . . I can't imagine it. (Laughs)

ML: And as you say, it's an article of faith on the internet, and for everyone who writes about *The Sopranos*, that Tony Soprano's mother is your mother, that there is a strong degree of identification.

DC: I would say a strong degree of identification, yeah. I mean more of my relatives saw it right away. It didn't have to be pointed out to them. As soon as they saw the show, they went, 'Oh my God! That's Aunt Norma.' My mother had always been a great source of amusement to most of the family because she was out of control. Or could easily go out of control. And she had no governor on her motor as to what she would say to people. And she was funny. And sometimes I thought to myself that she did this on purpose. But I'm not sure. I mean that she knew that she was being funny. No. But she did it to attract attention, I'd say that.

ML: So what kind of thing would she do?

DC: She would flip out. I mean we've done some of it on the show. For example, this is a woman at the age of 50, if things weren't going her way, she would actually stamp her feet and go, 'I don't want you to do that!' That kind of stuff. And we included a thing at one time, I remember I was home from school, it was a snow day, which is a great thing in the States. And I was being a real kind of an asshole. I was about 14 or so. And I wanted one of those . . . like a little electric organ because I was bored. And we didn't have a lot of money but I kept bitching and moaning about that organ. And finally she came out of the kitchen with a knife and put it up near my eyes. 'I'd like to stab your eyes out.' And she kind of meant it and I was really like, 'Whoa! Okay.' Not that she ever would have done it.

And I also remember another time when I was talking on the phone – I don't what it was. And the only phone was in the kitchen. And she was cooking. She was making veal cutlets, for veal parmigiana actually, I think. And she had a platter in one hand and a fork in the other and she got upset as she was talking to me and she started banging the platter and a chip came off of it and she just kept on going till the whole thing was destroyed. Ba-ba-ba-ba-ba! Down to this little nub in her hand. So that sort of thing. (Laughter)

ML: Because of the show there's so much emphasis on your mother. Your father very rarely gets mentioned. But what was his role in all this?

DC: My father was the guy who was: 'Poor Henry, he's saddled with Norma.' That was his role. Everybody thought she was a 'handful'. That's the way they used to describe it. And he sort of played on that. That he was, 'What could I do? There's nothing I can do.' My father, I think, was actually a very angry, bitter man. Which is fairly rare, I think, for the time. He was from a broken home – my grandmother had divorced – I don't know if they actually even officially divorced. My grandmother came to this country and she worked in a mill at the age of 13. A typical Italian immigrant story.

She was illiterate. She came from southern Italy. She worked in a mill in Rhode Island when she was 13 years old. That child labour stuff in the late nineteenth century. And probably, when she was probably 14 or 15, she married a guy and she had children with this guy. His name was DeCesare. I never wanted to tell this story because my last uncle was still around. But he's died. It's not that shocking. But he was an older man and he wouldn't have [wanted it talked about].

My father finally told me this later on. She was married to this older man. She probably married him at say, 14. By the time she was 26 or so, she had, I think, I don't know, four or five children by him. Then this boarder came over, a 19-year-old kid, sleeping upstairs. And she began an affair with this guy and had two kids with him. And then she and the second guy took off with all the children and left Rhode Island and went to New Jersey. And the reason our name was changed because the name was DeCesare. And the reason our name was changed is so that they couldn't be found.

As a boy, I never knew this. It seemed like all I ever knew was there was two names. There was Chase. That was like about four or five of my aunts and uncles were named Chase. The older ones. Then there were several younger ones named Fosco, who were the children of the second guy, Joe Fosco. But we all celebrated holidays and things together except there were very often schisms. And sometimes the Chase kids did not speak with the Fosco kids, although it didn't really break down along those lines. There was always someone taking my grandmother's part and other people who were loyal to my grandfather.

My grandfather, this guy, Joe Fosco, was a real prick. He was a bad guy. And he pitted those kids against each other. My aunt told me that. That he made the children of the first guy do piece-work at night. They had to do buttons and bows until 12, 1 o'clock, which he then sold. He had a contract with somebody who made them. They weren't his children. So he made them do this Dickensian sort of labour.

ML: And your parents' marriage – you're saying your father had come from what was called a broken home. But was their marriage happy, do you think?

DC: No. No, I don't think they were happy.

ML: It lasted, though?

DC: It did last. But I don't think it was – well, that's – it lasted. I don't know. They were constantly fighting. Or sulking. There was more sulking going on than fighting. It was long stretches where 'I'm not speaking to you.' That's how things were done in that house. 'I don't want you to speak to me for two weeks.' Okay. (Laughter)

ML: We're talking in the psychiatrist office, we're beside the couch, although you're only metaphorically on it. But Tony Soprano, he's haunted, daunted by his mother. She's the reason he enters therapy. Was that the case with you?

DC: Well, both my parents. Yeah. I was an only child so I was the complete focus of their attention. But a lot of it was not good. I mean they cared about me quite a bit. It's not that I was an abused child, or . . . neglected child. But they had their own demons and their own, I don't know what. But they just all sort of placed on me that I was going to somehow be their ticket to American respectability or something.

ML: And what were their ambitions for you. I mean, they wouldn't have wanted you to write a successful TV series about them. But what would they have wanted for you?

DC: They wanted me to, well, here's another thing is that we're Italian. There's a few people in our family, myself and my parents included, who are Protestant.

ML: That's very unusual. Everybody assumes it seems would be Catholic.

DC: Yeah. I know. The deal there was, and I'm not quite sure about this. My father's entire family is Protestant. And my aunt told me that, I think this starts off because there was a sect in the late 1800s called the Waldensians who came from Germany down into Naples for some reason. And that our family, their family had converted to this Waldensian religion. Then immigrated to the United States and I guess the closest thing that they could find to that was the Baptist Church.

My mother's father was a Socialist. And an atheist. And didn't bring his children up in any way, whatsoever. But I guess originally had been Catholic. And so the kids were free to like sort of find their way. Really what that meant was marriage, I think. I don't think they went to church as kids. And so most of my aunts married Catholics. But my mother found her way to this Protestant church for some reason. So that's where she met my father. At a youth group sort of thing. You know, I don't think she went there to go to church. I think they had like dances and stuff like that.

ML: So you were raised as a Baptist.

DC: Baptist and then Presbyterian.

ML: And does any of that remain?

DC: Well, probably. Yeah. I think I probably still have a tendency to see things in black and white.

ML: If we look at the textbooks around us in this psychiatrist's office, they would say about only children, most of them, that only children develop a very strong imagination. I mean quite a lot of them become writers. Are you aware of that?

DC: No. I was not. I'm not aware of that. I mean when I was in college and I studied psychology, there was a famous test that the United States Navy did. And they found out that fighter pilots in Korea with the most number of enemy kills were only children. Probably they were so angry. And then next was first-borns. And then down. That's the only thing I know about that whole thing.

ML: And what were your feelings? You talk about only children being angry. Did you feel isolated? Did you want to have had siblings?

DC: I did want to have a sibling. I think everybody wants an older brother or an older sister. Probably, if you're a boy, you want an older brother. And yeah, I wanted that. But then I saw like, for example, very close friends of ours, the kid that was a contemporary of me, had a younger brother and I saw that that didn't work at all. That the parents favoured the younger brother all the time. And my friend, Bobby, was always getting yelled at and his brother was getting away with murder. So then I didn't want a younger brother – that didn't seem to be too good. I'm the only one in the family. And most of my, well, I had another cousin who was an only child. But most of my cousins have siblings. And it seemed nice. It seemed nice to have sisters and brothers.

ML: You said of your father hadn't wanted you to have a TV. Why was that? He thought it was a bad influence?

DC: Yeah. No, he wanted me to concentrate on schoolwork.

ML: Were you a good student?

DC: At that time I was a very good student. I got really good grades in grammar in elementary school. Almost all As and some Bs. But I had always had bad grades for what was called deportment.

ML: And that was how you behaved.

DC: Behaviour.

ML: You were kept away from television in childhood. But you used to go to the movies?

DC: Yeah. It was two things that happened. There used to be Saturday matinees in America at that time in which they would run Westerns – mostly Westerns and sometimes like *Superman* serials and things like that. Or 'Knights in Armour' stories. Double bill usually. And it was really great. You'd spend an entire afternoon there eating candy, and getting this big sugar rush and watching (Laughs) some movies. And then afterwards, we'd walk home and sort of enact sword-fighting and stuff like that. It was really fun. And I used to go to that every Saturday. But there was also a thing in the New York metropolitan area, and I think Martin Scorsese has talked about this. There was a show on Channel 5 called *Million Dollar Movie* and they would run the same movie every night for five nights. In other words, for an entire week you could watch the same movie. You could watch it over and over again. And I mean I wouldn't say that I studied it but you got to be exposed more heavily to a film if you wanted to. And they were all black and whites. I think. Of course, the set was black and white. Mostly it was black and white. They were studio products of the 30s and 40s.

ML: Presumably they did it to save money. It's a fascinating bit of TV history because it's what people do now with DVDs, young directors are able to watch over and over again. You could do a version of that if you wanted.

DC: Right. It was difficult for me because I was supposed to be doing my homework at that time. It came on, I think, at 8 o'clock or 7. I forget. So I wasn't allowed to really do it all that often. But every time I could, I would. And that was the struggle was 'Go do your homework' and 'No, I want to watch TV.' And I can't say it was because I was in love with film. It's just I wanted to watch TV rather than do my homework.

ML: And were you conscious of who wrote and directed them?

DC: Not at all. Not in the least. I don't think I got that – it didn't really sink in until probably, strangely enough, probably 1965. I was never a film scholar. Actually I hadn't thought about this. In 1963, I went to a Baptist college – it no longer is Baptist – in North Carolina. And it wasn't because it had no religious connotation for me. My best friend was going there so that's – I made a mistake. I shouldn't have gone there. It was a college in the South. And it was very conservative. We had to go to chapel twice a week. And it was part of the Southern Baptist Convention. And in chapel they would play 'Dixie' and you're supposed to stand up. This is during the times of Civil Rights. I didn't like it. It was not – I didn't like it at all. But oddly enough, they had this Friday night film programme. And that's where I saw *8 1/2*. I don't know who was responsible for that. I saw two Fellini films there. I saw *Breathless*. And I think *Shoot the Piano Player*. At that place, which you wouldn't think – I think it was *Shoot the Piano Player*. I think it was. So I went to those and you're confronted with this thing called, this is a Fellini film. Wow. This is a Stanley Kubrick film. Oh. So some guy did this. It didn't come out of a factory. There's some single person who apparently is the chief of all this. (Laughs)

   And it really struck me when I went to see *Cul-de-Sac*, this Polanski film. By that time, I was going to school in New York. And I went in the daytime to see that film. And I walked out of there thinking, 'Okay, that's a Roman Polanski film. That means maybe that's a job I could do. Maybe that's a career for me.' And that was the first time that it really clicked that in some times, in some cases, somebody actually has responsibility for the vision of a film.

ML: Inevitably, because of what you went on to do with *The Sopranos*, the question arises of when you first saw gangster movies, Mafia movies?

DC: The first gangster film I saw was on *Million Dollar Movie*. It was *Public Enemy*, William Wellman's film with Jimmy Cagney. And that movie really scared me. And it just, I thought it was fantastic. I never saw anything like it.

ML: And while being careful about invoking an Italian-American stereotype, which you have been accused of, but in your childhood, were you ever aware of real mob activity?

DC: Yes. I mean, phew-w-w . . . you know, I grew up in New Jersey so those things were in the papers all the time. Mob hits and stuff like that. And I was always very interested in it. And there were some people in my family who were very tangentially connected. And then one guy who's a cousin of mine. My cousin married a guy who was actually, I think, fairly well connected. But I was told he was a bookmaker. That he was a bookie. But I think it might have gone deeper than that. But I don't know. And my parents didn't like that whole aspect.

ML: But you were vaguely aware of that going on?

DC: Uh-hm. Uh-hm. Yeah. Yeah. You couldn't, I don't think you could be living, being Italian-American in the North-East and not be aware of it. And that it wasn't that far away. And all these denials are ridiculous. (Laughs)

ML: The denials that it goes on.

DC: Yeah!

ML: Yeah. So when you're – we might as well raise it now, when you're accused, as you have been by some people, of invoking, perpetuating this stereotype of Italian-American life, your answer is that it's real.

DC: That's an answer I've given. And I suppose when there are no longer any Italian-American gangsters, then the American gangster film will go the way of the cowboy film.

ML: So the realisation coming out of the college in the South that there's this job – director, writer-director, whatever the next stage was – you then did think seriously about trying to get in . . .?

DC: I decided to go to film school. Right. I had been involved. I got struck with being, I don't know – somehow along the line I got this notion that I wanted to be an entertainer . . . well, a rock 'n' roll star first of all. I mean seeing The Rolling Stones on *Ed Sullivan* was a watershed event. And then we also had a lot of TV shows here called like *Shindig* and *Hullabaloo* . . . all these British bands. And that was very – that's all I wanted, cared about or thought about. And some friends of mine and I created a band together which never, we actually we were too good to ever play for people. We were kind of one of the first super groups out in New Jersey. (Laughter) No one ever heard of us because we just had to keep it for us until we ready to really go.

ML: What were you called?

DC: We never had a name.

ML: Band without a name.

DC: Yeah. Band without a name.

ML: You played what?

DC: I started out playing drums and then bass guitar and sang lead vocal. But I never really developed that well. Bass guitar. My fingers weren't really good at that. But literally, we never played a date. It was all theoretical. We were a virtual band.

ML: The rock period is interesting because breaking rules has been important to you and we'll soon get onto how you did that in television. But did that aspect of music in the 60s appeal to you? That it was rebellious? It was going against the grain?

DC: No doubt. No doubt. And it was also, I mean, all the style that went along with it. I guess it was the first time I really saw that this was like an art form. Actually, I didn't know how to draw so I couldn't be a painter. I didn't have the patience to be a writer. I sat down to write a novel once and I wrote three pages. And I had no idea when I sat down where it was going. I'd read novels. So I just started writing. After three pages I had nowhere to go. I went, 'What is this?'

ML: What age were you then?

DC: Probably 14.

ML: What was it about? Do you remember?

DC: It wasn't about anything. Actually it was about a guy who was the head dishwasher at a camp, a summer camp that I had been sent to work as a dishwasher because I'd gotten in trouble. My father had a hardware store. And on the last day of school of our sophomore year, I think, some friends and I went on this rampage and went up to this country club and threw all the pool furniture in the pool, and stuff like that. And we got caught and so my father said, 'You're going away. You're going to work in Pennsylvania this summer.' And so I worked there as a dishwasher and there was this African-American guy named Joe Bass who had a very beautiful daughter and the novel was going to be about him somehow. (Laughs) I don't know what. But it's just going to be about Joe Bass.

ML: Do they exist? Those three pages?

DC: No, they don't. No. When I was working – it's funny – when I was working on *The Rockford Files*, my mother came to visit us at Universal Studios. So myself and Meta Rosenberg, who was the executive producer, and Juanita Bartlett, who was one of our fellow-writers, we all went to lunch at the commissary. And so my mother said something, 'Oh, he used to write these things. This crazy stuff.' And they said, 'Well, do you have them?' And she said, 'Oh, no, we were moving. I threw them all away.' So that's my early work is gone.

ML: She said, 'These things.' So there was more than the three pages.

DC: Yeah. You know, in school, you have to write short stories and stuff like that.

ML: Poetry and so on?

DC: Oh, no. I tried poetry once. I couldn't. I didn't understand it. I didn't understand how to make that form or why it was like that. You know, I read a lot of it. And I was an English major but when it came time to actually practice it, I was clueless.

ML: And the 60s, a good time to go to film school because that's when modern American cinema began effectively?

DC: Well, it was a great time because also because a lot of really great people were at their prime. Bergman, Fellini. Kubrick. Polanski was starting. Scorsese, well, that was more like the 70s, I guess. It was a great time. Kurosawa.

ML: And at film school, what kind of work were you doing?

DC: You know, the truth is I never really – I was never focused enough on what I should have been focused on. So even though I was in film school, I was still kind of much more involved with, seriously, buying records and listening to records.

ML: You still wanted to be a rock star?

DC: I suppose so. I just was crazy about that music. And that's what I did more. I mean, I saw a lot of films in film school and I remember a lot of them and I learned a lot in film school. But I also picked a film school, Stanford University, which did not have a fictional tradition. It's not a place where you learn to make narrative films. It's dedicated to documentary filmmaking. But I got a fellowship there. This is graduate school. I got a free ride so I took it. My wife and I were newly married and we, just setting out and so we settled there. And I went to film school there.

ML: And then you went into television, but television was a second-best option?

DC: Yeah. I mean, yes, absolutely. I mean I really wanted – I fell in love with film during that time. But again, I'd have to say that, as I look at it now, I wasn't focused enough. You know, there are people like Quentin Tarantino and Martin Scorsese, they just know everything about every film ever made and they've seen every film. And Peter Bogdanovich. I wasn't like that. I just wasn't that focused.

ML: And so before you went to television, had you attempted to make a movie?

DC: I had written – what happened was that I'd written feature screenplays and the reason I got into television was because if I had been at UCLA, or USC, it might have been different. But we were up in Palo Alto. At Stanford, the number of visiting people from the business was not as great as those other schools would have. And so one of the guys that came up there was a guy named Roy Huggins. And I don't know why Stanford had a relationship with Roy Huggins but Roy Huggins was a TV producer and he had produced *Maverick* and *The Fugitive*. Pretty good stuff. All shows that I had really liked. But I wasn't interested in TV at all. However, because there was a relationship there, when I wrote a screenplay, Roy Huggins was someone that I sent it to. And Roy Huggins hired me to do my first TV job.

ML: Those early screenplays, what kind of thing were you writing?

DC: Oh, I don't know what they were. The one that actually got me the work was something I wrote with another guy. It was some bogus sort of attempt to be like Truffaut or something. It was some weak pathetic thing. Sort of like *Shoot the Piano Player*. Some piano player in New York, he's on the run from the mob and he ends up in New England and I don't even remember what it was about.

ML: Your first work in television was the horror genre?

DC: Yeah. I really did like, as a kid I really liked – I always did like horror films.

ML: And so *Grave of the Vampire* is your first credit.

DC: *Grave of the Vampire* is my first credit. That's right. Although that movie does not represent me as a writer at all. (Laughs) Actually, no, the truth is that was completely rewritten. I wrote a screenplay but there's almost nothing of that screenplay except the title. And it wasn't my idea. The idea of a woman who had been impregnated by a vampire, and then gave birth to a vampire, it was someone else's idea which I developed. But then they completely rewrote me.

ML: So there's very little of you in that film.

DC: Nothing.

ML: And so the first script you regard as yours would be what? Would be *The Night Stalker*?

DC: No. I worked for a while. A friend of mine and I from film school, this guy, Barry Pollack, I'd gone to film school with him. He established, you know we all came out of film school. He came down to LA as I did. And he got a job and directed two features for Gene Corman, Roger Corman's brother, one of which was a remake. What was called a blaxploitation film of those days. It was called *Cool Breeze*. It was a version of [John Huston's heist movie *The Asphalt Jungle*]. And then he did another one. And so he was really on his way. And then he brought me in to help. Gene Corman wanted to do a comedy about airline stewardesses. And we worked on this thing called *Fly Me*. Oh! Probably six months. And I made $600 on that. And it never went anywhere.

    And then I went off on my own. My wife was working supporting me and she really had a lot of faith in me, which I didn't have. But she did. And she went to work in a law firm. So I was at home all day long trying to write. And I wrote a screenplay that never got produced, which was like a psychological thriller. And that led to me actually being hired again. So I had done that one job in TV. Then I didn't work for two years. And in that time I did the stuff with Barry Pollack and then this other screenplay and that got me a job working with a guy and after that, that was like 1974, then I didn't stop working. It finally took. But it was TV.

And so once I got into TV, I'd never been able to write a feature script and have it be bought. So once I got established, or once I got a chance at the TV business, I just jumped on it because we had actually – remember this is like 1974 and right before Christmas, my wife and I, Denise, sat down and we said 'Maybe I need to stop.' You know, get a job as a teacher or something like that. That it wasn't happening.

ML: It was that close?

DC: Yeah. It was really that close.

ML: And your wife's faith in you as a writer, was it general love or was it based on reading and seeing the stuff?

DC: It was general love but I think she just – it was based on reading the stuff, I think. It was general love but I think she just felt, she's always felt that I was funny. And that I have a distinct view of looking at the world. And that some day, people would see that.

ML: And eventually they did. But you read a lot of books about American television where they say you're finished by 30. In fact, your huge success came in your 50s. So you were a late developer in that sense?

DC: I was. I was. I wasn't focused. I was not focused enough. I did not know how to go about it. I didn't know what I wanted to do for sure. And I didn't study enough. Something like that.

ML: And so you almost gave up. But then you got the job in TV?

DC: Well, that Christmas – what happened was is that in 1973 or four, I forget. '74 I think, the Writers' Guild went on strike. The Writers' Guild of America. And I had written this one TV show for this guy, Roy Huggins, an episode. It was a lawyer show called *The Bold Ones*, which I really didn't like doing and I didn't have any affinity for it. But it was a professional credit and was enough for me to have to be required to join the Writers' Guild. So I didn't work for two years. And I knew so little about the whole thing I said, 'What the fuck. What kind of guild is this where they don't even get me any work?' (Laughter) Shouldn't there be some sort of union hall for writers where you go down there and wait to be picked? Made no sense at all. But I didn't get any work through the union. So I was very annoyed about having to go stand picket duty when the strike happened. On picket duty, I met this man, British, actually been born in Britain. A man named Paul

Playdon, who was a young writer who had been a story editor on *Mission Impossible* and that was no small feat because those stories were very intricately plotted.

And he was about 30 I guess and I was maybe 28, 27. And he read a screenplay that I had written, a psychological thriller. He recommended that to his agent. The agent signed me as a client and then Paul got a job as a producer. They were changing administrations on a show called *The Magician*, with Bill Bixby. It was a magician who, you're probably going to be surprised, who solves crimes.

ML: Yeah. I saw one episode of that once in Britain. Yeah.

DC: (Laughter) And he would defeat the bad guys by throwing silk handkerchiefs and stuff like that. And so Paul took over the last nine episodes of that and brought me on as a staff writer. And then after that was over Paul was hired to be the producer of *The Night Stalker*, which had been a successful TV movie with [the actor] Darren McGavin, and when they went to make it into a series, they hired Paul to be the producer and he brought me along to Universal. I signed a contract with Universal, a seven-year contract, and I was a story editor on that show. So then I didn't stop working. I was always working. But I was entrenched in TV.

ML: And the interesting thing about *Night Stalker* or *Kolchak, The Night Stalker* as it's known some places is that it wasn't naturalistic, which I think is significant to what you went on to do. You've enjoyed the non-naturalistic aspects of television?

DC: I have, yeah. I suppose. I never thought of it that way.

ML: Well, I just thought looking at it, it's the only connection you can really see with your later work is the fact that it's very different. Like, *The Sopranos*, it breaks some of the rules of TV?

DC: Maybe you're saying the same thing. I've never been really that interested in those franchise shows and those political shows. It doesn't appeal to me at all.

ML: You've often spoken about the rules of network television and the importance of breaking them. What are the rules?

DC: What are the rules of network television? Well, there was a man whose name I forget. Herb something, who worked at, who was the president of NBC, who in the early 70s, I think, came up with a concept called LOP. Least Offensive Programming. That's the basic rule.

ML: And what are the rules?

DC: As little content as you can possibly have.

ML: Happy endings, sympathetic central characters.

DC: Happy endings. Yes. Happy endings. Sympathetic. Everyone's likeable. Seriously, I remember being involved with things where they wanted the villains to be likeable. (Laughter)

ML: And everything is resolved within one week. Perhaps if you're lucky – I think you did on *The Rockford Files* you can get a two-parter occasionally . . .

DC: That was because we would write those. It wasn't intentional. We would write them and they'd be too long and we'd have to split them in half. Yeah. Everything's resolved and I think it's dedicated to order. Everything, the order is not disturbed. And the order is always put back. Order is always restored.

ML: And what becomes crucial with *The Sopranos* is the rules about language. You just know as a writer that you can't have people speaking as they would speak on the street?

DC: No, you can't. You can't. So a totally psychotic pimp will sound fairly much like the guy who runs the delicatessen.

ML: *The Rockford Files*, which you wrote a number of scripts for. Was that a happy experience?

DC: It was great. That was great. Great experience. And my favourite part of the whole thing was in the mid- to late 70s, cowboy boots were back. I guess because of *Urban Cowboy*. Cowboy boots were back in style. Well, actually it had started in the early 70s, like with the Burrito Brothers and there was this, and The Eagles. There was a sort of cowboy chic. At least in California. Blue jeans, cowboy boots. So I, of course, was wearing cowboy boots. And I was in the producer's office. Meta Rosenberg. And Jim Garner came in to talk. And he had cowboy boots on. And I thought 'Holy shit! That's the guy that first made me want to wear cowboy boots when I was eight years old. That's Maverick!' And it was like it blew my mind. That it had come somehow full circle. You know? And I really enjoyed working with him. And there was a talented bunch of people. Actually, very fair. Very not back biting. Decent group of people. Stephen Cannell, Juanita [Bartlett], Meta – they were good people. Number one. And very talented. And I learned a lot.

ML: Also within the limitation of network TV, it was actually quite a quirky series, *The Rockford Files*.

DC: It was, yeah. [By the standards of] its day, he was not heroic. And he was kind of a coward. I mean in the end he would get there. He'd mix it up. But he didn't like to get into confrontations. And he didn't throw his weight around. And he was what they call self-deprecating. And he wasn't, Jim Garner was not afraid to look foolish. And it made for a very pleasant – I mean actually very – I still think, I haven't seen it in years. At the time I thought it was pretty good. And I remember when I first went over there to audition for the job, or to apply for the job they had me watch a couple of episodes. See, at that time it seemed like most TV shows, they took place in their time-slot. In some Nowhereville. Some generic time-slot for the universe. *The Rockford Files* seemed like it was taking place in Southern California, in a real place. And I thought, 'That's really good.' It felt like Southern California. It felt like Los Angeles.

ML: Something you said about network television once in an interview is that it's all dialogue. Now it's quite interesting to happen to talk about this at a time when the film of *Miami Vice* has just opened, because, apart from *Miami Vice*, most TV was not very conscious of it being a visual medium. It was very much a speech medium?

DC: Uh-hm. Yeah, well, I think it comes out of radio. I mean I guess it's part of it's because it comes out of radio. The same sponsors who used to sponsor *The Jack Benny Show* and *The Shadow*, which were radio shows, then just jumped onto the TV bandwagon. But the reason it's like that is because it's an economic thing. To have, as you should well know, to have you and I sitting here is not that expensive. Talking. But if you and I are going to get into a car and crash it, or if we're going to spend a certain amount of money to have you facing the sunset thinking, that costs money. But it's very cost effective to have people, two people going like that at each other in a room with lighting.

      Like *Marcus Welby* is the perfect television show. Right? It's all set on a stage. A patient comes in and he has the stethoscope, they talk. Nothing. No movement. No night. Night is expensive. So that's why it's like that.

ML: And very occasionally he'd do a home visit and we'd be amazed that he'd left the office?

DC: (Laughs) Right. Yeah. So there you go. You build a hospital set. You have a dolly. You know, you don't have to go up or down stairs. And you go from room to room talking with people about life and death situations. So allegedly it's gripping but you're not moving. It doesn't have any aspects of movement to it. And movement costs money.

ML: Were you conscious even on *The Rockford Files* as a writer of wanting to do things that you couldn't do?

DC: No. Things that I couldn't do. No. On *The Rockford Files* I became conscious that they were very character oriented. That what was important to them was not so much plot, although [creator] Steve Cannell really knew how to do a plot. And I learned a lot about plotting a show from him. We used to labour hard to come up with those stories beat by beat by beat. And he had some rules about stories which were actually good rules. But I think he felt that unless the story was working, it wasn't going to be good. That you needed a really solid story. Then you could have all the character beats you wanted. You could have all the quirks and interrelation. Intimacy or lack of intimacy. Misguided thoughts, passive-aggression. You could do all that stuff but you had to have a solid story.

ML: For the benefit of the aspiring writers watching this, what were Steve Cannell's rules of TV writing?

DC: The one that I remember – in fact, I had a plaque made for him for Christmas with it on, was: what are the heavies doing? And what that meant was: Rockford's in his trailer, there's a lot of noise outside. Cars are spinning around the parking lot and some body falls out and the car speeds away. And Steve would then make sure that 'Rockford' was locked into that for his own survival. That was one of his rules. 'So what are the heavies doing?' So in a detective story, so there's a body in the parking lot, so Rockford then finds, when people used to smoke, a book of matches in the guy's pocket. So he goes to the Nudies Western Wear store, where people buy cowboy suits and he interviews somebody there.

So it's all about finding information. You go here, you go there. And he would always say, 'What are the heavies doing?' because that means that the villains were not inactive. They were coming back at Rockford. So they would kick the action along. Otherwise, it's just a bunch of information gathering. It's like journalism or something. Or that's kind of a detective show. Like Hercule Poirot. This happened and then that happened and then some sort of ratiocenation which gives you the answer. That was not what he felt, and I thought he was right, that to make a show that was more interesting that had action in it, you needed to have people that were active. And a detective is really not active.

ML: And then becoming what is known in Hollywood as a hyphen: writer-director, writer-director-producer. That began with *Alfred Hitchcock Presents*, which is the first thing you directed. Had you been thinking about directing?

DC: I wanted to direct when I was in film school. And then I got sidetracked into TV. And I lost that. I became, I don't know. It didn't look like a lot of fun. It didn't look like a lot of fun to be directing episodic television, number one. I became nervous about telling people what to do, working with actors, telling cameramen 'I want this shot over here.' I lost confidence in some way.

And also I guess I was enjoying myself without it. I enjoyed working. *Rockford* was fun to work on as a producer, you were really getting to shape the material because you were a producer. There wasn't a need to direct. So I enjoyed that aspect of it. And I had let my feature ambition fall by the wayside because I was having a nice life.

ML: And so then how did the *Alfred Hitchcock* offer come about?

DC: What happened was that Chris Crowe, who was another guy at Universal under contract, wanted to make an anthology series. So what really appealed to me was the idea that the story would be self-contained with new actors every week. In other words, you would cast your own story and it wouldn't have recurring characters, so you wouldn't have to be involved with this crap, like 'Well, my character doesn't do that.' Coming in as a visiting professor and having someone saying, 'Well, why don't you draw the sketch?' [and another writer says], 'Well, he doesn't know how to draw. My character does all the drawing.'

So that appealed to me, the idea that it would be like doing a movie. You know, and the name Hitchcock carried a lot of weight with me. Even though he was dead, but still. I felt there was some connection to one of the greats of cinema.

ML: And you said you'd lost your confidence earlier as a director. But when you directed that did it come back quickly?

DC: No. No, it didn't come back quickly. No, I was petrified. It was difficult. It was a five-day schedule. And it was too ambitious. But it finally did come back. After about the second or third day. You know, Hollywood crews are tough. And they're tired. A TV crew is a tired bunch of people. They've been working usually for months and months and months. With this director, that director, and the directors have different levels of personal skills and different levels of talent and the crew has to take what they're given. And sometimes they have to carry a guy through that, or a woman. Or sometimes they're led, which I think they respect more.

And so they are very suspicious when someone comes around, first-time director. It's like, 'Here we go. You know what? Here goes my week. I'm getting home late every night.' But fortunately, I guess they began to see me as someone with a vision. That crew. And I was delighted. It was just a big event in my life.

The big event was finally like the operator said to me, like on day three or four, 'Boss, how do you want this?' And I thought to myself, 'Holy Jesus, this is Hollywood. And I'm the boss.' (Laughter)

ML: And the first show in which you took that brand of quasi-religious title, creator, which is one that everyone wants, was *Almost Grown*, which is a very hard show to track down now. But how did that come about?

DC: That came about because I had a deal – the pattern of my life was, post-*Rockford Files*, I would make development deals with studios or with independent production companies and what that means is I would be paid, this is a part of my life that I kind of regret. I would be paid money, a weekly salary, so I had a secure job for anywhere from, usually they were two-year deals. I told you my first job at Universal was a seven-year contract. They used to do that. (Chuckles) It's insane.

But usually I signed a two-year deal so I was guaranteed a weekly income for two years. In return for that, I would have to come up with TV ideas and try to get a series on the air.

None of which was interesting to me. I didn't want to have a series on the air. And the reason I did it was I would then take the time . . . while I was doing those deals. I'd write a pilot. Then I'd also be writing a feature at the same time. And my hope always was that one of those features would happen and I would be transported magically out of this television hell into the wonderful world of motion pictures. But it never happened.

So one of those deals was working at Universal, and a really smart guy named Robert Harris was running the place then. And because I had achieved some . . . I won an Emmy. Because I won that Emmy, I began to be seen as somebody that people at the networks wanted to have meetings with. I began to be – actually I'd won two Emmies. I forgot. I shared an Emmy with *The Rockford Files* people, for Best Drama one year.

But that didn't really do it. That helped. But then I got an Emmy for a movie for TV, a writing Emmy. So that this is the beginning of branding, right? The David Chase brand. So that's the way people look at it. Like, 'Oh, that guy. So that guy's responsible. Let's talk to him.'

So because of that movie, I got meetings to create series. And that landed me this deal at Universal. And this guy Robert Harris teamed me up with another writer named Larry Konner, who's a feature writer. And we were both sort of lifers. We were kind of sort of doing this TV deal with our left hand while trying to write movies. And that's where I met Larry. And Larry and I co-created that show together. Because there was pressure. You had to come up with something. You couldn't just sit there and write movies all the time because you were paid to write television.

So there was pressure to do something all the time. And so we came up with this idea of doing a story which would use rock 'n' roll and pop music from the 50s, 60s, 70s, 80s as a storytelling and thematic device. And . . . we pitched that to Robert Harris. And he added something to it. He added something smart and I can't remember what it was.

Oh, he added this idea of doing the framework, that it would start in the present but would go back to the past. Would go back and forth in time, which is what the show did. So it followed, the story was about a couple who had met in high school. Like my wife and myself. Also like Larry and his wife although they met a little bit later.

A couple who met in high school, went through all the changes of the 60s. [The music] was post-Elvis – The Chiffons, and the Four Seasons. All that from that era through the advent of British rock 'n' roll, soul music, FM-radio, all the way into the 80s at that time. And he had started out as a college disc jockey and he was at the end of it, he was a station manager. So we went back and forth between their life now, which they were divorced, and when they first met in various periods in their life. It really was cool. It was really nice.

ML: So again, non-naturalistic, which . . .

DC: I suppose so. Yeah. But they didn't dream these things or anything. It just went back and forth in time.

ML: And you referred once in an interview to the 'numerous sell-outs I've done during my life'. That would be this period?

DC: Yeah. Yeah. I mean it's been a while. I didn't have the nerves to actually just go out and freelance. To like not take that studio pay cheque and go out and sit in a garret and try to write feature screenplays and try to become a writer-director, which is what I really wanted. I couldn't wean myself away from the creature comforts. This is the negative way of looking at it. I could also say, 'Well, by that time I had a child.' . . .

ML: It's always a question with late developers, had you started to think that it wasn't going to happen, you weren't going to be the kind of success you wanted to be?

DC: Uh-hm. Yes. I sort of think that. Yeah. Because I had a bad reputation. A reputation was always . . . you know, 'He's very talented. But he's too dark. His material is too dark.' And that was both in movies and in TV. You know, it's that thing out there that once you're in the club it takes you a while to wash out. And so even though I had deal after deal after deal, in which nothing happened, I still kept getting hired because something had happened once.

ML: Therapy, as we've said, was an important part of your life. At what age had you started?

DC: About 32.

ML: And what had triggered that move?

DC: I was depressed a lot of the time. I was angry a lot of the time. But the actual trigger was my wife's younger sister died. And my wife was devastated by this. As was I. But nothing like her, of course. And we went back East for the funeral and as upset and sad as she was, and as stricken with grief as she was, I tried to be there for her. I was also overly concerned with my parents' reactions to things that were going on. I was just too hung up about my parents . . . about pleasing my parents. And I thought, 'Something's out of whack here. Why do I think about these people so much. They drive me crazy. What am I so – what is this little seed they planted in my brain as a kid that I just can't shake their – you know, "What are they going to say?" and I don't want to have to listen to them about this.' So that was what finally did it. It was making me into this sort of selfish, self-involved person, who wasn't really there for this other situation enough.

ML: You said your mother came to the *Rockford* set once. But your career as a writer in TV, that hadn't pleased your parents, or it wasn't enough for them?

DC: Oh, it was. Well, it was enough for my father. They were a strange pair. My father was actually very proud but he never let me see that. My mother never understood it. And could have cared less. In fact, probably hated it. She just didn't get it. It was too out of her ken, you know. At one point I had said I wanted to be an actor. This was like in my late teens. And my father said, 'You can be a clown in the circus but I want you to finish college first. You finish college first, and then you can be a clown in the circus if you want.' Which was an improvement over my mother, who said, for some reason, 'People like Frank Sinatra will eat you alive.'

ML: (Laughs) Good line that.

DC: Yeah. Oh, she was talented. (Laughter) She didn't realise she was talented. Why Frank Sinatra? I don't know. I never said I want to work with Frank Sinatra. (Laughter) Frank Sinatra was not even in my radar. I don't know. (Laughs)

ML: Did therapy change your writing or help your writing?

DC: I don't know. I don't know the answer to that. I don't think so.

ML: We're getting to the stage where you start to do the kind of work you really wanted to do. I wonder if the therapy had stabilised you, changed . . .

DC: It stabilised me. It helped ... yeah. It helped me having someone to talk to. It helped me. And I learned a lot about my growing up and the forces at work there. It didn't really cure the sort of depressive tendency, or the anger. But at least I had some, I wasn't like just spinning out, like 'Why do I feel this way? What is wrong with me?' That's what I used to feel a lot. 'What is wrong with me?' I mean I began, I learned what was wrong with me. But didn't really cure any of it.

ML: Particularly given your relationship with your parents, I'm interested in your reaction to their deaths. Was that a release or...?

DC: A release. I came back from (Chuckles) my father's funeral and my wife and I stayed in my old bedroom in the house. It's crazy when I think about it. And so we were leaving and we were straightening up the bed so my mother ... we were stripping the beds, so my mother wouldn't have to do it. Or making the bed, I forget. This was like 1976. And we were back there a total of like two or three days. I remember we were working and I was working and making the bed and singing to myself (Sings) 'You can go your own way. Hm-hm-hm.' And I realised, 'What the hell was going on?' You know. And she started laughing because it was obviously very telling. But I wasn't aware of what I was singing. I was just sort of humming to myself.

And I realised I felt good. That this, that some sort of oppressive control was gone. And the problem was my father was really, he was proud of me, but he – they came to visit me one other time at the studio. And I had a big office. Universal had built this new suite of offices. And there was an office problem. The office, for some reason, probably twice the size of this with a patio outside and expensive patio furniture.

A lot of people had these offices. But my parents were not prepared for this. And my father got there and he was like stunned. And they had their picture taken in Clint Eastwood's parking space with his name on the curb. They were very excited. And we went home for dinner that night and some other relatives joined us. And my father said, 'Well, we saw David's pretentious office today.'

And I thought, 'You prick. You lying hypocritical bastard.' And I was really upset and annoyed and hurt. And I don't know why he couldn't enjoy it or why he couldn't say ... I didn't care about . . . nobody cares about the office. But he did. But he didn't like it on some level. And I guess it was his, that was his, maybe that was his way of bragging. I don't know. Some backwards way of bragging.

ML: So you could go your own way after your father's death but then, after your mother's death, you were entirely free to do what you wanted?

DC: Well, I mean they never changed my behaviour. I never did or didn't do anything because of them, I don't think. I was in a state of rebellion against them fairly early on. But I always felt bad about it. That's what it was. It's amazing I could have forgot. They had been able to instil a sense of guilt that was very strong in me. I did what I wanted to but I always felt bad about it. So after he was gone, I wouldn't have to feel guilty about anything anymore. And my mother was, I don't know . . . it wasn't the same. I mean, now that I think about it, she did not exert the same kind of control that he did.

ML: What came next was *I'll Fly Away, Northern Exposure*. Looking back – because we know what's going to happen, which is *The Sopranos* – you were getting towards the kind of work you wanted to do?

DC: I would have to say that I have been very lucky my entire career in that I always got to work with talented people. I don't think, I mean there was a . . . I worked in a TV show called *Switch*, which is really no good. A Glen Larson show, it was garbage. Other than that, I've worked – I think I've been, despite of the way I complain about television, I think I've worked on shows that were pretty good. And I would include *Rockford* in that and *I'll Fly Away*. *Northern Exposure*, I never had any feeling for. I actively disliked it.

ML: Given what *The Sopranos* became in your life and in television history now, the moment of inspiration becomes important. When had the seed for that come?

DC: The seed of that had come – I change agencies. This was like in the late 80s or something like that. Early 90s. I changed agents. And I had a meeting with my new agents. They said, 'What kind of things do you want to do?' And so I told them it was all about movies. So I told them my feature ideas, one of which was about – my wife, Denise, had told me since forever, 'You need to write about your mother. Your mother is money in the bank. (Laughter) She's like really funny and people will enjoy it just the way your relatives do. Just the way all your cousins and your aunts and uncles get a laugh out of her, other people will too.'

And I couldn't figure out how that would work and why would anybody care? And then someone who worked with me on *Almost Grown* said the same thing. Said something like, 'You should do a story about a TV producer with this mother like yours.' And I thought, 'Why would anybody want to see that? A TV producer with a sort of crazy overbearing mother.' I couldn't. I never paid it much thought. Then something made me think about that it might be funny to do a story about a guy who was a lot tougher than me. A lot more masculine tough, savage. All those things with a mother like that.

And I was always interested in Italian-American mob shows. And so I thought it could be interesting if the guy was a mobster who puts his mother in a nursing home and she wants to have him killed for that . . . and through therapy, he realises that his real enemy is his mother. That that would be a good comedy.

So I pitched this when I changed agencies. And they said, 'Mob comedies. Mob movies. Please, no way. No way. And mob comedies. Never gonna happen.' And so I listened to them and then when I signed this deal with Brillstein Gray, another company, they said that they wanted to do a series that pressed the envelope. And they said, 'You're a guy who likes to press the envelope and we think you have a series in you that would be different. For example, how about *The Godfather* for television?' I said, 'No. That doesn't interest me.' And driving home that night, I remembered this feature story that I had about the gangster in therapy and all that. And I pitched that and went to Fox with it and they bought it. And a script was developed. And then, of course, then it lay fallow for two years. And then, as I was about to leave Brillstein Gray, HBO changed their business plan. They decided to do original series.

And I had been saying, 'Why can't we go to HBO? Why don't we go to HBO?' And they said, 'Oh, they won't come up with the money for this.' But, right at the end of my deal they changed their business plan, we submitted the script to them and they decided to go ahead and do it. Then we shot it, we made it, did the whole thing. And as we're about to go on the air, along comes a movie, *Analyze This*. It was a mob comedy. Now I still have this agent who said to me, 'Mob comedy. Forget it.' (Laughter) He's still my agent.

ML: A mobster and his shrink. Yeah.

DC: Hm-m. And I thought, 'Oh my God! What a bad thing – if that movie comes out before we do, because it's TV, we'll be seen as somebody who copied it.' And fortunately, we came out first. But, when I heard about it, I thought, 'Oh, no. How could this possibly be?' But theirs turned out to be, I guess, I've never really seen it – less psychological. There's no mother dynamic. There's nothing like that.

ML: So you deliberately didn't see it?

DC: Right. Right. I didn't want it – actually because then we were going on to the series and in the second season, and I didn't want any ideas to spill over from there.

ML: I'm interested. Your wife had told you to write about your mother. Had your therapist ever told you to write about her?

DC: No. I don't think so.

ML: You could have saved a lot of money.

DC: I suppose so. I suppose so. (Laughs) No, she'll tell you that.

ML: (Laughs) And when, again, given what *The Sopranos* has become, when you wrote those first scripts, did you have a sense that something was happening?

DC: Well, it's an interesting way to put it. I had a sense that something was happening. I felt I really enjoyed working on it. And it was something I could really sink my teeth into. But, you know, television, the schedule for American TV, is that usually in network television, you're bought for 13 episodes. The shows are purchased, the ideas are purchased say, in June of any given year. May or June. You put a staff together, you start to make the show over the summer. The show debuts in September.

So you're still working on the show. You still have like eight episodes to do as the show debuts. And people are reacting to it. That's not the way it was with *The Sopranos*. We had all the shows finished and in the can before anybody saw anything. And all of us, I think everyone would agree, James Gandolfini, Edie Falco, all the writers, I believe the directors, we'd had such a satisfying experience and HBO had been so great to work with, and it had been such a different kind of experience that we thought, 'Well, it's been too much fun. It's been nice knowing you. We had a good time. This'll never happen. This will be rejected by the audience. Or it won't be successful enough for HBO to continue it.' And we were wrong.

ML: You talked about the mantra at NBC: 'least offensive programming.' But HBO was the opposite. I mean it's almost the most offensive programming. They didn't care about who they . . .

DC: No. I think that needs to be corrected about HBO. Or at least a lot of their programming. They don't set out to do the most offensive programming. And I don't think they set out to like break down taboos. I mean I know they have shows that are sort of high, *Taxicab Confessions* and stuff like that. But they're really not out to make waves. I don't think they are now. They're out to do different kinds of shows that are good in and of themselves.

And I remember [them] saying to me the first season, 'Don't do something just because you can do it over here. Don't have like strange sex scenes just because you can. Don't have like gratuitous violence just because you can.' And I thought that made a lot of sense. I thought that was really – I was glad to hear that. They're not into, at least with us, they weren't into sensationalism.

ML: We talked earlier in the interview about the network's television rules. Now, at HBO, many of those you're able to break. A crucial one is language. I mean, for example, in the story you told earlier about your father coming back from your office at the lot, where you said 'prick' and 'bastard.' Now, a network would say, 'Does he have to say that?' 'Can't he say other words?' On HBO, you can use both words, you can use stronger words.

DC: Can you use them, by the way? I mean, I assume you could, but.

ML: Yeah, we can. On BBC4. It would be difficult in other areas of the BBC. But you'll be allowed to say it.

DC: Well, thank fucking Christ for that, huh? (Laughter)

ML: Freedom of language has been important to *The Sopranos* . . .

DC: It has been. You know, the problem with the other way of doing it is that you can't speak the way a career criminal would speak. It's these other words that you put in there, and so instead of saying 'ass', you say 'butt'. 'Oh, I'm gonna kick your butt.' And they're just terrible; they're weak and they're vague. Instead of saying 'scumbag', you have to say 'dirtbag'. And it makes you feel dirty that you're doing that, that you're not being true to the English language, not being true to humanity. It's a human, human life, you know, as it's really lived.

ML: Another thing that is crucial to say about it is the, that in mainstream television, the characters cannot get away with bad behaviour, except in a jokey way, J.R. Ewing, for example [in *Dallas*], but in general, in network television, the bad are punished, the good are rewarded ultimately. You can abandon all of that?

DC: Yes, we can abandon all of that. I don't watch [network television], so I'm really not up to date with it, but I believe that's still the case. It's a very simplistic moral. It's, you know, good versus evil, bad versus good. And the problem with it is that it's all about order. There's something fascistic about it. It's this corporate fascism that seems like it's all about making you feel you are living in the best country on Earth that all the problems here are created by these troublesome outsiders and people who don't get it. In the end, what it's saying is that all of our authority figures have our best interests at heart. They may have foibles. They may be crusty, and sometimes moody and cantankerous. And, sometimes, they may even wanna curse. But basically, they're looking out for us, and they'll come through. Doctors. Judges. Lawyers. Cops.

ML: Presidents, in . . . in *The West Wing*.

DC: Presidents. There you go.

ML: I'm interested in the question of being a writer-director-producer. Normally, a writer will write something and somebody else will say, 'We can't have night shooting. Gandolfini is off making a film, so we can't have him for as many scenes. And so on.' Because you do all three, when you're writing, are you conscious – at the writing level – of what you can do and what you can't do later?

DC: Yes. Oh, absolutely. Maybe we're not conscious enough, and as the show has gone on, I think that every show that runs for a long time gets sort of a little bit bloated. Especially if it's successful, there's a little bit of indulgence for the way you do things, and no one is saying to you, 'Take that out, you can't do that.' But I think even in situations where people are saying that, 'Take that out, you can't do that,' I think that it just grows by its own, there's nothing you can do about it. More characters are added in order to do newer and different things. We are very aware of the restrictions because, in the end, it just only hurts you that you have to take the script apart and, and make it doable. 'Cause you can't spend the rest of your life shooting this thing.

ML: The other thing that most normally happens with successful programmes and series, especially in America, is that the actors accumulate more and more power, they can ask for more and more money. Now you have the power that you could drive them out, I suppose, but does that become a problem?

DC: Yes, the actors ask for more money, and they're entitled to more money. This is a huge success. And I think everybody understands it, and, uh, they've helped make it, they've made it a success. So, why shouldn't they get more money?

ML: Because of the DVD market, and even more so the internet, TV shows are subjected to kind of a level of scrutiny that was never the case before. There are these chat rooms, thousands of pages of theories about *The Sopranos*. For example, eggs. There's apparently an obsession with the theme of eggs in *The Sopranos*. Very bad idea to eat an omelette or step over cracked eggs in *The Sopranos*, because you will normally die, it's said. Is any of this conscious?

DC: I just heard about that this week; I have no, it's completely, uh, unless, you know, unless there's some greater power working through, through the writers of the show. And I'm not, I don't know, if there is, I don't know what the greater power is trying to say, but no, it's, it's completely, um, coincidence.

ML: This has fascinated me because these sites they list 15, 20 scenes where someone eats an omelette, then has a stroke, or steps over an egg and . . .

DC: Steps over an egg. When did someone step over an egg?

ML: Oh, I think Tony steps over broken eggs just before he decides to kill his cousin.

DC: Oh yes, he's, yes, he's got, he's at the garbage thing, and he's ... Right, that's right. He steps in eggs and he has to get it off his shoes. No, it's completely unconscious. It's surprising to me because mostly people eat Italian food on the show, and there aren't a lot of big egg dishes. So I don't know what that's about.

ML: The other one, we'll do one more, because I'm fascinated by this. (Laughter) A lot of weird things. The significance of the time 3 o'clock. The websites trace the fact that there are various messages, in dream sequences as well, about 3 o'clock. Very ambitiously, someone has pointed out that it's the moment in Catholic belief at which Christ dies. 3 o'clock is seen as a deliberate patterning in the series.

DC: Well, it's deliberate in the case of Paulie Walnuts. 3 o'clock is significant to him. And Michael Imperioli wrote that. Maybe Michael knew that 3 o'clock is significant in the Catholic, um, religion, but I don't think any of the rest of us knew. We don't use it for any particular reason. Uh, it's not intentional in any of the other characters' lives. Maybe we do it because 3 o'clock in ... in the morning is, uh, kind of a scary time or a lonely time.

ML: But when, when you're on a series that is getting this level of scrutiny, there must be a temptation for writers to think, 'We might throw something to the chat rooms and the internet crowd.' But you would never do that, there's no deliberate symbolism?

DC: No. No, I don't believe so.

ML: Guilt is an important theme in *The Sopranos*. Have you ever felt any guilt about using your, your mother in that way?

DC: Uh, little ... little pangs. I thought people would say, 'What kind of person would write about his mother that way?' But it never did happen. Uh, little pangs of it. But you know ... now, my mother never tried to have me killed. But she was more than willing to sort of sacrifice me to the Vietnam war machine. That was okay. So that she wouldn't be embarrassed by having a son who resisted the war. It turns out I didn't have to, 'cause I had a medical deferment. But it was more important that she not be embarrassed by that.

ML: She would rather you had gone and died there?

DC: She said, 'I'd rather see you dead than avoid the draft.' She was a patriot. I'm being facetious; my mother was totally uninvolved with politics. But, anyway, aside from that connection, I presented this sort of comic view of my mother. I presented it on the air, and she became this beloved character, so I never felt guilty. Everyone loved Livia. They loved her. She – and just as my wife predicted – she was funny, she was outrageous, she said any ridiculous thing that came into her head, and I can't tell you the number of people, thousands of people who said, 'God, my aunt Mary's like that, my mother's like that, my grandmother's like that. I've never seen anything like it, you really caught my aunt. You really caught my mother.' So I didn't feel guilty, 'cause obviously I tapped into something about a certain kind of woman.

ML: You presumably fantasised about what, had she lived to see it, her reaction might have been?

DC: Um, well, she would have hated it, 'cause of all that cursing, for one thing. And, uh, she would have felt that the Sopranos were low class. But it was amazing to me how little my mother (Laughs), how little my mother got out of anything that I ever wrote. She never really understood anything I ever wrote. She would always miss the point.

ML: But she would watch them on the TV?

DC: She would watch them. She would watch them, but it was something about the fact that other people, her relatives, were excited by the fact that my name was on a screen somewhere bothered her tremendously. She … bragging was the worst thing you could do, in my mother's book. And in fact, succeeding wasn't a good idea. She wanted me to succeed, but only so high. It wasn't a good idea to be too visible.

ML: All writers, all creative people, I think, want to have a big success, but when you get to the level of this – critics have said the best TV series ever, you just won a poll in Britain for the best television drama ever. There must come a point where that, it starts to seem scary, that the level of praise is so high?

DC: Yeah, I try unsuccessfully not to listen to it, the good or the bad. I'm not successful. I just can't not hear it. But what we try to do is re-create as much as possible the conditions of that first season, when we were working, and no one had seen it, and we knew nothing about what people would react to. And it is scary because you've got this reputation, you don't wanna lose it. You know? But at the same time, I hate myself for saying that. Who cares about reputation? It's not what it's about. You know? It should be about the work and, if it pleases oneself, and the few people that one cares about, that's enough. And who cares what anybody else says? Who cares what a thousand critics say? That's the way it should be, but I guess it's just human nature; it's hard to turn away from that. You know, I also go out seeking the bad stuff. Look, he didn't like it. You know, I don't know what that's about.

ML: There's a probably over-quoted thing that the screenwriter William Goldman said: that 'nobody knows anything'. That's the cruel truth. We don't know why *The Sopranos* has worked so well, we, we couldn't reproduce it if we set out to.

DC: No. And it's true nobody knows anything, but some people know less than others.

ML: You are now considered someone who knows more than others. You could probably make anything you want next. What is it that you want to do?

DC: I'm not sure I'd like to do anything. Frankly, I'd like to take time off and just enjoy life. If I was going to work, I wouldn't do any more television. I've always wanted to do a movie. So I'd like to maybe do a motion picture, write and direct a motion picture.

ML: And would it be a *Sopranos* film or . . .?

DC: Oh, no, no, I . . . no, I think that's . . . I've done enough of that.

ML: And would you go back to those earlier scripts, or would you . . .?

DC: No, I think not. I think I probably shouldn't. I'd like to try something different. But, if I got lazy, I might go back to them. Because writing is hard and I've never really looked at myself as a . . . I . . . I know I've achieved a reputation as a writer. But I've never really looked at myself as a . . . as a writer. I don't . . . I don't think I'm a real writer. A friend of mine just . . . actually he . . . we went to film school together, and he, uh, he's written some of the books about *The Sopranos*. Allen Rucker. And Allen was, uh, hit with this disease, I don't know, maybe eight years ago, in which he was . . . he woke up and he was paralysed from the waist down, and he still is. So he just wrote a book about it. And it's really a . . . and I . . . and I read this book and I thought, he's really a writer. I mean, he can . . . he can write a book. And it was so well written. It was so funny, and the thoughts were expressed so well, and things interwove so well, and I just know I could never do that. Writing screenplays is not really writing. I don't think.

ML: Are we talking about being late because, you know, the years of not being recognised, not getting screenplays made, do you feel fulfilled now?

DC: Mmm . . . no . . . yes. I've . . . I've . . . it's been . . . it's . . . I've been very lucky. I've . . . It's . . . it's been . . . it's been great. And I . . . and I really, you know, that's the other thing is you have to . . . maybe that's why when you say it's really scary, uh, it must be really scary to have all those things said about you, so much of it is luck that in a way if you . . . I . . . I think . . . I never thought this before but if you . . . if you do . . . if you do feel that lot of it's luck, kind of liberating. Because it had nothing to do with you. So it's not you. It's just stuff happened. And, um, and I . . . I've really been . . . this has been a great experience. Um, will . . . your question was?

ML: Whether you were fulfilled?

DC: Oh, the . . . well, the . . . the area where I'm not is . . . is that I . . . I have not had the experience of making a film. And it's . . . it's a dif– . . . it's an experience of size. And that's not . . . it's not like, you know, Joseph E. Levine presents, dah-dah, dah-dah. I don't mean that. I just mean that there's the viewing experience in a movie theatre of a large screen wh– . . . where . . . where the vistas are really large, where the sound is really nuanced. Where you can hear every line of dialogue and every sound effect works, and the . . . and . . . and . . . and . . . and the close-ups are 20 feet high. That's an overwhelming, magical experience, and you don't get that on television. Even just technically. You know, we do our sound mixing out in LA. And we do it on the same stages, smaller ones, but the same dubbing stages that they make movies on. It's the same board, it's all that. And so sometimes it's on the big screen, and the close-ups are 20 feet high, and there's big vistas and all that, our show. But then in the end, we have to turn to this little television screen and watch it there, with two little dinky speakers because that's the way most people see it. And it's . . . you go like, oh, God. And you can't hear on those . . . you can't hear half of what . . . all the work you just did, all day long, which you're hearing, it's fantastic, it's so subtle, and little crickets and stuff like that. No.

ML: And it's perhaps becoming even more. The future of TV it seems will be people watching on mobile phones, people watching on laptops.

DC: Yeah, it's true.

ML: Does that depress you?

DC: No, I'm not going to be part of it, so I don't care. I mean, if that's the way they want to watch, that's the way they want to watch.

ML: The obvious final question, as we sit in this office beside this couch, is now, after all this success, with *The Sopranos*, are you still in therapy?

DC: No. I thought of going back recently, but I'm not.

ML: Why would you go back? To deal with all this?

DC: I'm still . . . Eh, frankly, I mean . . . I mean here I am in a psychiatrist's office, and I'm actually talking where it's . . . sounding stupidly like therapy. I'm still . . . I'm too angry. I . . . I shouldn't be this angry. I shouldn't be this volatile for my age and for the . . . for, basically what's been a really great life. I have a great family. I have a great career. And I . . . you know, and what am I so pissed off about?

ML: How does the anger come out? Do you shout at people? Fire people?

DC: Well I don't . . . no. I . . . I just, I'm always, I don't know. Just blowing up, you know.

ML: It's there inside.

DC: Yeah, just blow up at things all the time. Uh, and you see what you've seen on the screen. It's (Inaudible) type *Sopranos* behaviour. That's kind . . . it's kind of like that. Just pissed off and irritable, and it's . . . there's no reason for it.

ML: David Chase, thank you very much.

DC: Thank you.

15
Writing Music for Quality TV

An Interview with W.G. 'Snuffy' Walden

Peter Kaye

• •

W.G. 'Snuffy' Walden is probably one of the most recognised names working in contemporary American TV. Making his TV theme-writing debut back in 1987 with *thirtysomething*, he has since scored the music for some of the most high-profile shows in the last 20 years. Series like *The Wonder Years, Roseanne, I'll Fly Away, My So-Called Life*, and more recently for *The West Wing, !Huff* and *Studio 60 on the Sunset Strip*. I spoke to Walden in Los Angeles immediately following the cancellation of *The West Wing* in 2005 to discuss his working practices and ideas of quality in terms of scoring and musical composition. But before turning to what Walden has to say I want to situate him within the context of scoring for contemporary US television.

Walden and Notions of 'Quality' Music

'Snuffy' Walden landed at ground zero of 'quality television' (as defined by Robert J. Thompson 1996: 13–16), with his debut television scoring *thirtysomething*. ABC gave latitude to producers to hire composers whose backgrounds were in popular records and not television music (135). With co-composer keyboardist Stewart Levin, and along with his experience as a virtuoso, pop/rock guitarist for hire (having toured with Chaka Khan, Eric Burdon and Donna Summer), Walden is responsible for creating a new style of dramatic, non-diegetic underscore, notable for its use of instrumentation and idioms derived from contemporary popular music.

Such musical innovation served to fulfil ABC's ambitions for their new show about a group of thirtysomethings living in Philadelphia struggling with adult angst. Furthermore, and more importantly for me, it appealed to an audience defined by Thompson as an 'upscale, well-educated, urban-dwelling, young viewers advertisers so desire to reach' (14). This blue-chip demographic – namely, the baby-boom generation born between 1945 and the early 1960s – were the first generation weaned on television. This depth of experiential expertise, coupled with a strong sense of being special or different, bred a sensitivity to, or suspiciousness of, the obvious emotional manipulation that earlier more traditional forms of music underscore represented. Guitar, with all of its different cultural significations, was the instrument of their generation. Rich in the history of folk, blues, bluegrass and country that had rung through the halls of college dormitories in the 1960s and 1970s, the twangs and finger pulls on a steel string, flat-top guitar had become an integral part of popular music when the boomers were courting (The Eagles and Jackson Browne, for example). By *thirtysomething*, boomers were young, first-time homeowners with children and expanding incomes, but they still felt an ownership of this music that imbued it with integrity. It was Walden/Levin who figured out how to use these trusted elements as dramatic underscore, helping to align this desirable audience's emotions with the story.

thirtysomething made pop/rock the music of dramatic television. The holdouts were the small orchestral descendants of earlier 'must-see TV', such as *Dallas*, or hour-long night-time 'soaps' like *Knots Landing* and *Falcon Crest* that often tried using pop/rock for a few episodes, but went back to their earlier styles after complaints from their largely older audiences. Genres with historical underpinnings, such as fantasy (*Beauty and the Beast*) also retained the traditional elements. But by the 1990s, must-see TV (*Friends*, *Seinfeld*), not only had their prevailing formats changed back to situation comedies with music restricted to structural markers and punctuation, but any additional music would function to foreground meaning, as genre synecdoche or other form of cultural significance. Looking back at the iconoclastic score of the short-lived *Twin Peaks* composed by Angelo Badalamenti reveals that it failed to spawn any worthy successors. Its influence appears in isolated places, but just as *Twin Peaks* failed to move on, Badalamenti's score remains an intriguing cultural cul-de-sac.

Mike Post, also originally a guitarist, had injected pop/rock elements into the television music he wrote for dramatic, 'quality' predecessors of *thirtysomething*, *Hill Street Blues* and *L.A. Law*, but the core of his style was based on the traditional orchestral model, provided by his late partner Pete Carpenter. There had been a very successful cop/action genre usage of synthesised, contemporary music in *Miami Vice*, but the emotional elements were usually set to licensed pre-existing popular songs by artists boomers might recognise. Either way, they functioned to evoke a sense of nostalgia amongst the demographic. Often it was the textual or cultural elements, set into a music-video type of presentation that aroused the emotions.

Almost a generation on from *thirtysomething*, a new creeping social conservatism has brought back some of the older tastes in musical underscore that is illustrated by 'Snuffy' Walden's most recent high-profile score, *The West Wing*. Writing for orchestra, more closely associated with film scores, and working within a tradition far from where he made his mark, Walden walks a fine line between the grand, emotional style and a more conscious knowledge of how to move an audience. Now an old hand, his tone is perfect.

Walden: The Interview

I (PK) call 'Snuffy' Walden (SW) at his Los Angeles studio, only a few weeks after the news of *The West Wing*'s cancellation after seven seasons. I tell his assistant what the interview is about and she says she will ask if he can take some time to talk. Waiting on hold, quite suddenly, the phone starts ringing:

(ring, ring, click)

SW: There is no more quality in television. (Laughter ensues)
PK: Now that *The West Wing* is cancelled. (More laughter)
SW :   I say that jokingly, I've been blessed. I've had a lot of fun time in television. I can tell you this that when you are dealing with great film it makes my job a lot easier.

PK: Although *The West Wing* is a prominent credit included under the general rubric of quality television, I would not hesitate to imagine that *thirtysomething*, the show which first brought you to prominence as a composer, could be considered a predecessor in the genre. Yet it was such a change in *The West Wing*, going orchestral.

SW: It was a real switch. It cut through everybody. It threw me too, by the way.

PK: *The West Wing* has an *Air Force One*, Jerry Goldsmith, weight of the presidential office effect to it.

SW: A great compliment, thank you. If you really listen to it, it is a piece of gospel music. That is how I wrote it, on piano. Because I am not a piano player, I wrote it as a gospel-like piece. And it wasn't even meant to be the main title. I was working on something else when that actually happened.

PK: Although network television is not always prone to such ambition, especially involving the large orchestra, did you notice a drive for something better than usual from the start with this show?

SW: I'll tell you what the difference is. Sometimes you are asked to do a job that is a '911', you are doing some emergency work, some emotional surgery or something; and then there are shows like *The West Wing*, *thirtysomething* is another one. Not that I want to exclude any other shows, but there are certain shows, like *The West Wing*, where I learned so much, and at the same time I cut my teeth doing *thirtysomething*. Those guys taught me how to write music the way they were writing scripts – to look at the story and work with storyline. They beat me up for three or four years pretty hard. Marshall [Herskovitz, writer, producer and creator of *thirtysomething*] did, but it taught me so much that I am so grateful for. I learned something totally different from Aaron Sorkin [*The West Wing* writer and creator] and Thomas Schlamme [*The West Wing* producer and director] which was about a much bigger arc: not just the arc of a scene, but the arc of a show and the arc of a whole series.

PK: Are there any specific techniques that you might use for, let's say, all the scenes shot while walking through corridors as opposed to more emotional moments?

SW: Sometimes you are asked to use music to *pace* a scene or to *pace* a show. But for the most part when we first started doing *The West Wing* we had 15 to 20 minutes of music sometimes in an episode. By the time we got to the middle of the second year we were down to around eight [minutes]. The stories themselves and the characters had been so well developed, and people understood these characters so well that they didn't need guidance from me.

One of the biggest problems with underscore, one of the hardest things to do I think, is to make sure you are letting the viewer feel what they feel about [the drama] rather than telling them what to feel. When you are doing something of what I call '911' work . . . you end up having to lead people a little bit. But when you have great film, it stands alone; and you respond to the film the way you do and really, that is what makes it so easy because I look at the film and I just respond to it. Many times I might get a certain direction that we want to play against the picture. The picture may be about a mom and her child, but they want me to recall a time when she was destitute or when her husband left her. So there is a lot of subtlety in what you play and when to play it.

PK: So working on quality television makes your job easier?

SW: You will find that with a very high-quality show the hardest thing to do, and what a great filmmaker will do, would be use restraint. You have to earn those moments. You cannot just have a moment to make you cry if you have not earned it. Something Thomas Schlamme used to talk to me about was that you couldn't make a promise that you can't deliver. I found over the years, as we got deeper and deeper into *The West Wing*, and my relationship with Thomas and Aaron got deeper and deeper, I found myself more and more in restraint mode . . . If I wallpapered it with music the music wouldn't mean anything anymore.

PK: And yet people I have talked to have the impression that there is plenty of music. It seems to have impact.

SW: *The West Wing* now is one of the lightest musical shows I do.

PK: Are you still using much orchestra?

SW: We haven't used the orchestra since episode six of the first year. Everything I do is orchestral emulation . . . Once we told people that we were going to be orchestral on those first six (or eight episodes, something like that) then the ear accepts it; and also, I am not trying to do the same kind of music as we were doing in the earliest shows and pilot where we were almost swashbuckling through the White House. In those early episodes we were just scrambling, moving through those rooms, and that was about the White House. As soon as we got into the characters you find that the music became smaller and smaller, more and more subtle.

PK: So, if not a soap opera, it is really a character drama about people.

SW: That is what they always wanted. Yeah, the particular situation we're in is a unique one in the world. But we are really dealing with these human beings. From a composer's point of view, I think when you are able to get in touch with that part of the story, or whatever the vision of the director is . . . for me, I like character-driven drama. That is what *thirtysomething* was [and] that is what speaks to me the most. That is where I feel the best fit for me. Although, right now I am doing a sci-fi show [*Surface*] that I just love doing. It is 25 minutes of music a week; and it is so much fun because I like the filmmakers and I think they have great ideas and make good film.

PK: And a change is as good as a rest?

SW: After I did a year on *thirtysomething*, the show I did next [*I'll Fly Away*] I bought a piano and wrote the score on the piano even though I didn't play piano. I knew if I just kept playing guitar I would be the guitar guy and I would never be anything else. We were going to do *The West Wing* as a guitar show. I had just done a show with Aaron and Thomas called *Sports Night* [and] we were still doing it with electric guitar. They called me up and said, 'We've been temping it with all this orchestral stuff. What do you think? Can you do that?' I said, 'Sure'. They knew I wasn't a classically trained musician – it is just a different world to work in – but you are still underscoring the emotion and the life of these characters. You are trying to suspend disbelief so that you involve people in the moment. Anytime I pull somebody out of the story or out of the character I have done a bad job.

PK: So you have to tread very carefully – the semiotic line – so as not to play anything that would distract the audience?

SW: Sometimes there is a moment for that. There is a place for everything in it. Scoring is so subjective that two composers could score the same scene totally differently, and they would both work. But they would both do different things.

PK: Is there a show currently on television that you do not score but would want to because of its quality?

SW: I think *Lost* is really great. I think it is a wonderful TV show for what it is. Personally, I don't know what I would do different because I really like what Michael Giachinno has done. I find him a delightful composer. He uses a wonderful amount of restraint, and I think he does something that is ideal for that show. I worked with J.J. Abrams [creator of *Alias* and *Lost*] on *Felicity*. The filmmaking is just good. Anytime you are working with good filmmaking, it doesn't matter the genre. I may be doing four or five shows at one time, but I try to keep the palettes all different so when I step into the emotional realm the colours are different. So I'm not going to sound like I'm just moving from one show to the next with the same music. I am very particular about that.

I am working on a thing right now (he starts some music in the background, very modern, orchestral textures, it plays for a while) . . . this is all a sci-fi thing, an eight-minute action sequence. I am working in realms like this and then sometimes I am working on a show that is nothing but solo piano or solo guitar. It just depends.

PK: Thank you for your time and music.

SW: Thank you. Glad to be of service.

16

Read Any Good Television Lately?

Television Companion Books and Quality TV
David Lavery

What are the requirements for transforming a book or a movie
to a cult object? The work must be loved, obviously, but this is not
enough. It must provide a completely furnished world so that its fans
can quote characters and episodes as if they were aspects of the fan's
private sectarian world, a world about which one can make up quizzes
and play trivia games so that the adepts of the sect recognize through
each other a shared expertise.

Umberto Eco (1986: 197–8)

With the advent of box sets of television on DVD, it is now possible
for bibliophiles (I am one) to commingle on their library shelves
television books – from Robert Allen's *Channels of Discourse,
Reassembled* to Glenn Yeffeth's *Seven Seasons of Buffy* – and very-
book-like-in-size-and-shape TV DVD sets – *Alias* to *The X-Files*.
Those gorgeous non-Region One *Buffy the Vampire Slayer* sets (the
ones that Region One's extreme fans, incapable of waiting until
the collections came to America, were tempted to purchase), were
they not meant to look, and beguile, exactly like books? Books and
television are supposed to be incompatible, even adversarial. The
highbrow, literate culture of the book and the low-brow/no brow
(Seabrook 2000), illiterate television culture are assumed to be
strange bedfellows, and yet I doubt my mixed-media 'book' shelf
is at all out of the ordinary. Indeed, quality television, inherently

'literary and writer based' (according to Robert J. Thompson 1996: 15), may be naturally sympatico with the book.

Twenty years ago, John Fiske reminded us (in *Television Culture*) that TV series are, at least potentially, 'activated texts', generating much more than the individual episodes that constitute a series' actual on-air presence. Both secondary (criticism, publicity) and tertiary (discussion and commentary occurring at the fan level) texts follow in the wake of many TV shows, and the meaning and significance that both spawn are ploughed back into the primary texts themselves, becoming part of how viewers 'read' them. That *Entertainment Weekly* guide to *Seinfeld* enhanced our appreciation of a show about nothing. Those fanfics we discovered on the internet, imagining/slashing Kirk and Spock, or Buffy and Spike as lovers (long before they became such in the narrative itself), lead us to see *Star Trek* and *Buffy the Vampire Slayer* in a new light. That book of 'fantasy blueprints of classic TV homes' (Mark Bennett's 1996 *TV Sets*) enhanced our grasp of the 'textual geography' of the Clampett mansion or Gilligan's island.

Activated American television has spun-off a wide variety of *official* tie-in books, 'commodity intertexts' (James Collins' coinage) intended to market the show, earn extra income, tell new, non-televisual tales, and satisfy the often cultic needs of television fans to know more – much more – about their favourite programmes. Bookshop shelves have long been strewn with hastily written novels (in which a series' characters have adventures that never make it to air) and dull, expository compendia of information about the series in question, but like the series that 'inspire' them, TV tie-in books can sometimes be 'quality' offerings, wonderfully imaginative extrapolations that become for those who read them instrumental factors in how serious viewers 'read' the show. Not surprisingly, my focus in this chapter will be on such quality books on quality television and, in particular, on the companion book.

Companion Books

In its 'Platonic' form, if you will, the television companion book is likely to contain sketches of the major (and perhaps minor) characters, profiles of the lead actors and actresses and of the series' creators and probably interviews with them, and, of course, an episode guide. In addition to being displayed on coffee tables, it is put to a variety of uses by serious viewers, fan-scholars and scholar-fans (an important distinction made by Matt Hills, referring to two similar types of dedicated television viewer), who may seek within its pages new tidbits to be shared around the water cooler, particulars about missed episodes or misunderstood narrative developments, and inside knowledge about a series' creative life. Although companion books to non-quality television series have appeared (*Hogan's Heroes*, *The Flying Nun*, *Baywatch* and *Full House* have all had their own), quality television as described by Thompson (1996: 13–15), rich in memory, genre-bending, literary, 'self-conscious', controversial, obviously lends itself to extrapolation into book form.

For many, awareness of quality ties began in the early 1990s. *Twin Peaks*, a show that was supposed to change television (Rodman 1989: 139–44) but did not, did change the nature of the tie-in book. It had a shorter than two-season run and those who could not get enough of the series were given not only the companion book *Welcome to Twin Peaks: Access Guide to the Town* (1991) but two intriguing 'fictions': *The Secret Diary of Laura Palmer* (1991), written by Jennifer Lynch, daughter of series' co-creator David Lynch, and *The Autobiography of F.B.I. Special Agent Dale Cooper: My Life, My Tapes* (1991), by the son of Mark Frost, *Twin Peaks'* other creator.[1] CBS's *Northern Exposure* likewise inspired several books (Weiner 1992, 1993; Chunovic 1993, 1994), as did Fox's *The X-Files* (Lowry 1995, 1996; Meisler 1998, 1999, 2000; Shapiro 2001). In the last decade, quality series like *Buffy the Vampire Slayer* (Golden and Holder 1998, 1999; Golden et al 2000; Ruditis 2004), *Alias* (Vaz 2002), *Lost* (Vaz 2005) and *Desperate Housewives* (2005) have also been companioned, though none memorably.

Somewhat more successful is *24: The House Special Subcommittee's Findings at CTU*, the first and only companion book to the Fox Television 'real time' series, now in its sixth season, which professes to be the work of 'investigative journalist' Marc Cerasini (2003).[2] As the book's introduction explains, 'You hold in your hands a classified document leaked to this reporter by an anonymous source' (ix). The infamous *Pentagon Papers*, which made public US policy in Vietnam, leaked to the press by Daniel Ellsberg, are evoked as precedent for the book which, as the title suggests, is made up of the report of a secret investigation by the US House of Representatives.

Although presented in a metafictional format, much of the book's contents are typical for a companion book. The profiles of major and minor characters sprinkled throughout the book not only provide useful summaries for viewers trying to keep *24*'s numerous personae straight, but also surprising biographical details and backstories not part of the TV text. The baffling revelation that the series' ultra-violent superhero Jack Bauer (Kiefer Sutherland) was an English major in college, as I have commented elsewhere (Lavery 2006a) is no doubt revealing and significant new information, but did we really need to know that minor character Janet York (Jacqui Maxwell) was kicked off the cheerleading squad when her grade point average fell below 2.5? (Cerasini 2003: 84). We are also provided with the de rigeur episode guide, though again in a non-traditional format (the transcripts of the committee's interviews are arranged, as are the series' individual episodes, hour by hour). An uncomplicated glossary ends the book.

Cerasini's book is by no means a simple linear rendering of Jack Bauer's first 'worst day'. The interviews (mostly with Jack) that comprise most of the text are interrupted by 'Reporter's Notes' providing additional information, complicating 'Political Corrections' in which 'Pundits and insiders have a few things to say', and disconcerting autopsy reports on *24*'s rapidly-multiplying dead. Cerasini's split-screen approach is hardly as exciting as the TV version, but it does succeed in enticing the reader into new paths through the text.

For exquisite detail, no other companion book can match the (to date) five volumes produced to accompany Fox's perpetually subversive *The Simpsons*, the adult animated series now in its eighteenth season (Richmond and Coffman 1997; Gimple 1998, 1999; McCann 2002, 2005). *Simpsons* companions may not enlarge the diegesis, but they do succeed, in their ingenious, comprehensive and snarky translation of the Simpsonsverse into a book world, in becoming something special. Each and every episode of the first 14 seasons receives a graphically rich two-page spread that offers not only sample images from that week but just about everything needed to play back everything memorable. For example, the entry for an episode selected at random, 'Lisa the Tree Hugger' (12: 4) offers us (a partial list only) a concise plot summary; an image of Bart's blackboard punishment ('I am not the acting president'); a comprehensive list of 'The Stuff You May Have Missed' (for example,

Homer's hilariously sick reference to the food at Kentucky Fried Panda as 'Finger Ling-Ling good'); an in-depth Dewar's Profile-style look at a single character (Jesse Grass – the ecologically-minded Springfield teen who convinced the prison to opt for a solar-powered electric chair); and a 'Movie Moment' (Bart homaging *The Matrix*). One of the richest texts (and intertexts) in the history of television, as Jonathan Gray demonstrates in a recent study, *The Simpsons* has got the companion books it deserves.[3]

Not TV Books

The many original, quality series – *Sex and the City, The Sopranos, The Wire, Six Feet Under, Deadwood, Curb Your Enthusiasm, Entourage, Rome* – produced by the American premium channel HBO are branded as 'not TV'. So it should not surprise us that such shows have inspired not TV companion books.

Though teeming with exclusive information and insights into the HBO shows they accompany, Rafael Álvarez's *The Wire: Truth be Told* (2004) and Amy Sohn and Sarah Wildman's *Sex and the City: Kiss and Tell* (2004) do not push the boundaries of the genre. The HBO companion books to *The Sopranos* and *Six Feet Under*, on the other hand, are brilliantly conceived.

Beautifully designed (by Dan Newman), *The Sopranos: A Family History* (2000) purports to be the by-product of author Allen Rucker's assignment to organise a massive archive on the Soprano family assembled by an expert on organised crime named Jeffrey Wernick, humbly presenting itself as 'little more than journalistic housecleaning' compared to 'Wernick's Herculean efforts' (Rucker 2000: preface). At the outset we find a list of contributors, a group that includes all the people Wernick and Rucker supposedly spoke to, from ex-gangsters now in the witness protection programme to Tony Soprano's favourite teacher, to Livia Soprano's briefly employed geriatric caregiver. Jeffrey Wernick (Timothy Nolen), of course, is actually a character on *The Sopranos* (as are many of the other contributors), appearing on television in 'The Legend of Tennessee Moltisanti' (1: 8) sharing his knowledge of the New Jersey mob with local media. One day, we are told, Wernick will tell all, but 'the Sopranos story is a long way from over' (the series is still ongoing), and in the meantime we will have to make do with his assistant's pastiche assemblage of Sopraniana.[4]

False modesty is part of Rucker's fiction, of course. The book offers all the givens of a TV companion volume: an interview with series creator David Chase (who, the official *Sopranos* website tells us, 'was instrumental in developing the look and content of the book'), profiles of each of the major players, and an authoritative episode summary,[5] and it is hard to imagine a book of its kind any more original than this. 'As the Bible is to Western thought', David Chase proclaims on the website, 'so is *The Sopranos: A Family History* to the field of companion books'!

In 10 chapters Rucker presents us with deep background on the series in a variety of registers. We are privy to FBI emails detailing what is known about both of Tony's families; insights into New Jersey's immigrant population from a Newark Public Library expert; family photos (some from the old world); the crudely conceived family trees of AJ (Anthony Soprano, Junior); FBI surveillance transcripts; probation reports; a 1975 letter on Tony's behalf by an English teacher seeking to prevent him from being expelled; a college letter from Tony to Carmela; Johnny Boy Soprano's arrest record; a page from Christopher Moltisanti's awful unfinished screenplay ('You Bark, I Bite'); confidential reports on Tony's mother (including complaints filed by fellow residents) from the Green Grove Retirement Home; a letter from Carmela to her interior decorator declining an offer to have her home featured in *New Jersey Today*; a list of materials found in the Sopranos' trash; Carmela's 10 favourite movies (from a contest at her video store); an 'abridged dictionary of Northeastern regional mob patois'; a diagram of the Sopranos' cashflow; a 'body count' roster of those who have (allegedly) died at the hands of the Sopranos; transcripts of Meadow Soprano's visits to an online chat room; Meadow's Discover Card bill; Joan O'Connell Scrivo's equivocal letter of recommendation for Meadow to Georgetown (written as a result of Carmela's mob-mom encouragement). The result of this polyphony of voices is a simulated oral history in which the series' already rich, multidimensional characters and its meticulously genuine milieu are realised even further. There is so much even a faithful watcher of the series would never have known: that Tony hates Bruce Springsteen (because the music of his fellow Jerseyite is too depressing); that Livia's father was a Eugene Debs-style socialist; that Tony subscribes to *Waste News*; that Livia had an annoying neighbourhood dog whacked; that the yearly income of Paulie Walnuts is between $60,000 and $100,000 a year; that at

Seton Hall Tony hired another student to write his English paper for him ('Symbolism in *Cat on a Hot Tin Roof* – it received a B+); that Janice Soprano's estranged son Harpo may have changed his name to Hal after being beaten up on the playground . . .

In 2002 a second *Sopranos* companion book appeared, this time a parody of a popular genre. Again written by Allen Rucker, though purporting to be 'compiled by Artie Bucco', the hapless, pathetic chef (played by John Ventimiglia) of Nuovo Vesuvio Ristorante, *The Sopranos' Family Cookbook* offers authentic, beautifully presented Italian recipes while simultaneously extending our knowledge of several key characters and the rich New Jersey locale of the series. Throughout the book, Artie interviews several Sopranos family and crew: Uncle Junior blows hard about eating in the old days; muscle Furio Giunta insists, insultingly, that Italian-Americans eat like Germans; Carmela espouses her conviction that food is a language, convenient, say, for subtly threatening a prominent lawyer into writing a letter of recommendation. Others speak in their own voice (or rather Rucker ventriloquises, more or less, for them): the clueless, anal-compulsive sociopath Paulie Walnuts gets sentimental about his beloved Nucci, mothers and Italian cuisine; the seriously obese, dim-witted Bobby Bacala offers a piece hilariously entitled 'If I Couldn't Eat, I'd F**king Die'; the (now whacked) Adriana La Cerva gives us advice on food and romance; her ex, the illiterate aspiring screenwriter Christopher Moltisanti, catalogues his favourite food scenes from mob movies.

Of course, *The Sopranos' Family Cookbook* is as darkly humorous as the show itself and Rucker's earlier book. The inside cover, front and back, offers the appealing sight of the late Livia Soprano trying to douse a raging fire on her kitchen stove (a scene from '46 Long', 1: 2), and Tony's own chapter on grilling is illustrated by an equally tempting photo of a backyard grill exploding in flame – the result of the panic-attacked mob boss's spilling of a can of lighter fluid on hot coals.

If *The Sopranos: A Family History* is the bible of companion books, *Six Feet Under: Better Living Through Death* (2003) is the *Bhagavad-Gita* (Johnson 2004) or *Tao Te Ching* (Tzu 1990) – books quoted (along with Thomas Lynch's *Bodies in Motion and at Rest* [2001], C.S. Lewis' *A Grief Observed* [2001], *The Tibetan Book of the Dead* [Jinpa and Coleman 2006] and Carlos Castaneda's *Tales of Power* [1992]) in transitional epigraphs. Issued in a red, white and clear plastic case, edited by series creator Alan Ball and executive producer Alan Poul and written by a variety of *Six Feet Under* screenwriters, this atypical book is intended, as a glance at its binding reveals, to look like a kind of scrapbook. And so it is; a multi-generic assemblage of documents from the prehistory and history of *Six Feet Under*, it includes: an invitation to the marriage of Ruth Elizabeth O'Connor and Nathanial Samuel Fisher; letters back and forth from Vietnam by the newlyweds; Ruth's desperate letter, written at 19, to a newspaper advice column; advertisements for embalming fluid;[6] Ruth's annual Christmas letter (and poem); childhood photos of Nate, David and Claire; 'actual' chapters from *Nathaniel and Isabel* and *Charlotte Light and Dark*; David's first-grade report card; Brenda Chenowith's pre-adolescent poetry; the troubling report of Nate's high-school guidance counsellor; Ruth's angry note to sister Sarah (after Nate lost his virginity at 15 to a family friend during a visit to his aunt's); letters from David to his Russian pen pal and actor Matt Dillon; Lisa Kimmel's column in the Seattle Co-op newsletter; Claire's alarmingly violent but brilliant rejected submission to her high-school literary magazine; David's 'Call to Arms' for independent funeral directors in *Mortuary Advocate*; Claire and Billy Chenowith's instant messenger conversation while he was in a mental hospital; Nate's MRI report on the arterial venous malformation that will eventually kill him; pages from Brenda's lurid, heavily researched novel; Claire's application to LAC Arts; Olivier's caustic/praising evaluation of Claire's work in his 'Form and Space' class.

Like Rucker's *Sopranos* books, *Better Living Through Death* extends and deepens the diegesis of the series that inspired it, and it does so while breaking with companion-book conventions. Other than an introduction by Ball, we find not a word about or directly from cast and crew; no episode guide is offered, we are not taken behind the scenes of the series. The series finale of *Six Feet Under* (screened in 2005) transports us into the far future of the series diegesis, or at least one possible future, as we witness the family's deaths, imagined by Claire (Lauren Ambrose) on an American history-reversing journey east in her new car, of Ruth (Francis Conroy), Keith Charles (Mathew St Patrick), David (Michael C. Hall), Brenda (Rachel Griffiths), Federico Diaz (Freddy Rodriguez) and, finally herself. *Better Living Through Death* takes us in the opposite direction – to the beginning.

In a classic essay on 'cult movies and intertextual collage', Umberto Eco (see the epigraph to this chapter) suggests that one given of a cult work is its ability to 'provide a completely furnished world so that its fans can quote characters and episodes as if they were aspects of the fan's private sectarian world, a world about which one can make up quizzes and play trivia games so that the adepts of the secret recognize through each other a shared experience' (1986: 198). Eco's observation is obviously of relevance as well to our understanding of the symbiotic relationship of quality television and quality television books.

Any companion book worth the price of purchase offers the sort of insider knowledge of its show that serious fans need to know to distinguish themselves from the not-so-serious. But only quality companions like *The Sopranos: A Family History* and *Better Living Through Death* hail readers as 'adepts of the secret', inviting them to exhibit all the care and imagination with which they watch, to immerse themselves in an expanded, broadened, deepened – in time and in space – multimedia diegesis, existing now in print and on screen.

This essay incorporates and expands upon an earlier review of *Buffy the Vampire Slayer* and *Sopranos* companion books in *Television Quarterly*, 2001: 89–92.

Defining Quality
Into the Future

17

Lost in Transition

From Post-Network to Post-Television
Roberta Pearson

. . . .

The crash of Oceanic Flight 815 maroons 48 survivors on a desert island in uncharted waters far from shipping lanes and flight paths. The island lures them with tropical beaches and stunning sunsets, mystifies them with 16-year-old messages and enigmatic hatches and terrifies them with a gigantic but invisible beast. The threats and opportunities of a rapid reconfiguration of the media landscape similarly lure, mystify and threaten television producers and network executives who daily face uncertainties far scarier than a pilot-munching monster.

In her introduction to *Television After TV*, Lynn Spigel lists factors that are altering the channel scarcity and mass-audience landscape of broadcast television; the demise of the American three-network system, the rise of multi-channel cable and global satellite delivery, multinational conglomerates, internet convergence, changes in regulation policies and ownership rules, and the innovation of digital television systems like TiVo. Says Spigel, 'If TV refers to the technologies, industrial formations, government policies, and practices of looking that were associated with the medium in its classical public service and three-network age, it appears that we are now entering a new phase of television – the phase that comes after TV' (2004: 3). The mega-global hit *Lost* emerged from the relatively stable industrial conditions of the post-network era of the last part of the twentieth century, when television, even if no longer broadcasting to mass audiences, still retained its centrality as a domestic medium. But *Lost* also reflects the increasingly unstable industrial conditions of the post-television era of the early twenty-first century, when the continual convergence of platforms and fragmenting of audiences morphs the medium into something rich and strange.

Lost – owned and funded by Touchstone Television, made by Bad Robot, the production company of co-creator and executive producer J.J. Abrams, and aired on ABC – typifies the post-network vertical integration of content production and distribution within a vast multinational conglomerate, in this case the Disney Corporation. Jennifer Holt tells us:

> The quintessential New Hollywood marriage of product and pipeline was achieved in 1995 when Disney bought ABC for $19 billion. This was the first merger of the post-Fin Syn landscape between a studio and broadcast network . . . At the time, the new conglomerate represented the promise of boundless synergy for a brave new Magic Kingdom (2003: 19).[1]

The promised synergy failed to deliver. 'ABC took a nosedive and languished in third place almost losing out to Fox at one point' (19). Writing in 2003, Holt offered a gloomy prognosis for ABC's future. 'The long-term prospects for ABC are unsteady at best, presently resting on a very narrow strategy of reality-based programming . . . The company has yet to create any new ideas of visionary programming for their properties' (20).[2] But in that same year development began on *Lost*. Lloyd Braun, then president of ABC Entertainment, had an idea about the survivors of an air crash on a tropical island. 'I want to do *Castaway* as a series,' he told fellow executives at a network retreat in the summer of 2003. Finding support for his idea from Thom Sherman, head of drama, Braun commissioned a script from writer Jeffrey Lieber, who still retains a co-creator credit on *Lost* (Vaz 2005: 19). Finding the script unsatisfactory, Braun passed it to J.J. Abrams, who had already produced the fruitful *Alias* for the network, to see what he could do with it. Abrams wrote the successful pilot script together with co-creator Damon Lindelof (Stewart 2005: 485–7). *Lost* premiered in the autumn of 2004 and, together with *Desperate Housewives*, 'is credited with raising formerly beleaguered ABC to the top of the US network ratings chart' (Vaz 2005: 10). In January 2006, the *Hollywood Reporter* praised *Lost* as 'the rare combination of a critical and commercial hit for ABC, earning a rabid worldwide following, the Emmy last year for best drama series and the drama series Golden Globe last week' (Andreeva 2006).

Lost Revealed, a making-of programme shown on Channel 4 in conjunction with the show's UK premiere, says that *Lost* 'is the creation of two of Hollywood's hottest young producers, Damon Lindelof and J.J. Abrams' (*Lost Revealed* 2005). The prominence in *Lost* publicity of the two men specifically credited as the show's creators, Abrams and Lindelof, obscures the complex industrial arrangements behind the show's origins and subsequent commercial and critical success. The post-network era highly values the creating, writing and executive producing of television shows, assigning authorship to the individuals who fulfil these functions. This is a significant departure from the industrial practices of the network era in which executive producers, even those who were also creators, kept a low public profile in keeping with their relative lack of power. In her 1971 book, *The Hollywood TV Producer: His Work and his Audience*, Muriel Cantor says 'Even when a man owns, creates, and produces his own show, the network retains the right to *final* approval of scripts, casts and other creative and administrative matters' (9). Executive producers achieved far greater creative freedom and the public prominence attendant upon it in the post-network era because their names proved more attractive to demographically desirable audiences than did the network brand, diluted by the new technologies of the remote control and the video recorder, together with the proliferation of new networks and satellite channels. Michele Hilmes says of Steven Bochco, perhaps the most fabled of all the post-network executive producers, or, in *Variety*-speak, hyphenates:

> As one of television's premier auteurs in a fragmented business that provided few forms of continuity, his name had begun to mean more in terms of genre, quality, style, and audience than did the name of the network his shows appeared on. The stamp of an author – even when actual authorship was somewhat removed by the production practices of television – gave a program a degree of authenticity and legitimacy absent from television's earlier decades (2002: 312).

Lost's authenticity and legitimacy stemmed not from the struggling ABC network but from its creators Abrams and Lindelof. Abrams is undoubtedly the more highly valued Hollywood player, called by *The Los Angeles Times* 'the hottest young producer in television' (James and Eller 2005: C1). Industry insiders confirm his importance. Speaking of the need to find someone to rewrite the unsatisfactory first script, Thom Sherman said, 'Anytime we had an idea at ABC that we were having trouble with the first idea that popped into our head was what would J.J. do with it?' ('The Genesis of *Lost*'). Harold Perrineau, who plays Michael, recalls that at the time of the casting call, 'There was great buzz about the show. J.J. Abrams is creating this great new show. You should go [read for a part]' ('*Lost* at the Museum of Television and Radio'). ABC's faith in the Abrams brand radically curtailed the usual lengthy process of commissioning a script and then a pilot for a new show. According to Mark Cotta Vaz, '*Lost*, in practically every respect, was an anomaly in the business of launching a television series' (2005: 18). The development of a new show normally takes a year, starting in June when networks begin accepting scripts for potential pilots. The networks greenlight the lucky ones in January, at which point the producers must quickly assemble cast and crew and wrap production of a pilot within two weeks. Over the next few months network executives screen the pilots and make the final selections. After the schedulers have determined time-slots, the new shows are presented to the advertisers in May.

The *Lost* pilot was given the go ahead simply on the basis of a treatment within a week of Abrams being called in by the network. The overall time between Braun's initially contacting Abrams and the delivery of the pilot was less than four months. That pilot, rather than being shot rapidly on a relatively restricted budget on a studio back-lot, had a production schedule of eight weeks, a budget that various estimates put at $5 million or $10 million and an exotic location on the Hawaiian island of Oahu. Says Bryan Burke, one of the first season's five executive producers, 'It was amazing that the network and the studio took a chance and decided that if they were going to do it, they were going to do it right, regardless of the expense. Everyone made a leap of faith with an immense project, before there was even a script. They had complete faith in J.J. and Damon' (quoted in Vaz 2005: 31). Burke speaks of the network's faith in Abrams and Lindelof, but ABC had brought in the latter simply to guarantee that the overcommitted Abrams, who was writing another pilot, would be able to produce a script. Abrams himself seems happy to share the credit:

> It became apparent that Damon . . . was not just running the show but as much or more the creative vision as I was. . . I got a lot more credit for the show, incorrectly, just because people are more familiar with the work I did on *Alias* than what Damon did on *Crossing Jordan*. I always feel a little guilty when I hear, 'Wow, I love J.J's show'. I'm happy to be a part of it, but I'm certainly not entirely responsible for it (quoted in Vaz 2005: 76).

Abrams may generously try to put the record straight, but industrial conditions may in the future militate against his or other creators' too selflessly sharing the credit. The multiplication of channels, which diluted the network brand during the transition from the network to the post-network era, placed increased importance upon the brand of the author. As the multiple platforms available for digital distribution (of which more below) further dilute network brands in the transition to post-television, the author brand may become an even more important marker of the quality now expected by demographically desirable viewers. Might *Lost*'s anomalous conditions of production, the short-circuiting of a usually tortuous process, presage the reconfiguration of the industry's standard production practices to accommodate ever more powerful executive producers who will be granted ever more creative freedom (as long, of course, as they continue to boost that bottom line)?

The attribution of authorship to the executive producer has been one of the most striking aspects of a post-network television era that saw the emergence of so-called quality television and the concomitant increase of the medium's cultural value. For much of its history, television was the Cinderella of the entertainment industries, left in the kitchen with the servants while the theatre and the cinema went to the ball and mingled with the aristocracy. Like any new medium, television made strident bids for respectability in its infancy, mimicking its older sisters in the anthology programmes of the so-called 'golden age' of the 1950s. But the stability of the three-network hegemony largely freed the medium from concerns about cultural value, the overriding goal was the simple one of retaining roughly one-third of the mass audience. The 1980s and

1990s' reconfiguration of that hegemony, which resulted in the post-network era, entailed new discourses of quality, many of which now circulate around *Lost*. But the quality discourse concerning the respective cultural values of television and cinema looks ahead to a post-television era in which these two media may become all but indistinguishable. As Vaz puts it, 'the medium has traditionally been looked down on by the movie side of the entertainment industry. But many in the business feel that television is finally getting some respect' (55). Playing Prince Charming, cultural critics have fitted the glass slipper, daring to suggest that television equals its glamorous older sister in accomplishment (and perhaps even occasionally surpasses her). Take, for example, Stephen King, who knows a thing or two himself about shifting cultural hierarchies and critical re-evaluations. In his *Entertainment Weekly* column at the start of the 2005 television season, King wrote 'Maybe one of the reasons this summer's movie offerings looked so cheesy was that they came after a particularly brilliant TV season, starring . . . *Desperate Housewives*, *24*, *The Wire*, *The Shield* and *Lost*' (2005: 150).

Jack Bender, Hawaiian executive producer of *Lost*, asserts that, 'Episodic television has changed, thanks to cable. There's no more "it's good enough for television" . . . It's the quality – episodic television has to look like a feature film' (quoted in Vaz 2005: 53). Bender sees cable competition, a key driver of the post-network era, as pushing the networks toward a quality programming that is as visually appealing as the cinema. Others in the production crew perceive the convergence of film and televisual technology and personnel, a key driver of the post-television era, as generating *Lost*'s high production values, which – at least in terms of location and visual effects – surpass the cinematic look of such quality predecessors as *The Sopranos* and *Six Feet Under*. First assistant director Allen DiGioia boasts that 'we're using the same elements, the same equipment and cameras [as in film]' (quoted in Vaz 2005: 161). Director of photography Michael Bonvillain is proud that 'our crew is all A-list feature guys. Paul Edwards, our A-camera operator, has done a ton of features' (quoted in Vaz 2005: 56). Perhaps as a result of the presence of so many feature guys, the *Lost* crew employs shooting techniques more characteristic of film than of television, the time and budgetary constraints of the latter medium often imposing standardisation and routinisation. According to director Tucker Gates, 'Some shows have very strict rules about how to shoot things, what's expected in terms of coverage, how scenes are approached. *Lost* seems to be more film-oriented in its style, that's something J.J. and Jack [Bender] have instilled in the show' (quoted in Vaz 2005: 65).

Both production personnel and critics particularly lauded the cinematic look of the pilot, which production designer Mark Worthington thought resembled a '$100 million feature' ('Designing of a Disaster'). Dominic Monaghan (Charlie Pace), who has gone from hobbit in the mega-film hit *The Lord of the Rings* to failed rock god in the mega-television hit *Lost*, claimed that the pilot,

> looks like a film. I'd been immersed in the film industry for so long I got confused and thought we were making a film. I thought at some point ABC were probably going to say 'Let's try to release it in the cinema and turn this into a feature film.' It was that grand in scale and ambition ('Making of the Pilot').

The critics agreed. Interviewed in 'Lost Revealed', Boyd Hilton of *Heat* magazine was 'struck by how much like a really good film it is. It's brilliantly directed, it looks amazing.' On the same programme, E! Entertainment's Kristen Veitch praised the quality of the plane-crash scenes as 'just as good if not better than anything seen in the cinema'. The crash scenes looked so good because the pilot, said to be the most expensive ever made, availed itself of visual effects more often seen in a summer blockbuster than a television pilot. Vaz reported that,

> the pilot was a major visual effects effort, with close to 200 shots ... There were twenty-five to thirty shots alone required for the digital removal of the crane and wires holding up an airplane wing. A dramatic scene in which a live engine sucked in a bystander and explodes was a heavily visual effects number (2005: 31).

Lost's production values, no matter how cinematic, could not alone have guaranteed favourable critical reception or the quality label. Since *Hill Street Blues*, *thirtysomething* and other shows of the early 1980s demonstrated the appeal of dense serial storytelling to viewers with the desirable demographics, narrative complexity has become a hallmark of the quality television of the post-network period. In an article in the online television studies journal *Flow*, Jason Mittell claims that '*Lost* is the best show on American broadcast television'. Mittell, himself part of that desirable demographic to which quality television has been primarily marketed, not surprisingly values the narrative even over the very impressive production values.

> For a show with such a high-budget and elaborate visual style, the most impressive special effects are accomplished within the writing itself – sophisticated and surprising twists, reveals, and structures offer what we might consider storytelling spectacles, a contemporary 'television of attractions' that asks viewers to marvel at the sheer bravado of the creators (2005).

Lost's 'sophisticated and surprising twists, reveals, and structures' occur within the overarching serial narrative of a 22-episode per-year television season; if the programme runs for the minimum of four to five years necessary for successful syndication that seriality may well encompass 88 to 110 episodes and, if for the seven or more years enjoyed by many ratings-toppers, 154 or more episodes. In an act of creative bravado unequalled in any other contemporary medium, *Lost*'s creators had to devise a narrative premise and group of characters capable of sustaining audience involvement over tens of episodes until an ultimate resolution that probably, given the show's current success, lies years in the future.

J.J. Abrams, speaking of his previous creation, *Alias* 'once likened the start of a season to driving through a fog towards a distant mountain with landmarks to aim for along the way, the fog clearing the deeper one went on the journey' (quoted in Vaz 2005: 55). Unlike their castaways, *Lost*'s creators knew their exact location, even at the very start of the journey when the mountain may have been entirely obscured by fog. Bryan Burke describes a meeting with Abrams and Lindelof very early in the pre-production of the pilot.

> We started talking about what the show was, who these people were and where they had landed . . . and the big picture of where we were going. At the end of an excited conversation of 20 to 30 minutes we had discussed where the show was going over the next five or six years. We realised we know what this show is ('Genesis of *Lost*').

But, as the myriad disappointed fans of *The X-Files* know all too well, producers may claim to know the way but still drive endlessly through the fog and in the end completely bypass Resolution Mountain. *Lost*'s producers, aware of this public scepticism, insist that they've got a very good map; they're just not ready to show it to the audience. Lindelof asserts, 'We have the answers to what the monster is or where does the polar bear come from but we're just not at the point yet where we need to answer' ('*Lost* Revealed').

They have some of the answers but by no means all of them; the evolution of a dense serial narrative, with multiple character storylines and lengthy narrative arcs, constitutes what Vaz refers to as the 'little miracle of episodic television' (2005: 17). Like many creative endeavours, a television show to some extent takes on a life of its own, moving in unpredictable directions. Carlton Cuse, another of the show's five original executive producers, likens the ongoing development of a television series to a 'two-way street'. 'A show is a very organic entity and you don't just force your will upon it . . . We get feedback watching an actor's performance and the qualities they bring to a character, there's the dynamics we discover when two actors are paired and we see how they interact' (quoted in Vaz 2005: 55). Lindelof acknowledges that the show's organic nature may look rather like making it up as they go along:

> The 'making it up' part is just our acceptance that this is a collaborative process, that the show is about writers and actors and directors and all these voices. There's a jazz-like quality to *Lost* . . . That's the sense in which we're making things up. It's all about trusting each other (quoted in Vaz 2005: 83).

It might seem that television's intensely pressurised production conditions – episodes penned by multiple writers and shot in a few days on relatively small budgets – would forever culturally disadvantage the medium in relation to the cinema. But *Lost's* producers imply that it is precisely the pressurised, continual and collaborative process that produces the multilayered and complexly woven narratives of serial television drama. Like many critics, Stephen King believes that these new narrative forms make post-network television drama superior to the dramas of the 1950s, 1960s and 1970s:

> The perfect critique of the old TV is offered in Rob Reiner's *Stand by Me*. Gordie Lachance asks his buds if they've ever noticed that the people on *Wagon Train* . . . never seem to get anywhere. 'They just keep on wagon-training' . . . He knows that stories should resemble life and life has a beginning, a middle and an end (2005: 150).

Cinema reaches the ends rather too rapidly for those of us who prefer our resolutions almost infinitely delayed, our imaginary worlds almost infinitely expanded and our middles almost infinitely elaborated. Since cinema's industrial conditions of production and reception preclude multi-year narratives constructed over hundreds of episodes, television may now be the superior medium, at least for some kinds of storytelling.

Since the early 1980s, increasingly high production values and increasingly dense serial narratives have boosted television several rungs up the cultural hierarchy. In this respect *Lost* typifies much post-network television drama accorded the quality label, but perhaps also looks forward to a post-television era in which the medium may be perceived as not only equalling but perhaps even surpassing cinema's cultural status. *Lost*'s sharing many characteristics with what those within the industry call 'genre shows' and those without call 'cult shows' may also presage the post-television era. Said Lindelof, 'We were aiming for that *Alias*-type audience. We knew it was a little bit weird. It has a huge cast, it's serialized, and it requires the audience's attention. It's everything procedural crime drama's aren't' (quoted in Armstrong 2005: 30). *Lost* accords almost precisely with the definition of cult television given by Matt Hills:

> Cult TV series like *Angel, Babylon 5, Blake's 7, Buffy the Vampire Slayer, Doctor Who, Monty Python's Flying Circus, The Prisoner, Star Trek, Twin Peaks* and *The X-Files* . . . tend to be marked by sustained enigmas, and by ongoing or unresolved mysteries about their characters, character relationships, or aspects of their invented worlds. Regardless of how TV narratives progress . . . there is a sense in which what we see on screen is only a part of a much wider narrative world, always implying further events and developments (2005: 190).[3]

Genre shows construct their wide narrative worlds within dense webs of precedent and intertextuality, laying bare the device in a deliberately self-conscious manner designed to appeal to the knowing viewer eager for clues to the show's mythology. *Lost* has a legion of obvious literary, filmic and televisual ancestors: desert island stories (*Robinson Crusoe, Mysterious Island, Swiss Family Robinson, Lord of the Flies, Gilligan's Island*); science fiction/fantasy television (*The Twilight Zone* in particular); and reality television shows (*Survivor*). The Wikipedia entry for *Lost* features a helpful discourse on the show's intertexual references. Character names allude to Enlightenment philosophers who theorised about man's natural state and the relationship among nature, civilisation and government: John Locke to the eponymous English philosopher and Danielle Rousseau to Jean-Jacques Rousseau. *Lost* Locke's father Anthony Cooper shares his name with Enlightenment Locke's political mentor and patron, Lord Anthony Ashley-Cooper. Locke's protégé Boone Carlyle shares his name with Thomas Carlyle, who spoke of the 'organisation, structure and leadership of society'. Books prominently displayed or mentioned include *Heart of Darkness*, *Lord of the Flies*, *Turn of the Screw*, *The Brothers Karamazov*, *An Occurrence at Owl Creek Bridge*, the Bible and *Alice in Wonderland*. The reference to *Alice in Wonderland* takes place in the first season's third episode 'White Rabbit', when Locke mentions the book, although Jack's supposedly dead father appearing and disappearing like the titular white rabbit should make the Lewis Carroll connection abundantly obvious. The *Star Trek*-conversant viewer like myself may also think of the original series episode 'Shore Leave' (1: 15), which features various creatures seemingly spontaneously generated by the planet: Alice and a large white rabbit straight out of the Tenniel illustrations as well as people from the characters' pasts. This intertextual frame leads me to speculate that the ghosts, polar bears and other mysterious phenomena on *Lost* Island might be, as on the *Star Trek* planet, of alien manufacture. *Lost's* multiple precedents and references are designed precisely to engender such speculation and to appeal to the specialised knowledge and puzzle-solving propensities of many genre fans.

Lost may look like a genre show, but it has achieved greater commercial and critical success than any of its precursors. Genre shows benefited from the increasing audience fragmentation of the post-network era by attracting small, but dedicated and demographically desirable, niche audiences. In its seventh season (2002–3), the very successful (by genre standards) *Buffy the Vampire Slayer* often ranked below 100th place and in 2003 achieved a highest rating of five, representing approximately five per cent of all households. *Buffy* and other genre shows such as *Star Trek: The Next Generation* and *The X-Files* have garnered the occasional critical accolade and even the occasional award from Viewers for Quality Television, but not industry awards (except in technical categories) or very large audiences. *Lost* has achieved top ratings, Emmies and a Golden Globe. Its producers, obviously keen to retain the show's broad critical and commercial appeal, resist the potentially damaging genre/cult label. ABC Entertainment president Steve McPherson invokes the mantra of the quality drama: 'I'm constantly telling [the producers] "Character, character, character." If you just had the machinations of the mythology it would be a cult show' (quoted in Vaz 2005: 32). The executive producers get the message. Carlton Cuse, another of the first season's five executive producers, credits the characters' backstories with the show's wide appeal. 'The flashback stories are the emotional core of the series and give a much broader audience access. There's a genre audience that enjoys the mythology, but the broader audience wants to know more about the characters and the flashbacks and go back to the seminal events in their lives' (quoted in Vaz 2005: 55). Says Burke, 'These are real people in extraordinary situations. If [fans] are sticking around hoping to find out what this crazy monster thing is . . . then, fine, stick around. But that's not what this show is about' (quoted in Vaz 2005: 17). The producers may deny *Lost*'s cultness, but a 'host of new sci-fi series' appeared at the beginning of the 2005 season, as, in accordance with usual industry practice, other networks, clearly having categorised the show as cult, tried to imitate its success (Armstrong 2005: 30).

Do *Lost*'s big audiences, prestigious awards, its positioning as quality television and a host of would-be imitators indicate that genre shows will play an increasingly important role in the future? The vast narrative worlds and complex narrative enigmas of genre shows engender an intense viewer involvement in a programme's virtual world that has benefited producers in the post-network era.[4] Fan studies has established that keen genre viewers are more likely to be repeat viewers and to purchase DVDs and licensed products, as illustrated by Abrams's previous show *Alias*, now cancelled after five years. Referring to the show as 'cult-fave spy-fi drama', the *Hollywood Reporter* said that it 'was among the first of a new breed of TV series that can be sustained for multiple seasons of modest primetime numbers on the strength of such ancillary businesses as DVD sales and video games' (Anon 2005). Might genre shows, particularly if they equal *Lost*'s mainstream success, offer business models particularly appropriate for the post-television age? I have speculated above that the value of the author's brand may increase as multiple platforms further dilute the network brand. Might the author's brand hold even more value for genre fans, who attribute the origins of their beloved virtual worlds to Chris or Joss or J.J.

and Damon? Paramount-Viacom's listing of the deceased Gene Roddenberry as the creator in *Star Trek* credits is one marker of the value of authorship to a genre audience. Does the need for immersion in and speculation about the virtual world drive genre fans to create more internet sites and engage in more internet chat than their non-genre counterparts, giving rise to the internet buzz that is increasingly important to a show's success? Will genre fans seeking immersion be more eager to download episodes to their hard drives or iPods or to purchase supplementary texts constructed for their mobiles?

As I flipped through a recent *New Yorker*, I came across an advertisement appealing to those desiring a media-immersed life, offering a range of content-to-go on the new visual iPod: music; audio books; podcasts; photos; music videos and TV shows. The TV show is, of course, *Lost*, its presence on the iPod the result of a deal between Apple and Disney that makes the studio a Hollywood leader in exploiting current television programmes across multiple platforms. Reported *Television Week*:

> In one fell swoop, The Walt Disney Co. was transformed . . . from the staid media company it had been known as under former Chairman and CEO Michael Eisner into a technologically innovative first mover under current CEO Robert Iger, according to many technology analysts. Disney and Apple unveiled a deal last Wednesday to make episodes of some of Disney-owned ABC's most popular television series – including 'Desperate Housewives' and 'Lost' – available for download on Apple Computer's popular iTunes Music Store (Sherman 2005: 26).

Michael McGuire, research director at technology consulting firm Gartner, is quoted in the article as saying, 'This is an inkling of the steps of large media companies coming to grips with the issue of broadband distribution . . .' (26).

Coming to grips with the issue of broadband distribution entails media industries rethinking their basic organisations and strategies. Jennifer Holt, quoted above, attributes Disney's 1995 purchase of ABC to the 'promise of boundless synergy'. That promise has failed to pay off not only for Disney but also for the other mega-companies created to maximise the profits from one product across all divisions. Part of the failure stems from the fact that not all products lend themselves to synergy. Paramount-Viacom could market *Star Trek* television, *Star Trek* films, *Star Trek* books and *Star Trek* theme parks but it's difficult to see how Disney could do the same with *Desperate Housewives* or even, perhaps, with *Lost*. Even when synergy works it cannot last forever; franchises inevitably age past their sell-by dates, as did *Star Trek* with the failure of the fifth series, *Enterprise*, and the tenth film, *Nemesis*. Another reason for the failure lies in the clash of organisational cultures created by mergers; it's hard to maximise profits across divisions when those divisions cannot work together. All those divisions also made companies just too big to respond flexibly to a rapidly changing business environment. Whether coincidentally or not, soon after the *Star Trek* franchise timidly went, Paramount-Viacom split into two separate companies, CBS Paramount Television and Viacom Media. Industry executives no longer worship at the alter of synergy but rather adhere to what John Caldwell calls the 'gospel of "repurposing content" and "migrating content" to this or that "platform"'. He says:

> The rhetorical shift from talking about productions as 'programs' to talking about them as 'content' underscores the centrality of repurposing in industrial practice. The term 'content' frees programs from a year-long series and network-hosted logic and suggests that programs are quantities to be drawn and quartered, deliverable on cable, shippable internationally, and streamable on the Net (2004: 49–50).

Rather than seeking long-term synergies, media industries now seek hot properties, which enable the extraction of maximum profits in minimum time through simultaneous distribution across multiple platforms and across the globe.[5] As one of the hottest of hot properties, *Lost* epitomises the repurposing of content and globalisation that lie at the heart of the transition to a post-television era.

I will return to global distribution in a bit, but for now let us consider the transformative potential of multi-platform distribution. Will the direct-to-video, viewing-on-demand models now emerging threaten the decades-old distribution arrangement of networks and affiliates? ABC's affiliates, reported *Television Week*, were 'up in arms' about the iPod deal, fearing that it threatened ratings and advertising revenues. The network issued a placatory press release. 'Through our arrangement with Apple, we are not only taking advantage of new technology, but hoping it will bring increased interest to the first-run broadcasts of 'Desperate Housewives,' 'Lost' and 'Night Stalker' on our affiliates . . .' (Greppi 2005: 5). Some network executives believe that downloading may actually help to build audiences for serialised shows, which may otherwise fail to attract viewers who miss the first few episodes or lose viewers who miss mid-season episodes. *Broadcasting and Cable* reported that the iPod deal turned an executive from a rival network into a *Lost* fan, 'I downloaded all the old episodes, caught up, and am now hooked and I'll watch it on ABC when the next first-run comes out so I can be part of the social experience . . . So that platform has created a viewer that would never have been' (Grossman 2006: 16). Viewership for *Lost* and *Desperate Housewives* increased by 17 per cent and 8 per cent after episodes were made available for downloading (ibid). The fact that *Lost* increased its audience by more than double that of *Desperate Housewives* would seem to support my hypothesis about the suitability of genre shows to the post-television era; a *Lost* viewer seeking clues to the narrative's hermeneutic may be more fearful of missing an episode and more inclined to repeat viewing than a *Desperate Housewives* viewer. Said one 15-year-old *Lost* fan:

> I make sure to watch every episode on TV because the screen is bigger and the stereo is better and it's a more fun experience . . . But if I'm talking to people about episodes on the forums and we decide to go back and look at one or want to screen-capture something, I will go and watch them from the computer (quoted in Fernandez 2006: E1).

Multi-platforms have implications for narrative as well as for industrial organisation, enabling what Spigel refers to as 'transmedia storytelling': 'content . . . designed to appear across different media platforms so that we can now access our favorite media "franchises" and characters in multi story-telling universes' (2004: 6). *Lost's* transmedia storytelling is well adapted to the post-television age. A headline in *The Los Angeles Times* declared: '*Lost* is easy to find, and not just on a TV screen; Fans can get fixes from iPods, blogs, podcasts, and soon, cellphones. It's a new media model' (quoted in Fernandez 2006: E1). The article reports that The *Lost Video Diaries*, two-minute episodes about castaways who do not appear on the show, is available on Verizon cellphones. ABC is also 'developing an interactive website to delve into aspects of the show's mythology that will never be explored on air', with content created by a staff writer (Fernandez 2006: E1). Fans, or at least fans with sufficient disposable income, will be able to spend many happy hours lost in a *Lost* virtual world created by the programme's producers. Said yet another of *Lost's* executive producers, Carlton Cuse, 'The show is the mother ship, but I think with all the new emerging technology, what we've discovered is that the world of "Lost" is not basically circumscribed by the actual show itself' (quoted in Fernandez 2006: E1). Fans, of course, have known for years that a show's metaverse expanded far beyond the confines of a weekly episode, but might media producers' commercial and authorised expansions of programme metaverses decrease the non-commercial, non-authorised, bottom-up expansion of fan fiction and other fan-created texts? That is a question for another article, but clearly these new modes of distribution and narrative have profound implications for audience reception in the post-television age. Might multiple platform distribution and transmedia storytelling perhaps take us ever closer to the totalising vision of the Frankfurt School?

Lost also offers a model for the global distribution so crucial to a post-synergy strategy of the maximisation of profits. Caldwell says that 'syndication possibilities and foreign distribution in particular are now always very much on the minds of producers and executives, so much so that such perspectives encourage a "collage" approach to series development and a penchant for aggregating an ensemble of actors and story lines that will travel across national boundaries' (2004: 48). The desire to cross national boundaries has resulted in Paramount working with the British Sky network during the development of the science fiction series *Threshold* and in Twentieth Century Fox's top development executives regularly consulting with foreign broadcasters (Brennan 2005c). I have no evidence that any such consultation took place during *Lost's* development, but the producers certainly aggregated an ensemble of actors with appeal to a global audience. Said a *Lost* executive consultant, Jeff, 'We knew early on we were going to have an international cast. It was an international airline and it wasn't going to be a bunch of Americans' ('Before They Were Lost'). The first season cast included two Korean-born actors (Yoon-jin Kim and Daniel Dae Kim), an Asian-British actor (Naveen Andrews), a British actor (Dominic Monaghan), an Australian (Emilie de Ravin), a Canadian (Evangeline Lilly), two African-Americans (Harold Perrineau and Malcolm David Kelley) and an American of Chilean descent (Jorge Garcia). Not only was the cast multinational and multicultural, but two of the actors (Kim and Kim) actually spoke to each other in a foreign language translated only by subtitles. Even more surprisingly, one of the actors (Andrews) played an Iraqi and former member of the Republican Guard as a hero rather than a villain. Abrams wrote the character consciously thinking about 'what's going on globally. Let's take an Iraqi and make him an heroic character on an American television show.' Andrews professes astonishment at this decision: 'I couldn't believe that a major network was going to have an Iraqi character who was also from the Republican Guard' ('Lost Revealed').

Lost has been seen in Britain, Germany, Russia, Australia, the Philippines, Ireland, Sri Lanka, India, Greece, Japan, Italy, France, Spain, Belgium and more than a hundred other countries, its global success so striking that some have credited it and its ABC stablemate *Desperate Housewives* with reviving the erstwhile flagging fortunes of American television drama abroad. At the beginning of 2006, *Broadcasting and Cable* reported that 'since 2000 or so, foreign content providers quit leaning as heavily on American shows' (Winslow 2006: 16), but the article offers evidence that overseas sales have by now rebounded. Belinda Menendez, president of NBC Universal International Television Distribution, says, 'There is more interest in US shows and willingness to schedule them in prime time' (quoted in Winslow 2006: 16). Tom Toumazis, executive vice-president of Buena Vista International Television, Disney's overseas television distribution division, said that the last fiscal year was the 'biggest in our history by some margin' and, 'The most obvious examples' of this upward trend, 'are "Lost" and "Desperate Housewives," two shows that are racking up record ratings around the world' (quoted in Winslow 2006: 16). The *Hollywood Reporter* concurs: 'The international success of such shows as "Desperate Housewives," "Lost" and the "CSI" franchise has been helping to drive Hollywood programming back into primetime slots abroad . . .' (Brennan 2005b). Hans Seger, chief programme officer at leading German pay TV company Premiere, attributes American television drama's renewed international success to the signifiers of quality discussed above – production values and narrative complexity. 'Last year with "Lost" and "Desperate Housewives" . . . we saw a real jump in quality – in the storytelling and in the production look. The money was on the screen' (quoted in Brennan and Turner 2005). Buena Vista has licensed *Lost* to more than 180 international territories, making it the 'fastest-selling TV series' in Disney's history, outstripping even *Desperate Housewives'* (Brennan 2005b). On Britain's Channel 4, *Lost* achieved the best-ever ratings for a US series, with a viewership of 6.4 million and a 28 per cent share of the audience, overturning the record previously held by *Desperate Housewives* (Kemp 2005). *Lost's* premiere on Russian public service broadcasting's First Channel attracted 42 per cent of the 18-plus audience, 50 per cent higher than the channel's primetime average for January–May 2005 (Holdsworth 2005). *Lost* has also been a major hit in Germany and in Australia (Brennan 2005a).

I have likened the plight of media industry executives to that of *Lost's* castaways, both faced with the uncertainties of unknown environments. Television studies scholars face similar uncertainties, as the post-television era transforms the well-known industrial landscapes of the network and post-network ages out of all recognition. *Lost*, the programme that represents the culmination of industrial trends of the post-network era and may presage many of the industrial trends of the post-television era, illuminates some areas of a largely uncharted new landscape. But the case study has produced more questions than answers: will the post-television era see an increased valuation of authorship, a further re-evaluation of cultural hierarchies, with television seen as cinema's equal or superior, a rise in the critical and commercial stock of genre shows, even more emphasis upon international distribution? Just as *Lost's* viewers must wait several years to solve the mysteries of the island, television studies scholars must wait several years to solve the mysteries of the post-television landscape. But while J.J. Abrams and Damon Lindelof may have the answers to some of the viewers' questions, no one as yet has the answers to ours.

This article grows out of discussions with several of my colleagues in the Institute of Film and Television Studies at the University of Nottingham about a potential collaborative research project on *Lost*. My thanks to Paul Grainge, Gianluca Sergi, Julian Stringer and Peter Urquhart for their input.

TV and Film Guide

· ·

Television

Alfred Hitchcock Presents (NBC, 1955–62; 1985–7)
Alias (ABC, 2001–6)
All in the Family (CBS, 1971–9)
Ally McBeal (Fox, 1997–2002)
Almost Grown (CIC, 1988–9)
Andy's Gang (NBC, 1955–60)
Angel (WB, 1999–2004)
Angels in America (HBO, 2003)
Apprentice, The (NBC, 2004–7)
Arrested Development (Twentieth Century Fox, 2003–6)
Avengers, The (ITV, 1961–9)
Babylon 5 (CFMT, 1994–8)
Bachelor, The (ABC, 2002–5)
Band of Brothers (BBC/HBO, 2001)
Baywatch (NBC, 1989–2001)
Beauty and the Beast (CBS, 1987–90)
Beverly Hills, 90210 (Fox, 1990–2000)
Bewitched (ABC, 1964–72)
Big Love (HBO, 2006–)
Blake's 7 (BBC, 1978–81)
Bob Newhart Show, The (NBC, 1961–2/CBS, 1972–8)
Bold Ones, The (1969–72)
Bonanza (NBC, 1959–73)
Border Patrol (TV One, 2002–4)
Boomtown (NBC, 2002–3)
Boston Legal (ABC, 2004–)
Boston Public (Fox, 2000–4)
Buffy the Vampire Slayer (WB, 1997–2001; UPN, 2001–3)
Butterflies (BBC, 1978–83)

Cagney and Lacey (CBS, 1982–8)
Campbell Live (TV3, 2005–)
Carnivàle (HBO, 2003–5)
Carol Burnett Show, The (CBS, 1967–78)
Chappelle's Show (Comedy Central, 2003–6)
Charlie's Angels (ABC, 1976–81)
Chicago Hope (CBS, 1994–2000)
China Beach (ABC, 1988–91)
CHiPS (NBC, 1977–83)
City of Angels (CBS, 2000)
Close Up @ 7 (TV One, 2005–)
Colbert Report, The (Comedy Central, 2005–)
Cold Case (WB, 2003–)
Cold Feet (Granada/ITV, 1997–2003)
Columbo (NBC/ABC, 1968–2003)
Cops, The (BBC, 1998–2000)
Coronation Street (Granada/ITV, 1960–)
Cosby Show, The (NBC, 1984–92)
CrossBalls (Comedy Central, 2004)
Crossfire (CNN, 1982–2005)
Crossing Jordan (NBC, 2001–)
CSI: Crime Scene Investigation (CBS, 2000–)
CSI: Miami (CBS, 2002–)
CSI: New York (CBS, 2004–)
Curb Your Enthusiasm (HBO, 2000–)
Daily Show, The (Comedy Central, 1996–)
Dallas (CBS, 1978–91)
Dancing with the Stars (TVNZ, 2005–)
Deadwood (HBO, 2004–6)
Dead Zone, The (Sci-Fi Channel, 2002–)
Designing Women (CBS, 1986–93)
Desperate Housewives (ABC, 2004–)
Dharma and Greg (ABC, 1997–2002)
Dr. Quinn Medicine Woman (CBS, 1993–8)
Doctor Who (BBC, 1963–81, 2005–)
Dynasty (ABC, 1981–9)
EastEnders (BBC, 1985–)
Ed Sullivan Show, The (CBS, 1948–71)
Ellen (ABC, 1994–8)
Entourage (HBO, 2004–)
ER (NBC, 1994–)
Everybody Hates Chris (CBS Paramount, 2005–)
Fair Go (TV One, 1977–)

Falcon Crest (CBS, 1981–90)
Family Affairs (Channel 5, 1997–2005)
Family Guy (Fox, 1999–)
Fantasy Island (ABC, 1998–9)
Felicity (Touchstone, 1998–2002)
1st & Ten (HBO, 1984–91)
Flying Nun, The (ABC, 1967–70)
Frasier (NBC, 1993–2004)
Friends (NBC, 1994–2004)
Fugitive, The (ABC, 1963–7/CBS, 2000–1)
Full House (ABC, 1987–95)
Gilligan's Island (CBS, 1964–7)
Grace Under Fire (NBC 1993–8)
G-String Divas (HBO, 2000)
Heroes (NBC, 2006–)
High Chaparral, The (NBC, 1967–71)
Hill Street Blues (Fox, 1981–7)
Hitchhiker, The (HBO, 1983–91)
Hogan's Heroes (CBS, 1965–71)
Holmes (TVNZ, 1989–2004)
Homicide: Life on the Street (NBC, 1993–9)
Honeymooners, The (CBS, 1955–6)
House, M.D. (NBC, 2004–)
Howdy Doody (Canadian Broadcasting Company, 1954–9)
!Huff (Showtime/FX, 2004–)
Hullabaloo (NBC, 1965–6)
I Love Lucy (CBS, 1951–7)
I'll Fly Away (NBC, 1991–3)
Jack Benny Program, The (CBS, 1950–65)
Joan of Arcadia (CBS, 2003–5)
Jon Stewart Show, The (Paramount, 1993)
Judging Amy (CBS, 1999–2005)
K Street (HBO, 2003)
Kid Notorious (Comedy Central, 2003)
Kingpin (NBC, 2003)
Knight Rider (NBC, 1982–6)
Knots Landing (CBS, 1979–93)
Kolchak: The Night Stalker ((ABC, 1974–5)
L.A. Law (NBC, 1986–94)
Larry Sanders Show, The (HBO, 1992–8)
Late Late Show, The (CBS, 1999–2004)
Law & Order (NBC, 1990–)
Law & Order: Criminal Intent (NBC, 2001–)

Leap of Faith (NBC, 2002)
Little Angels (BBC, 2004–)
Lost (ABC, 2004–10)
Lost Uncovered (Sky One, 2006)
Lost Revealed (Noblesgate, 2005)
Lou Grant (CBS, 1977–82)
Love Boat, The (ABC, 1977–86)
MacGyver (ABC, 1985–92)
Magician, The (CBS, 1973–4)
Man Show, The (Comedy Central, 1999–2004)
Marcus Welby, M.D. (ABC, 1969–76)
Mark Lawson Talks to . . . (BBC, 2006–)
Martha Raye Show, The (NBC, 1955–6)
Marty (NBC, 1953)
Mary Tyler Moore Show, The (CBS, 1970–7)
*M*A*S*H* (CBS, 1972–83)
Maude (CBS, 1972–8)
Maverick (ABC, 1957–62)
Medical Investigations (NBC, 2004–5)
Miami Vice (NBC, 1984–9)
Million Dollar Movie (KHJ Los Angeles, 1955–66)
Mod Squad, The (ABC, 1968–73)
Monk (NBC, 2002–)
Monty Python's Flying Circus (BBC, 1969–74)
Moonlighting (ABC, 1985–9)
Murder, She Wrote (CBS, 1984–96)
Murphy Brown (CBS, 1988–98)
My Name is Earl (NBC, 2005–)
My So-Called Life (ABC, 1994–5)
Mystery Science Theater 3000 (Comedy Central, 1991–6)
Nash Bridges (CBS, 1996–2001)
Nine, The (ABC, 2006–7)
Nip/Tuck (FX, 2003–)
Northern Exposure (CBS, 1990–5)
NYPD Blue (ABC, 1993–2005)
NZ Idol (TVNZ, 2005–)
Off the Rails (RTE, 2000–)
Once and Again (ABC, 1999–2001)
Outrageous Fortune (TV3, 2005–)
Over There (Fox, 2005)
Oz (HBO, 1997–2003)
Patterns (NBC, 1955)
Pennies From Heaven (BBC, 1978)

Persuasion (BBC, 1995)
Piha Rescue (TV One, 2005–6)
Police Tapes, The (ABC, 1977)
Politically Incorrect (ABC, 1994–2002)
Practice, The (ABC, 1997–2004)
Prison Break (Fox, 2005–)
Prisoner, The (ITC, 1967–8)
Providence (NBC, 1999–2002)
Quincy M.E. (Universal, 1976–83)
Real Sex (HBO, 2001–)
Rescue Me (FX, 2004–)
Rockford Files, The (NBC, 1974–80)
Rome (BBC/HBO, 2005–7)
Roseanne (ABC, 1988–97)
Russell Simmons Presents Def Poetry (HBO, 2002–5)
Saturday Night Live (NBC, 1975–)
Scrubs (NBC, 2001–)
Secret Agent (Darlow Smithson Productions, 1998)
Seinfeld (NBC, 1990–8)
Sex and the City (HBO, 1998–2004)
Shield, The (FX, 2002–)
Shindig (ABC, 1964–6)
Short Attention Span Theater (Comedy Central, 1989-94)
Shortland Street (TVNZ/RTE, 1992–)
Simpsons, The (Fox, 1989–)
Singing Detective, The (BBC, 1986)
Six Degrees (ABC, 2006–7)
Six Feet Under (HBO, 2001–5)
Six Million Dollar Man, The (ABC, 1974–8)
Soap (ABC, 1977–81)
Sons and Daughters (7 Network, 1982–7)
Sopranos, The (HBO, 1999–2007)
South Park (Comedy Central, 1997–)
Spin City (ABC, 1996–2002)
SportsCenter (ESPN, 1979–)
Sports Night (ABC, 1998–2000)
St. Elsewhere (Fox, 1982–8)
Stand Up, Stand Up (HBO/Comedy Central, 1992–5)
Star Trek (NBC, 1966–9)
Star Trek: Deep Space Nine (CBS, 1993–9)
Star Trek: Enterprise (CBS, 2001–5)
Star Trek: The Next Generation (CBS, 1987–94)
Star Trek: Voyager (CBS, 1995–2001)

Starsky and Hutch (ABC, 1975–9)
Strictly Come Dancing (BBC, 2004–)
Studio 60 on the Sunset Strip (NBC, 2006–7)
Sunday (Nine Network Australia, 1981–)
Surface (NBC, 2005–6)
Survivor (CBS, 2000–)
Switch (CBS, 1975–8)
Tanner '88 (HBO, 1988)
Taxicab Confessions (HBO, 1995–)
thirtysomething (ABC, 1987–91)
Threshold (CBS, 2005)
Trapper John, MD (CBS, 1979–86)
21 Jump Street (Fox, 1987–91)
24 (Fox, 2001–)
Twilight Zone, The (CBS, 1959–64, 1985–9/UPN, 2002–3)
Twin Peaks (ABC, 1990–1)
Upright Citizen's Brigade, The (Comedy Central, 1998–2000)
Upstairs Downstairs (LWT/ITV, 1971–5)
Veronica Mars (UPN, 2004–7)
Very Social Secretary, A (Channel 4, 2005)
Wagon Train (ABC, 1957–65)
Walker, Texas Ranger (CBS, 1993–2001)
War, The (in production)
Weeds (Showtime, 2005–)
West Wing, The (NBC, 1999–2006)
Whine Gums (BBC3, 2006)
White Shadow, The (Fox, 1978–81)
Whitey Show, The (MTV, 1999)
Who Wants to be a Millionaire? (ABC, 1998–)
Winky-Dink and You (Barry and Enright Productions, 1953–7)
Wire, The (HBO, 2002–)
Your Show of Shows (NBC, 1950–4)
X-Files, The (Fox, 1993–2002)

Films

All That Jazz (Bob Fosse, 1979)
American Beauty (Sam Mendes, 1999)
Analyze This (Harold Ramis, 1999)
Apocalypse Now (Francis Ford Coppola, 1979)
Armageddon (Michael Bay, 1998)
Asphalt Jungle, The (John Huston, 1950)
Avalon (Barry Levinson, 1990)

Black Hawk Down (Ridley Scott, 2001)
Breathless (Jean-Luc Godard, 1960)
Cool Breeze (Barry Pollack, 1972)
Cul-de-Sac (Roman Polanski, 1966)
Days of Thunder (Tony Scott, 1990)
Days of Wine and Roses (Blake Edwards, 1962)
Deer Hunter, The (Michael Cimino, 1978)
Deliverance (John Boorman, 1972)
Diner (Barry Levinson, 1982)
Dr. Zhivago (David Lean, 1965)
8 1/2 (Federico Fellini, 1963)
Fly Me (Cirio H. Santiago, 1973)
Goodfellas (Martin Scorsese, 1990)
Grave of the Vampire (John Hayes, 1974)
Lord of the Rings: The Fellowship of the Ring, The (Peter Jackson, 2001)
Marty (Delbert Mann, 1955)
Miami Vice (Michael Mann, 2006)
Mission Impossible (Brian de Palma, 1996)
Mysterious Island (Spencer Gordon Bennet, 1951)
Mysterious Island (Cy Endfield, 1961)
Network (Sidney Lumet, 1976)
Patterns (Fielder Cook, 1956)
Pearl Harbor (Michael Bay, 2001)
Public Enemy, The (William A. Wellman, 1931)
Rashômon (Akira Kurosawa, 1950)
Requiem for a Heavyweight (Ralph Nelson, 1962)
Robinson Crusoe (Luis Buñuel, 1954)
Robinson Crusoe (Rod Hardy, George Miller, 1997)
Seventh Seal, The (Ingmar Bergman, 1955)
Shoot the Piano Player (François Truffaut, 1960)
Stand by Me (Rob Reiner, 1986)
Star Trek: Nemesis (Stuart Baird, 2002)
Swiss Family Robinson (Ken Annakin, 1960)
Swiss Family Robinson (Edward Ludwig, 1940)
Tin Men (Barry Levinson, 1987)
Top Gun (Tony Scott, 1986)
Urban Cowboy (James Bridges, 1980)

Notes

1 Is Quality Television Any Good?

1   It is important to stress that I am not suggesting that the determination of 'good television' is completely subjective; I am not conflating the practice of critical judgement with mere personal preference (like or dislike). As I will argue later, the qualities of the particular text are crucial in determining our evaluation of it.

2   For good accounts of British quality television, see John Caughie (2000) and Charlotte Brunsdon (1990a). Both scholars pinpoint two key features that may be found in British quality television: first, the claim of a 'privileged relation to the real', and second, the drawing of legitimacy from other, revered art forms (e.g. theatre or literature). They also note that such television displays a commitment to high production values, carefully planned composition and set design (whether in pursuit of realism or sumptuousness), and the use of established British actors who are able to achieve simultaneously a high level of realism (social and emotional authenticity) and yet also a visible 'performance', influenced by longstanding British theatrical traditions.

3   Scholars' fraught relationship with 'quality' texts, especially when those texts are understood as middle-brow, can also be found in other British scholarly contexts. Within cinema studies, for example, Andrew Higson's work on the heritage film exhibits the same concerns (see for instance Higson 1993). In person and in retrospect, Higson is refreshingly honest about his awkward relationship with his material.

4   See Caughie (2000), Brunsdon (1990a, 1990b, 1997) and Jacobs (2001). Christine Geraghty (2003) has also tackled the subject.

5   I use the term 'value' here in the sense of its relation to the process of 'evaluation', rather than in its more prosaic economic sense.

The latter understanding of value can be found in television scholarship such as Simon Frith (2000b); my use of the word echoes its deployment in aesthetics and art criticism rather than in media studies and sociology.

6   The reasons for the differences in approach to British and American quality television might be partly explicable in terms of scholars' national affiliations. While American writers seem willing to take a positive attitude towards both British and American quality programmes, British writers appear more comfortable praising American quality television rather than British quality television, taking up a rather traditionally British stance of self-effacement.

7   A fuller analysis would need to consider not just the 'meaning' of this moment but its mood, its tone and its relationship with the rest of the credits, programme and serial.

8   I am not claiming that these qualities are either sufficient or necessary to produce good television, but that they are more likely to be correlated with good television.

9   In *Andrew Davies*, I make a similar observation regarding the work of Davies and how his best work arises when his creative freedom is somehow contained by a structured form; I compare this with a poet using the sonnet form (Cardwell 2005a: 73).

10   I would propose that an ideal approach to the interpretation and evaluation of an artwork is 'disinterested and sympathetic attention', following Noël Carroll (2000: 195); this is an idea also utilised in *Andrew Davies* (Cardwell 2005a). In the next paragraph, this is what I refer to when I mention an 'appropriate attitude'.

11   To some extent, what I am calling for here is an 'aesthetics of television'. For a fuller elucidation of this, and an examination of the role of close analysis, interpretation and evaluation within television aesthetics, see Cardwell 2005b.

12   I am drawing for inspiration on the tradition exemplified in Victor F. Perkins's work on film (1972).

3 Quality TV Drama

1   For historical background on policy see, for example, Michele Hilmes (2003a), and on evaluation, Charlotte Brunsdon (1990a), John Corner (1994) and Robert J. Thompson (1996).

2   Taking an approach based on industry economic structures, Behrens (1986) coined the terms TVI and TVII as shorthand for the network era of television in the USA (roughly 1948–75) and post-network era (roughly 1975–95). Following Behrens, Rogers, Epstein and Reeves have proposed 'TVIII' to cover the post-1995, digital global context. They prefer this means of distinction to the

'broadcast', 'cable' and 'digital' characterisations of eras since, as they rightly point out, 'broadcast and cable television continue to exist in the "digital era"' (Rogers, Epstein and Reeves 2002: 55).

3   The idea of a 'common culture' is associated with the writing of seminal cultural commentators in Britain, Raymond Williams (1981) and Richard Hoggart (1958).

4   In a paternalistic founding policy for the early BBC, director-general John Reith famously proposed to bring the public what it needed, not what it wanted.

5   The more populist BBC policy was introduced in the 1960s by director-general Hugh Carleton Greene; see Hilmes 2003a: 41–2.

6   Now chairman of the board of BBC governors, Michael Grade has worked in both the commercial and public-service sectors of British television for over 30 years.

7   As part of a hierarchy in which he installed knowledge above reasoning, belief and illusion respectively, Plato in *The Theaetatus* (1987) located the animal drives, passions, emotions and desires in the lowest part of the soul and intellect in the highest part.

8   Film directors, who formerly eschewed television as beneath their dignity in the traditional Hollywood industrial film/TV hierarchy, have been drawn into television first to make commercials (Martin Scorsese, Francis Ford Coppola, David Lynch) and subsequently to make series, Lynch with *Twin Peaks* (1990) serving as a landmark. Some film producers such as Jerry Bruckheimer on *CSI* have taken control of entire series, with guest directors such as Quentin Tarantino making occasional contributions. Guest director slots have long been common for other 'high-end' products such as *ER*.

9   For an account of the rise of Fox Television, see Daniel Kimmel (2004).

10   For an account of the 'screen debate', which advocated frame-breaking 'Brechtian' devices in place of classic narrative realism, see Tony Bennett (1981).

11   Pierre Bourdieu's (1992) seminal account of shifting taste formations would construct this emphasis in terms of the preference of the emerging taste formation of the 'new petite bourgeoisie' that favours, 'all the forms of culture which are, provisionally at least on the (lower) boundaries of legitimate culture – jazz, cinema, strip cartoons, science fictions' (1992: 360).

12   See Jeanette Steemers (2004: 158).

13   The focus of the *Screen* conference Glasgow, July 2006 was on television aesthetics.

6 Quality Control

1 Both citations are taken from the Peabody Awards website at http://www.peabody.uga.edu.
2 http://www.comedycentral.com/shows/the_daily_show/about_ the_show.jhtml
3 In the mid-1990s, Comedy Central struggled with where to place *MST3K* on the schedule, particularly as the network's other programming options expanded. The avid fanbase for the show was becoming a problem for the network.

11 HBO and the Concept of Quality

1 Nor is this the first or only homage to Potter in US quality drama. *Chicago Hope*, for example, did an entire episode, 'Brain Salad Surgery' (4: 3), in the form of a Potter-like musical. They even had a guest character named Dr Denise Potter (Tasha Smith).

13 Quality and Creativity in TV

1 This was evident from our interviews with craft workers such as Dan Curry, visual effects producer on the series, who told us:

> One of the things that's fed into *Star Trek* is my years of living in Asia, especially with Klingon architecture and culture. For one episode, I needed to come up with a sword for [the Klingon character] Whorf [this turned out to be the 'ba'atleth'] and I went to Rick and the other producers, and said, hey, why don't you come up with something that's totally unique, never been seen before, and I can make a whole martial arts style around it. And that's what we did. And sadly I never had it copyrighted, I gave it to the show, and it's become an icon of the Klingons, and everybody makes money from them but me.

2 See note 1.
3 Threats to the integrity of the self are a popular theme in *Star Trek*, and, as Thomas Richards points out, they usually come not from within but from outside, from some sort of 'alien' interference; Richards suggests that 'alien forces are often standins for the dark forces of the mind' (1997: 88).
4 Here, the holodeck is an invaluable invention – one of the few ingenious production ideas not anticipated by Roddenberry.

16 Read Any Good Television Lately?

1 For a fuller consideration of all three *Twin Peaks* books see my 'The Semiotics of Cobbler' (Introduction to Lavery 1994: 6–10).

2   Several original *24* novels have also appeared, two written by Marc Cerasini. In reality Cerasini is a prolific author (Amazon lists 53 Cerasini titles) of novelisations (*Wolverine, AVP: Alien Vs. Predator, Jimmy Neutron, Boy Genius, Cinderella Man*), television and movie tie-in books and original novels (for *Godzilla, 7th Heaven*), children's books, and books on the military (*The Complete Idiot's Guide to U.S. Special Ops Forces*).

3   Any discussion of *Simpson* tie-in books would be incomplete without a mention of *The Simpsons Guide to Springfield* (Groening 1998), a parody of a Chamber of Commerce tourism guide offering an inside look at everytown's dining, nightlife, shopping, and worship ('Come for the Fun, Stay for the Guilt').

4   *The Sopranos: A Family History* has been revised and updated throughout the series' first five seasons, but the format has remained basically the same.

5   I did find three errors in the episode guide. We are told that, after the Junior-ordered, unsuccessful hit (in 'Isabella', 1: 12), Tony crashes 'his Suburban into a tree', when in fact he smashes into some parked cars. In 'Guy Walks into a Psychiatrist's Office' (2: 1) Philly Parisi 'runs into Gigi Cestone (working for Tony) at the airport and gets summarily whacked'. In fact, Parisi had unwittingly gone to the airport specifically to pick his killer up. And Sandra Bernhard's name (she appears in 'D-Girl', 2: 7) is spelled wrong (Bernhardt). Picky, picky? Perhaps, but this is, after all, an 'official' companion.

6   These ads recall the satiric live-action commercials that punctuated the *Six Feet Under* pilot.

17 Lost in Translation

1   Post-Fin Syn refers to the FCC's relaxation of rules governing the networks' ownership of the shows they aired.

2   Thanks to Paul Grainge for this reference.

3   I must admit to being a bit baffled by the inclusion of *Monty Python's Flying Circus* in Hills's list.

4   For academic speculation about viewer involvement in virtual worlds, see Gwenllian Jones (2002).

5   I am grateful to Graham Murdock for explaining the failure of synergy to me.

Bibliography

Akass, Kim and McCabe, Janet (eds) (2005) *Reading Six Feet Under: TV To Die For*, London: I.B.Tauris.

Akass, Kim and McCabe, Janet (eds) (2004) *Reading Sex and the City*, London: I.B.Tauris.

Akass, Kim and McCabe, Janet (2002) '"Beyond the Bada Bing": Negotiating Female Narrative Authority', in David Lavery (ed), *This Thing of Ours: Investigating The Sopranos*, London and New York: Wallflower/Columbia University Press: 146–61.

Alley, Oskar (2003) 'TVNZ Goes from Cash Cow to Milking Taxpayers for Millions', *Sunday Star-Times*, 12 October: A7.

Alvarez, Rafael (2004) *The Wire: Truth Be Told*, New York: Pocket Books.

Andreeva, Nellie (2006) 'Touchstone Offers *Lost* Cast a Raise', *Hollywood Reporter*, 23 January (accessed through Lexis/Nexis Executive).

Anon (2005) '*Alias* Ends Mission with Fifth Season', *Hollywood Reporter*, 29 November (accessed through Lexis/Nexis Executive).

Anon (2002) 'Sorkin Wings It', International Movie Database: 29 October: http://www.imdb.com/news/sb/2002-10-29#tv2

Armstrong, Jennifer (2005) 'Love, Labor, *Lost*', *Entertainment Weekly*, 838–9, 9 September: 30.

Ball, Alan and Poul, Alan (eds) (2003) *Six Feet Under: Better Living Through Death*, New York: Melcher Media.

Bankston Douglas (2001) 'Searching for Clues', *American Cinematographer*, May: 58–65.

Bart, Peter (2003) 'The Hunt For Hits', *Variety*, 13 January: 8.

Behrens, Steve (1986) 'Technological Convergence: Towards a United State of Media', *Channels of Communication 1986 Field Guide*: 8–10.

Bennett, Mark (1996) *TV Sets: Fantasy Blueprints of Classic TV Homes*, New York: TV Books.

Bennett, Tony (2003) *Formalism and Marxism (New Accents)*, London: Routledge.

Bennett, Tony (ed) (1981) *Popular Television and Film*, London: bfi Publishing.

Bianco, Robert (2003) 'Once Powerful *West Wing* Falls from Grace', *USA Today*, 23 September: http://www.usatoday.com/life/television/reviews/2003-09-23-west-wing_x.htm

Bianco, Robert (2002) 'Boomtown is All in the Telling', *USA Today*, 23 July: D9.

Bianculli, David (1999), *Daily News* (New York), 8 January: 116.

Bianculli, David (1994) *Tele-Literacy, Taking Television Seriously*, New York: Touchstone.

Bibb, Porter, (1993) *It Ain't as Easy as it Looks: Ted Turner's Amazing Story*, New York: Crown.

Bignell, Jonathan (forthcoming) 'The Police Series', in John Gibbs and Douglas Pye (eds), *Close Ups, 3*, London: Wallflower.

Bignell, Jonathan and Lacey, Stephen (eds) (2005) *Popular Television Drama: Critical Perspectives*, Manchester: Manchester University Press.

Billen Andrew (2002a) 'Why I love American TV', *Observer*, 28 July: www.observer.guardian.co.uk

Billen, Andrew (2002b) 'Cops, Docs and Lawyers', *Prospect*, August: 62–5.

Billen, Andrew (2001) 'Cops Without Frontiers', *New Statesman*, 18 June: www.newstatesman.com

Blanchard, Simon and Morley, David (eds) (1982) *What's this Channel Four?: An Alternative Report*, London: Comedia.

Blum, David (2004) 'Millennium Cowboys', *New York Sun*, 19–21 March: 16.

Bourdieu, Pierre (1986) *Distinction: A Social Critique of the Judgement of Taste*, trans. R. Nice, London: Routledge; reprinted 1992.

Bozell, Brent (2006) 'TV's Ickiest Moments of 2005', 5 January 2006: http://www.parentstv.org/PTC/publications/lbbcolumns/2006/0105.asp

Bozell, Brent (2004) 'Prepared Witness Testimony for the House Committee on Energy and Commerce', 28 January: http://energycommerce.house.gov/108/Hearings/01282004hearing1165/Bozell1844.htm

Bradberry, Grace (2002) 'Swearing, Sex and Brilliance', *Observer*, 20 October: Review section, 8.

Brennan, Steve (2005a) *Hollywood Reporter*, 20 May (accessed through Lexis/Nexis Executive).

Brennan, Steve (2005b) *Hollywood Reporter*, 23 May (accessed through Lexis/Nexis Executive).

Brennan, Steve (2005c) *Hollywood Reporter*, 26 May (accessed through Lexis/Nexis Executive).

Brennan, Steve and Turner, Mimi (2005) *Hollywood Reporter*, 20 October (accessed through Lexis/Nexis Executive).

Brunsdon, Charlotte (1998) 'Structure of Anxiety: Recent British Crime Fiction', *Screen*, 39.3: 223–43.

Brunsdon, Charlotte (1997) *Screen Tastes: Soap Opera to Satellite Dishes*, London: Routledge.

Brunsdon, Charlotte (1990a) 'Problems with Quality', *Screen*, 31.1: 67–90.

Brunsdon, Charlotte (1990b) 'Television: Aesthetics and Audiences', in Patricia Mellencamp (ed), *Logics of Television*, London: bfi Publishing: 59–72.

Buckland, Warren (1999) 'Between Science Fact and Science Fiction: Spielberg's Digital Dinosaurs, Possible Worlds and the New Aesthetic Realism', *Screen*, 40.2: 177–92.

Caldwell, John T. (2004) 'Convergence Television: Aggregating Form and Repurposing Content in the Culture of Conglomeration', in Lynn Spigel and Jan Olsson (eds), *Television After TV: Essays on a Medium in Transition*, Durham, NC: Duke University Press: 49–50.

Caldwell, John T. (1995) *Televisuality: Style, Crisis and Authority in American Television*, New Brunswick, NJ: Rutgers University Press.

Cantor, Muriel G. (1971) *The Hollywood TV Producer: His Work and his Audience*, New York: Basic Books.

Cardwell, Sarah (2005a) *Andrew Davies*, Manchester: Manchester University Press.

Cardwell, Sarah (2005b) 'Television Aesthetics and Close Analysis: Style, Mood and Engagement', in John Gibbs and Douglas Pye (eds), *Perfect Strangers. Style and Meaning: Studies in the Detailed Analysis of Film*, Manchester: Manchester University Press: 179–94.

Cardwell, Sarah (2002) *Adaptation Revisited: Television and the Classic Novel*, Manchester: Manchester University Press.

Carroll, Noël (2000) 'Art and the Domain of the Aesthetic', *British Journal of Aesthetics*, 40.2: 191–208.

Carter, Bill (2002a) 'Calibrating Next Step for *The Sopranos*', *The New York Times*, 7 October: Business section, C1, C4.

Carter, Bill (2002b) 'He Lit Up HBO. Now he Must Run It', *The New York Times*, 29 December: Business section, E1, E10–E11.

Carter, Bill (2000) 'He Engineered a Mob Hit, And Now It's Time to Pay Up', *The New York Times*, 11 January: Arts section, E1, E10.

Castaneda, Carlos (1992) *Tales of Power*, New York: Washington Square Press.

Caughie, John (2000) *Television Drama: Realism, Modernism, and British Culture*, Oxford: Oxford University Press.

Caughie, John (1984) 'Television Criticism: A Discourse in Search of an Object', *Screen*, 25.2: 109–20.

Cerasini, Marc (2003) *24: The House Special Subcommittee's Findings at CTU*, New York: Harper Entertainment.

Chater, David (2004) 'TV Choice', *The Times*, 24 January: www.thetimes.co.uk

Chunovic, Louis (1994) *The Northern Exposure Book*, New York: Citadel Press.

Chunovic, Louis (1993) *Chris-in-the-Morning: Love, Life, and the Whole Karmic Enchilada*, New York: Contemporary Books.

Clash, James M. (1995) 'Mr. Hatfield, Meet Mr. McCoy', *Forbes*, 30 January: 73–4.

Cole, G.D.H. (1946) 'Introduction', in Karl Marx, *Capital*, London: Everyman.

Collini, Stefan (2000) 'From Clubmen to Clubbing', *Guardian*, 4 November: http://www.guardian.co.uk/dumb/story/0,,391877,00.html

Collins, James (1992) 'Television and Postmodernism', in Robert C. Allen (ed), *Channels of Discourse, Reassembled: Television and Contemporary Culture*, Chapel Hill: University of North Carolina Press, 2nd edn: 327–53.

Comedy Central, http://www.comedycentral.com/shows/the_daily_show/about_the_show.html

Cooke, Lez (2005) 'A "New Wave" in British Television Drama', *Media International Australia Incorporating Culture and Policy*, 115: 23–32.

Corner, John, (1994) 'Debating Culture: Quality and Inequality', *Media, Culture and Society*, 16: 141–8.

Curtin, Michael (2003) 'From Network to Neo-Network Audiences', in Michele Hilmes (ed), *The Television History Book*, London: bfi Publishing: 122–5.

Davis, Mike (1986) *Prisoners of the American Dream: Politics and Economy in the History of the U.S. Working Class*, London: Verso.

Deans, Jason (2006) 'Channel Five Bags First HBO Show', *Guardian*, 13 February: http://media.guardian.co.uk/broadcast/story/0,,1707280,00.html

Dempsey, John (2002) 'HBO High on Wire', *Variety*, 4 June: http://www.variety.com/article/VR1117867981.html

Dempsey, John (2001) 'It's Lonely At The Top', *Variety*, 10–16 September: 1, 75.

Dempsey, John (1994) 'Cable Channel Seeks a "Beavis"-Style Boost: Comedy Central Aims for Firstrun Future', *Variety*, 14 February: 27–8.

Desperate Housewives: Behind Closed Doors, New York: Hyperion, 2005.

Dicker, John (2005) '*Sex & The City*: Secular Filth and Hot! Hot! Hot!', *Huffington Post*, 6 October: http://www.huffingtonpost.com/john-dicker/sex-the-city-secular-f_b_2419.html

Douglas, Susan J. (1994) *Where the Girls Are: Growing Up Female with the Mass Media*, New York: Three Rivers Press.

Dow, Bonnie J. (1996) *Prime-Time Feminism: Television, Media Culture, and the Women's Movement since 1970*, Philadelphia: University of Pennsylvania Press.

DTI/DCMS (2002) *The Draft Communications Bill – The Policy*, London: Stationery Office.

Eco, Umberto (1990) *The Limits of Interpretation*, Bloomington: Indiana University Press.

Eco, Umberto (1986) '*Casablanca*: Cult Movies and Intertextual Collage', in Umberto Eco, *Travels in Hyper Reality*, trans. William Weaver, New York: Harcourt, Brace Jovanovich: 197–211.

Ellis, John (1983) *Visible Fictions: Cinema, Television, Video*, London: Routledge and Kegan Paul.

Epstein, Michael M., Reeves, Jimmie L. and Rogers, Mark C. (2006) 'Surviving "The Hit": Will *The Sopranos* Still Sing for HBO', in David Lavery (ed), *Reading The Sopranos: Hit TV from HBO*, London: I.B.Tauris: 15–25.

Faludi, Susan (1991) *Backlash: The Undeclared War Against American Women*, New York: Anchor Books.

Fanthome, Christine (2003) *Channel 5: The Early Years*, Luton: Luton University Press.

Fernandez, Maria Elena (2006) 'ABC's *Lost* is Easy to Find, and Not Just on a TV Screen', *The Los Angeles Times*, 3 January: E1.

Feuer, Jane (2005), 'Discovering the Art of Television's Endings', *Flow TV*, 8 July, http://idg.communication.utexas.edu/flow/?jot=view&id=819

Feuer, Jane (2003) 'Quality Drama in the US: The New "Golden Age"?', in Michele Hilmes (ed), *The Television History Book*, London: bfi Publishing: 98–102.

Feuer, Jane (1995) *Seeing Through the Eighties*, London: bfi Publishing.

Feuer, Jane, Kerr, Paul and Vahimagi, Tise (eds) (1984) *MTM 'Quality Television'*, London: bfi Publishing.

Fish, Stanley (2005) *Is There a Text in this Class?: The Authority of Interpretive Communities*, Cambridge, MA: Harvard University Press.

Fiske, John (1996) *Media Matters: Race and Gender in U.S. Politics*, Minneapolis: University of Minnesota Press.

Fiske, John (1987) *Television Culture*, New York: Routledge.

Ford, Jeff (2004) Interview with Ian Goode, 15 April.

Foucault, Michel (1998) *The Will to Knowledge: The History of Sexuality, 1*, trans. Robert Hurley, London: Penguin.

Foucault, Michel (1989) *The Archaeology of Knowledge*, trans. A.M. Sheridan Smith, London and New York: Routledge.

Friend, Tad (2001) 'The Next Big Bet', *New Yorker*, 14 May: 80–91.

Frith, Simon (2000a) 'The Black Box: The Value of Television and the Future of Television Research', *Screen*, 41.1: 33–50.

Frith, Simon (2000b) 'The Value of Television and the Future of Television Research', in Jostein Gripsrud (ed), *Sociology and Aesthetics*, Kristiansand: Høyskole Forlaget, Norwegian Academic Press: 109–30.

Frost, Scott (1991) *The Autobiography of F.B.I. Special Agent Dale Cooper: My Life, My Tapes. A Twin Peaks Book*, New York: Pocket Books.

Gardam, Tim (2006) 'Media', *Evening Standard*, 15 February: 39.

Geraghty, Christine (2003) 'Aesthetics and Quality in Popular Television Drama', *International Journal of Cultural Studies*, 6.1: 25–45.

Gerrold, David (1973) *The Trouble with Tribbles: The Birth, Sale and Final Production of One Episode*, New York: Ballantine Books.

Gibson, Owen (2005) '*Lost* Finds Record Audience', *Guardian*, 12 August: 5.

Gimple, Scott (ed) (1999) *The Simpsons Forever: A Complete Guide to Our Favorite Family . . . Continued*, New York: HarperPrism.

Gimple, Scott (1998) *Matt Groening's The Simpsons' Guide to Springfield*, New York: HarperPerennial.

Gitlin, Todd (1983) *Inside Prime Time*, New York: Pantheon Books; reprinted 2000.

Golden, Christopher and Holder, Nancy (1998) *Buffy the Vampire Slayer: The Watcher's Guide*, New York: Pocket Books.

Golden, Christopher and Holder, Nancy (1999) *Sunnydale High Yearbook*, New York: Pocket Books.

Golden, Christopher, Holder, Nancy, Bissette, Stephen R. and Sniegoski, Thomas E. (2000) *Buffy the Vampire Slayer: The Monster Book*, New York: Pocket Books.

Goldman, William (1983) *Adventures in the Screen Trade*, London: Abacus; reprinted 2001.

Grant, Frances (1997) 'Soap Gets Up a Lather', *New Zealand Herald*, 24 May: B8.

Gray, Jonathan (2005) *Watching with The Simpsons: Television, Parody, and Interextuality*, New York: Routledge.

Grego, Melissa (2002) 'Feared Yet Respected', *Variety* (Special on HBO at 30), 4 November: A1–2, A5.

Greppi, Michele (2005) 'ABC Affils Remain Uneasy; Network Does Little to Erase Concerns Raised by iPod Pact', *Television Week*, 24 October: 5.

Groening, Matt (1998) *The Simpsons' Guide to Springfield*, New York: HarperPrism.

Grossman, Ben (2006) 'The New Deal: How TV Executives Will Find Digital Dollars in the Coming Year', *Broadcasting and Cable*, 2 January: 16.

Gwenllian Jones, Sara (2002) 'The Sex Lives of Cult Television Characters', *Screen*, 43.1: 79–90.

Hallam, Julia (2005) 'Remembering *Butterflies*: the Comic Art of Housework', in Jonathan Bignell and Stephen Lacey (eds), *Popular Television Drama: Critical Perspectives*, Manchester: Manchester University Press: 34–50.

Hamit, Francis (2002) 'The *CSI* Shot', *Emmy Magazine*, 24.3, June: 101.

Harris, Paul (2006) 'America's TV Genius Strikes Gold Again', *Observer*, 24 September: 36.

Hettrick, Scott (1998) 'Get-togethers Make New *South Park* Cable's Best 18–49 Demo Flocks to See Christ vs. Satan', *Hollywood Reporter*, 11 February 1998 (accessed through LexisNexis Academic 1 February 2006).

Higson, Andrew (1993) 'Re-presenting the National Past: Nostalgia and Pastiche in the Heritage Film', in Lester Friedman (ed), *British Cinema and Thatcherism: Fires Were Started*, London: University College of London Press: 109–29.

Hills, Matt (2005) 'Cult TV, Quality and the Role of the Episode Programme Guide', in Michael Hammond and Lucy Mazdon (eds), *The Contemporary Television Series*, Edinburgh: Edinburgh University Press: 190–206.

Hills, Matt (2002) *Fan Cultures*, London: Routledge.

Hilmes, Michele (ed) (2003a) *The Television History Book*, London: bfi Publishing.

Hilmes, Michele (2003b) 'US Television in the Multichannel Age (Protectionism, Deregulation and The Telecommunications Act of 1996)', in Michele Hilmes (ed), *The Television History Book*, London: bfi Publishing: 62–7.

Hilmes, Michele (2002) *Only Connect: A Cultural History of Broadcasting in the United States*, Belmont, CA: Wadworth.

Hofler, Robert (2002) 'Noises Off: B'way Gets Patriotic', *Variety*, 12 August: http://www.variety.com/article/VR1117871014.html

Hoggart, Richard (1958) *The Uses of Literacy: Aspects of Working-Class Life with Special Reference to Publications and Entertainments*, Harmondsworth: Penguin.

Holden, Stephen (1999) 'Sympathetic Brutes in a Pop Masterpiece', *The New York Times*, 6 June: S2, 23.

Holder, Nancy with Mariotte, Jeff and Hart, Mary Elizabeth (2000) *Buffy the Vampire Slayer: The Watcher's Guide, Vol. 2*, New York: Pocket Books.

Holdsworth, Nick (2005) *Hollywood Reporter*, 16 July (accessed through Lexis/Nexis Executive).

Holquist, Michael (2002) *Dialogism: Bakhtin and his World*, London: Routledge.

Holston, Noel (2004) 'A Six-gun Saga in 4-Letter Words', *Newsday*, 21 March: C19.

Holston, Noel (2002) 'For Show's Creator, An Unexpected Run', *Newsday*, 13 September: B10.

Holt, Jennifer (2003) 'Vertical Vision: Deregulation, Industrial Economy and Prime-time Design', in Mark Jancovich and James Lyons (eds), *Quality Popular Television: Cult TV, the Industry and Fans*, London: bfi Publishing: 11–31.

Home Office (1989) *Report of the Committee on Financing the BBC* (The Peacock Report), London: HMSO; reprinted 1996.

Home Office (1988) *Broadcasting in the 1990s: Competition, Choice, Quality*, London: HMSO.

Jacobs, Jason (2001) 'Issues of Judgement and Value in Television Studies', *International Journal of Cultural Studies*, 4.4: 427–47.

James, Caryn (2001a) '*Sopranos*: Blood, Bullets and Proust', *The New York Times*, 2 March: E1, E30.

James, Caryn (2001b) '*The Sopranos*: Brutally Honest', *The New York Times*, 22 May: E1, E6.

James, Meg and Eller, Claudia (2005) 'Paramount Chief said to be Wooing Top TV Producer', *The Los Angeles Times*, 15 December: Business section, C1.

Jancovich, Mark and Lyons, James (eds) (2003) *Quality Popular Television: Cult TV, the Industry and Fans*, London: bfi Publishing.

Jaramillo, Deborah L. (2002) 'The Family Racket: AOL Time Warner, HBO, *The Sopranos*, and the Construction of a Quality Brand', *Journal of Communication Inquiry*, 26.1, January: 59–75.

Jarvik, Laurence (1999) *Masterpiece Theatre and the Politics of Quality*, Maryland: Scarecrow Press.

Jenkins, Henry and Tulloch, John (1995) *Science Fiction Audiences: Watching Doctor Who and Star Trek*, London: Routledge.

Jinpa, Thupten and Coleman, Graham (eds) (2006) *The Tibetan Book of the Dead: First Complete Translation*, trans. Dorje Gyurme, London: Penguin.

Johnson, Greg (1998) 'Kenny Watches his Mouth on T-Shirts', *Toronto Star*, 21 November: T04.

Johnson, Ted (2003) 'Risks and Rewards', *Variety*, 25–31 August: A6, A8.

Johnson, W.J. (trans.) (2004) *The Bhagavad Gita*, Oxford: Oxford Paperbacks.

Kan, Raybon (1993) 'Awards Make Relativity Seem Simple', *Dominion*, 23 March: 22.

Katz, Jon (1992) 'Rock, Rap and Movies Bring You the News', *Rolling Stone*, 625: 33.

Kemp, Stuart (2005) *Hollywood Reporter*, 12 August (accessed through Lexis/Nexis Executive).

Kimmel, Daniel, M. (2004) *The Fourth Network*, Chicago: Ivan R. Dee.

King, Scott Benjamin (1990) 'Sonny's Virtues: The Gender Negotiations of *Miami Vice*', *Screen*, 31.3: 281–95.

King, Stephen (2005) 'Lost's Soul', *Entertainment Weekly*, 838–9, 9 September: 150.

Kuhn, Annette (1988) *Cinema, Censorship and Sexuality 1909–1925*, London and New York: Routledge.

Lane, Christina (2003) 'The White House Culture of Gender and Race in *The West Wing*: Insights from the Margins', in Peter C. Rollins and John E. Conner (eds), *The West Wing: The American Presidency as Television Drama*, New York: Syracuse University Press: 32–41.

LaTempa, Susan (2002) 'The Women of *CSI*: Tough Girls Do Dance', October: http://www.wga.org/WrittenBy/1002/csi.html

Lavery, David (2006a) 'Afterword', in Steven Peacock (ed), *Reading 24: TV Against the Clock*, London: I.B.Tauris: 209–12.

Lavery, David (2006b) 'Climate Change: Television Books, the Series', *Critical Studies in Television: Scholarly Studies in Small Screen Fictions*, 1.1, Spring: 97–103.

Lavery, David (2005a) '"It's Not Television, It's Magic Realism": The Mundane, the Grotesque and the Fantastic in *Six Feet Under*', in Kim Akass and Janet McCabe (eds), *Reading Six Feet Under: TV to Die For*, London, I.B.Tauris: 19–33.

Lavery, David (ed) (2005b) *Reading The Sopranos: Hit TV From HBO*, London: I.B.Tauris.

Lavery, David (ed) (2002) *This Thing of Ours: Investigating The Sopranos*, London and New York: Wallflower/Columbia University Press.

Lavery, David (2001) 'Review Essay of *Buffy the Vampire Slayer: The Monster Book* by Golden, Bissette and Sniegoski; *Buffy the Vampire*

Slayer: The Watcher's Guide, Vol. 2 by Holder, Mariotte and Hart; and *The Sopranos: A Family History* by Alan Rucker', *Television Quarterly*, 31.4, Winter: 89–92.

Lavery, David (ed) (1994) *Full of Secrets: Critical Approaches to Twin Peaks*, Detroit: Wayne State University Press.

Lavery, David, Hague, Angela and Cartwright, Maria (eds) (1996) *Deny All Knowledge: Reading the X-Files*, New York: Syracuse University Press.

Lavery, David and Thompson, Robert J. (2002) 'David Chase, *The Sopranos*, and Television Creativity', in David Lavery (ed), *This Thing of Ours: Investigating The Sopranos*, London and New York: Wallflower/Columbia University Press: 18–25.

Lawson, Mark (2006a) 'Are You Sitting Comfortably?', *Guardian*, 2 November: G2 section, 4–7.

Lawson, Mark (2006b) 'Why Newspapers Should Stop Publishing TV Reviews', *Critical Studies in Television: Scholarly Studies in Small Screen Fictions*, 1.1, Spring: 104–7.

Lawson, Mark (2005) 'Foreword', in Kim Akass and Janet McCabe (eds), *Reading Six Feet Under: TV to Die For*, London, I.B.Tauris: xvii–xxii.

Lealand, Geoff (2001) 'Searching for Quality Television in New Zealand: Hunting the Moa?', *International Journal of Cultural Studies*, 4.4, December: 448–55.

Lealand, Geoff (2000) 'Regulation – What Regulation? Cultural Diversity and Local Content in New Zealand Television', *Media International Australia*, 95, May: 77–89.

Lealand, Geoff (1988) *A Foreign Egg in Our Nest? American Popular Culture in New Zealand*, Wellington: Victoria University Press.

Lealand, Geoff and Martin, Helen (2001) *It's All Done with Mirrors: About Television*, Palmerston North: Dunmore Press.

Leggatt, Timothy (1996) 'Quality in Television: The Views of the Professionals', in Sakae Ishikawa (ed), *Quality Assessment of Television*, Luton: Luton University Press: 145–68.

Levin, Gary (2002) 'West Wing Popularity is Slipping in the Polls', *USA Today*, 16 November: http://www.usatoday.com/life/television/news/2002-10-15-west-wing_x.htm

Lewis, C.S. (2001) *A Grief Observed (Collected Letters of C.S. Lewis)*, Missouri: Zonderran Publishing House.

Liddiment, David (2004) 'Time to Speak Up for Quality TV', *Guardian*, 23 August: Media section, 4.

Longworth, James L. (2000) 'David Chase "Hit" Man', in James Longworth (ed), *TV Creators: Conversations with America's Top Producers of Television Drama*, Syracuse: Syracuse University Press: 20–36.

Lowry, Brian (1996) *Trust No One: The Official Third Season Guide to The X-Files*, New York: HarperPrism.

Lowry, Brian (1995) *The Truth is Out There: The Official Guide to The X-Files*, New York: HarperPrism.

Lynch, David, Frost, Mark and Worman, Richard Saul (1991) *Welcome to Twin Peaks: Access Guide to the Town*, New York: Pocket Books.

Lynch, Jennifer (1990) *The Secret Diary of Laura Palmer*, New York: Pocket Books.

Lynch, Thomas (2001) *Bodies in Motion and at Rest*, New York: Vintage.

Lury, Karen (2005) *Interpreting Television*, London: Hodder Arnold.

McArthur, Colin (1980) 'Point of Review: Television Criticism in the Press', *Screen Education*, 35, Summer: 59–61.

McCabe, Janet (2005) 'Creating Audiences for *E.R.* on Channel 4', in Michael Hammond and Lucy Mazdon (eds), *The Contemporary Television Series*, Edinburgh: Edinburgh University Press: 207–23.

McCabe, Janet (2000) 'Diagnosing the Alien: Producing Identities, American "Quality" Drama and British Television Culture in the 1990s', in Bruce Carson and Margaret Llewellyn-Jones (eds), *Frames and Fictions on Television: The Politics of Identity Within Drama*, Exeter: Intellect: 141–54.

McCann, Jesse L. (ed) (2005) *The Simpsons One Step Beyond Forever: A Complete Guide to Our Favorite Family . . . Continued Yet Again*, New York: Perennial.

McCann, Jesse L. (ed) (2002) *The Simpsons Beyond Forever: A Complete Guide to Our Favorite Family . . . Still Continued*, New York: Perennial.

McLean, Gareth (2005) '*CSI*: Tarantino', *Guardian*, 11 July: New Media section, 12.

McLoone, Martin (1997) 'Boxed In?: The Aesthetics of Film and Television', in John Hill and Martin McLoone (eds), *Big Picture, Small Screen: The Relations between Film and Television*, Luton: John Libbey: 76–106.

Mann, Denise (1992) 'The Spectacularization of Everyday Life: Recycling Hollywood Stars and Fans in Early Television Variety Shows', in Lynn Spigel and Denise Mann (eds), *Private Screenings: Television and the Female Consumer*, Minneapolis: University of Minnesota Press: 41–70.

Marcus, Daniel (2003) 'Public Television and Public Access', in Michele Hilmes (ed), *The Television History Book*, London: bfi Publishing: 55–9.

Martel, Ned (2004) 'Resurrecting the Western to Save the Crime Drama', *The New York Times*, 21 March: 34.

Mediawatch (2004), Radio New Zealand National, 5 September.

Meisler, Andy (2000) *The End and the Beginning: The Official Guide to The X-Files*, San Francisco: HarperPrism.

Meisler, Andy (1999) *Resist or Serve: The Official Guide to the The X-Files*, San Francisco: HarperPrism.

Meisler, Andy (1998) *I Want to Believe: The Official Guide to The X-Files*, San Francisco: HarperPrism.

Messinger Davies, Máire and Pearson, Roberta (forthcoming) *Small Screen, Big Universe: Star Trek as Television*, California: University of California Press.

Miller, Jeffrey S. (2000) *Something Completely Different: British Television and American Culture*, Minneapolis: University of Minnesota Press.

Miller, Toby, Govil, Nitin, McMurria, John, Maxwell, Richard and Wang, Ting (2004) *Global Hollywood: No. 2*, London: bfi Publishing.

Millichap, Joseph (2006) 'Robert Penn Warren, David Milch, and the Literary Contexts of *Deadwood*', in David Lavery (ed), *Reading Deadwood: A Western to Swear By*, London: I.B.Tauris: 101–13.

Mittell, Jason (2005) 'The Loss of Value (or the Value of *Lost*)', *Flow*, 2.5, May 2005: http://idg.communication.utexas.edu/flow/?issue=Volume%202,%20Issue%205&jot=view&id=786

Monroe, Josephine (1999) 'Voice of a Nation', *Observer*, 6 June: Screen section, 2–3.

Morley, David (1992) *Television Audiences and Cultural Studies*, London and New York: Routledge.

NBC, *The Apprentice* website: http://www.nbc.com/The_Apprentice_4/about/markburnett/

Nelson, Robin (2006) '"Quality Television": *The Sopranos* is the Best Television Drama Ever . . . in my Humble Opinion', *Critical Studies in Television*, 1.1: 58–71.

Nelson, Robin (1997) *TV Drama in Transition*, Basingstoke: Macmillan.

Nelson, Robin (1996) 'From *Twin Peaks*, USA to Lesser Peaks, UK: Building the Postmodern TV Audience', *Media, Culture and Society*, 18 April: 677–82.

New Zealand On Air (2004) *Annual Report*, Wellington: NZOA, 2004.

Newcomb, Horace (1974) *Television: The Most Popular Art*, New York: Anchor.

Newman, Thomas (2005) interviewed by Gary Calamar on *Open Road*, Sunday 18 September: http://www.supermusicvision.com/frames.htm

Newman, Thomas (2003) *Filmtracks*, 1: http://www.filmtracks.com/composers/newmant.shtml

Nienhaus, Brian Jacob (1993) 'Lost Causes: Mass Media Exposure's Empirical Meanings in Survey Research. A Critique and Introduction to Commodity Relations', unpublished dissertation, University of Michigan.

Norrish, Merv (1995) 'NZ On Air Street Credibility', *Sunday Star-Times*, 19 February: C5.

O'Malley, Tom (2003) 'The BBC Adapts to Competition', in Michele Hilmes (ed), *The Television History Book*, London: bfi Publishing: 86–9.

Peabody Awards, http://www.peabody.uga.edu

Pearson, Roberta (2005) 'The Writer/Producer in American Television', in Michael Hammond and Lucy Mazdon (eds), *The Contemporary Television Series*, Edinburgh: Edinburgh University Press: 11–26.

Perkins, Victor F. (1972) *Film as Film*, Harmondsworth: Penguin.

Peyser, Marc (2001) 'HBO's Godfather: David Chase Created the Acclaimed *The Sopranos*. Now He Wants to Bump it Off', *Newsweek*, 5 March: 5.

Pirandello, Luigi (1921) *Six Characters in Search of an Author (Sei Personaggi in Cera d'Autore) A Comedy in the Making*, trans. Edward Storer, New York: E.P. Dutton.

Plato (1987) *The Theaetatus*, London: Penguin.

Poniewozik, James (2005) 'The Decency Police', *Time*, 20 March: http://www.time.com/time/archive/preview/0,10987,1039672,00.html

Poole, Mike (1984) 'The Cult of the Generalist – British Television Criticism 1936-83', *Screen*, 25 February: 41–61.

Postman, Neil (1987) *Amusing Ourselves to Death*, London: Methuen.

PR Newswire (2000) 'Comedy Central's *South Park* in Global Licensing Arena', 13 June (accessed through LexisNexis Academic 1 February 2006).

Reeves-Stevens, Judith and Reeves-Stevens, Garfield (1997) *Star Trek The Next Generation: The Continuing Mission*, New York: Pocket Books.

Richards, Thomas (1997) *Star Trek in Myth and Legend*, London: Orion Books.

Richmond, Ray (1998) '"South Park" May Warp to Bigscreen', *Daily Variety*, 20 January (accessed through LexisNexis Academic, 1 March 2006).

Richmond, Ray and Coffman, Antonia (eds) (1997) *The Simpsons: A Complete Guide to Our Favorite Family*, New York: Perennial.

Rixon, Paul (2003) 'The Changing Face of American Television Programmes on British Screens', in Mark Jancovich and James Lyons (eds), *Quality Popular Television: Cult TV, the Industry and Fans*, London: bfi Publishing: 48–61.

Rodman, Howard (1989) 'The Series that Will Change TV',
    Connoisseur, September: 139–44.
Rogers, Mark C., Epstein, Michael M. and Reeves, Jimmie L.
    (2002) '*The Sopranos* as HBO Brand Equity: The Art of Commerce in the
    Age of Digital Representation', in David Lavery (ed), *This Thing of
    Ours: Investigating The Sopranos*, New York: Columbia University
    Press: 42–59.
Rosett, Claudia (2002) 'TV: Much More Than a Mob Story', *Wall Street
    Journal*, 28 January: A13.
Rowland Jr, Willard D. (2003) 'The V-Chip', in Michele Hilmes (ed),
    The Television History Book, London: bfi Publishing: 135.
Rucker, Allen (2002) *The Sopranos' Family Cookbook, as Compiled by
    Artie Bucco*, New York: Warner.
Rucker, Allen (2000) *The Sopranos: A Family History*, New York: New
    American Library, reprinted 2001, 2002, 2003.
Ruditis, Paul (2004) *The Watcher's Guide, Vol. 3*, New York: Spotlight.
Schneider, Michael (2003) 'Viacom Takes Laughs to the Bank', *Variety*,
    28 April (accessed through LexisNexis Academic, 15 February
    2005).
Schrøder, Kim Christian (1992) 'Cultural Quality: Search for a
    Phantom? A Reception on Judgements of Cultural Value', in
    Michael Skovmand and Kim Christian Schrøder (eds), *Media
    Cultures: Reappraising Transnational Media*, London: Routledge:
    199–219.
Seabrook, John (2000) *Nobrow: The Culture of Marketing—The Marketing
    of Culture*, New York: Knopf.
Shapiro, Marc (2001) *All Things: The Official Guide to The X-Files*, New
    York: HarperPrism.
Sherman, Jay (2005) 'Disney Transformed: Other Media Companies
    Expected to Follow Technology Trail', *Television Week*, 17
    October: 26.
Simon, David (1991) *Homicide, A Year on the Killing Streets*, New York:
    Ballantine Books.
Slade, Christina (2002) *The Real Thing: Doing Philosophy With Media*,
    New York: Peter Lang.
Sohn, Amy and Wildman, Sarah (2004) *Sex and the City: Kiss and Tell*,
    New York: Pocket Books.
Solow, Herbert F. and Justman, Robert H. (1999) *Inside Star Trek: The
    Real Story*, Philadelphia: DIANE Publishing Company.
Spigel, Lynn (2004) 'Introduction', in Lynn Spigel and Jan Olsson
    (eds), *Television After TV: Essays on a Medium in Transition*,
    Durham, NC: Duke University Press: 1–34.

Spigel, Lynn (1992) 'Installing the Television Set: Popular Discourses on Television and Domestic Space, 1948–1955', in Lynn Spigel and Denise Mann (eds), *Private Screenings: Television and the Female Consumer*, Minneapolis: University of Minnesota Press: 3–40.

Steemers, Jeanette (2004) *Selling Television*, London: bfi Publishing.

Steinberg, Jacques (2005) 'The News is Funny, as a Correspondent Gets his Own Show', *The New York Times*, 12 October: E1 (accessed through LexisNexis Academic, 1 March 2006).

Stewart, James E. (2005) *Disney War: The Battle for the Magic Kingdom*, London: Simon & Schuster.

Stewart, Jon, et al (2004) *The Daily Show with John Stewart Presents America (The Book): A Citizen's Guide to Democracy in Action*, Clayton, Victoria: Warner Books.

Television New Zealand (2003) 'Charter': http://corporate.tvnz.co.nz/tvnz_detail/0,2406,11135-244-257.html

Thompson, Peter A. (2005a) 'Achieving Quality in Television Broadcasting: What Matters, What Measures, What Motives?', workshop discussion paper presented to the 'Taking Up the Challenges: Tomorrow's Television in New Zealand' Ministry of Culture and Heritage Seminar, Auckland, 2 June.

Thompson, Peter A. (2005b) 'Star Wars: The Empire Strikes Out?', *New Zealand Political Review*, 54, Autumn: 44–9.

Thompson, Robert J. (1996) *Television's Second Golden Age: From Hill Street Blues to ER*, New York: Continuum; reprinted 1997.

Time-Warner (2001) 'Comedy Central Soars Past 70 Million Subscriber Mark Adding over 1 Million Subscribers in the Past Month', 6 March: http://www.timewarner.com/corp/newsroom/pr/0,20812,668535,00.html

Troup, Gary (2006) *Bad Twin*, New York: Hyperion.

Twitchell, James (1992) *Carnival Culture*, New York: Columbia University Press.

Tzu, Lao (1990) *Tao Te Ching*, Boston: Shambhala Publications.

Variety (1999) 'Comedy Web Smiling Over Sub Increases', 12 April (accessed through LexisNexis Academic, 23 August 2005).

Vaz, Mark Cotta (2005) *The Lost Chronicles: The Official Companion Book*, London: Transworld Publishers and New York: Hyperion.

Vaz, Mark Cotta (2002) *Alias Declassified: The Official Companion*, New York: Bantam Books.

Wang, Onc (1988) '*Miami Vice*: Sex and Drugs and Rock & Roll in the TV Market', *Jump Cut*, 33: 10–19.

Weiner, Ellis (1993) *The Northern Exposure Cookbook: A Community Cookbook from the Heart of the Alaskan Riviera*, New York: Contemporary Books.

Weiner, Ellis (1992) *Letters from Cicely*, New York: Pocket Books.
Wells, Matt. (2003) 'Channel Five Programming Stripped Bare of Pornography', *Guardian*, 14 July: http://www.guardian.co.uk/uk_news/story/0,,997672,00.html
Wicks, Maggie (2005) 'Go West', *Sunday Star-Times*, 26 June: 3.
Wilcox, Rhonda and Lavery, David (eds) (2002) *Fighting the Forces*, Lanham, MD: Rowman & Littlefield.
Williams, Michael (2001) *Problems of Knowledge*, Oxford: Oxford University Press.
Williams, Raymond (1981) *Culture*, London: Fontana.
Williams, Raymond (1974) *Television, Technology and Cultural Form*, London: Fontana.
Wilson, Tim (1999) 'Street Cred', *Metro*, May: 72.
Winslow, George (2006) 'We Want Their Shows, They Want Ours: NATPE International Market is Vigorous for Content Providers', *Broadcasting and Cable*, 23 January: 16.

DVD

'Before They Were Lost', *Lost: The Complete First Season*, The Essential *Lost* Bonus Features, Buena Vista Home Entertainment and Touchstone Television, 2005.
Daily Show with Jon Stewart – Indecision 2004, The (Andy Barsh, Scott Preston, 2005)
'Designing a Disaster', *Lost: The Complete First Season*, The Essential *Lost* Bonus Features, Buena Vista Home Entertainment and Touchstone Television, 2005.
'Genesis of *Lost*, The', *Lost: The Complete First Season*, The Essential *Lost* Bonus Features, Buena Vista Home Entertainment and Touchstone Television, 2005.
'*Lost* at the Museum of Television and Radio', excerpt from salute to *Lost* held by the Directors' Guild of America at the 22nd Annual Paley Festival, *Lost: The Complete First Season*, The Essential *Lost* Bonus Features, Buena Vista Home Entertainment and Touchstone Television, 2005.
'Making of the Pilot', *Lost: The Complete First Season*, The Essential *Lost* Bonus Features, Buena Vista Home Entertainment and Touchstone Television, 2005.

Index